Unlocking English Learners' Potential

Praise for *Unlocking English Learners' Potential*

Much may be debated about what English learners need in order to be successful in school, but while that debate continues, teachers need access to sensible and accessible assistance to teach language and content to English learners right now. This new book by Diane Staehr Fenner and Sydney Snyder is the book to fill that need. In clear prose, accompanied by lively classroom examples and a series of engaging application activities, the authors target the topics of culturally responsive teaching, scaffolded instruction for oral language and reading, understanding academic language, and how to formatively assess student development in these areas. There is something here for both novice teachers and their more seasoned colleagues as Fenner and Snyder skillfully bring together the necessary ingredients to help teachers advance the language and content learning of their English learners.

Alison L. Bailey, Professor of Human Development and Psychology
Department of Education, University of California, Los Angeles

Fenner and Snyder have written a much-needed and illuminating text in the field of EL education that challenges educators to rethink language pedagogy in new ways that never dichotomize theory and practice. Not only do the authors provide numerous sound and exciting hands-on instructional recommendations but they impressively model for educators what it means to link theory to practice by anchoring their applications to a comprehensive equity and cultural wealth framework.

Lilia Bartolome, PhD, Professor of Applied Linguistics
University of Massachusetts Boston, College of Liberal Arts

There is so much to love about Unlocking English Learners' Potential. *Fenner and Snyder have created a truly readable text packed with practical suggestions for all educators who teach ELs! ESOL educators will find the focus on advocacy and leadership provides them with new ideas to take their practice to the next level. Content educators will appreciate the many easy-to-incorporate strategies for developing oral language and reading within their own academic content classes. And finally, the emphasis on teacher collaboration is vital to get everyone on board with an agenda that stresses equity and excellence for our culturally and linguistically diverse learners. This text will undoubtedly be a hit with school PLCs and teacher education programs.*

Tim Boals, WIDA Executive Director
University of Wisconsin–Madison

With so many resources available today and so little time to review them all, it becomes harder and harder for educators to know what to read and when to read it. What Fenner and Snyder offer to educators of English learners with this book is the unique opportunity to find in one resource a synthesis of the current research, examples of its impact in the classroom through authentic classroom vignettes, and a wealth of tools to get started in their own classrooms. Fenner and Snyder have successfully combined their own expertise with that of colleagues and educators to bring to the field a valuable tool for professional growth and collaboration. Thank you!

Mariana Castro, Director of Standards
WIDA Consortium at the Wisconsin Center
for Education Research

Continuing their advocacy for English learners to obtain an equitable education, Diane Staehr Fenner and Sydney Snyder offer a remarkable framework to guide teachers to better understand the complex nature of teaching diverse students. This book not only examines why a supportive school environment matters but also offers detailed, research-informed instructional strategies applicable to every class. It is a must-read for all teachers of English learners!

Maria G. Dove, EdD, Associate Professor and Coordinator
Molloy College, New York, Graduate Education TESOL Programs

Unlocking English Learners' Potential: Strategies for Making Content Accessible *offers a treasure trove of practical resources and ideas for all teachers— and not just those with ELLs in their classrooms.*

Larry Ferlazzo, Teacher and Author
The ESL/ELL Teacher's Survival Guide

Fenner and Snyder masterfully unravel the intricacies of teaching and supporting English learners (ELs). Seen through a series of guiding principles within an equitable educational framework, each chapter reveals an important theme in enacting effective instructional strategies that advance EL learning. Their focus on teacher collaboration in furthering students' language development and academic achievement provides insight into implementing their carefully delineated steps. With its many application activities, this book offers both content and language teachers a myriad of ideas for working with ELs integral to their classroom practices.

Margo Gottlieb, Co-founder and Lead Developer for WIDA
Wisconsin Center for Education Research,
University of Wisconsin–Madison

Fenner and Snyder have created a practitioner-friendly guide for educators of ELs to help create welcoming school and classroom environments, build cultural responsiveness, and increase educators' toolboxes for serving ELs. The authors speak with experienced teacher voices and have a gift for making the complex simple through explicit explanation, classroom examples, and use of tools for instruction and assessment. This is a must-read for preservice educators of ELs who are seeking authentic professional learning to meet the needs of their ELs.

Janet E. Hiatt, EL/Title III Consultant
Heartland Area Education Agency, Iowa

Unlocking English Learners' Potential: Strategies for Making Content Accessible *not only offers a fresh perspective on approaching the education of English learners, but also provides readers with practical and comprehensive guidance on how to ensure success for ELs. I am honored to endorse this new book from leading experts Diane Staehr Fenner and Sydney Snyder, who continue to demonstrate uncompromising dedication to and advocacy for ELs, while also offering ready-to-implement strategies and examples of successful practices.*

Andrea Honigsfeld, Associate Dean and
EdD Program Director
Molloy College, New York

In the current ESSA era, all teachers are charged with teaching both the language and content featured in standards-based instruction and assessment. This timely work, grounded in extensive EL vignettes and readily implementable examples of useful pedagogy, shines a welcome light on this topic, particularly for teachers of language who recognize the urgency to provide ELs access to the core curriculum. This comprehensive educator tool represents a significant contribution to the field and will be a well-used desk reference by K–12 teachers.

Stephaney Jones-Vo, English Learner/Title III Consultant
Heartland Area Education Agency, Iowa

Teachers and administrators often read books that later end up on the shelf covered in dust. Unlocking English Learners' Potential: Strategies for Making Content Accessible *is not one of them. It is a practical pedagogical guide that helps all teachers realize their role as a teacher of English learners. Teachers will especially love how it builds their background knowledge as well as provides actual strategies that work for ELs.*

Samuel Klein, Supervisor, ESOL/HILT
Department of Instruction, Arlington Public Schools

Unlocking English Learners' Potential *is a powerful and valuable guide for deepening all educators' understandings, practices, and beliefs that contribute to the success of English language learners. Fenner and Snyder provide a framework for educating ELLs explained with practical tools, helpful examples, scenarios, and activities that promote the implementation of best practices with this population of students. A must-have for schools looking to establish a shared schoolwide responsibility for educating ELLs.*

Jacqueline LeRoy, Director of ENL, World
Languages and Bilingual Education
Syracuse City School District

For anyone needing a blueprint for how to successfully work with and instruct English language learners, Unlocking English Learners' Potential *is a one-stop shop.*

This book is a beacon of light for schools and practitioners who are new to ELLs and want to implement exemplary practices.

Giselle Lundy-Ponce, ELL Policy Expert
American Federation of Teachers

Drs. Fenner and Snyder compile an impressive number of instructional strategies that work for emerging bilingual students. With clarity and relevant examples, strategies are brought to life for both practitioners and administrators. A very timely work that will help with the education of the fastest growing population in our schools.

David Nieto, Executive Director
BUENO Center for Multicultural Education,
University of Colorado Boulder, School of Education

Unlocking English Learners' Potential

Strategies for Making Content Accessible

Diane Staehr Fenner
Sydney Snyder

Foreword by Lydia Breiseth

CORWIN
A SAGE Publishing Company

FOR INFORMATION:

Corwin

A SAGE Company

2455 Teller Road

Thousand Oaks, California 91320

(800) 233-9936

www.corwin.com

SAGE Publications Ltd.

1 Oliver's Yard

55 City Road

London EC1Y 1SP

United Kingdom

SAGE Publications India Pvt. Ltd.

B 1/I 1 Mohan Cooperative Industrial Area

Mathura Road, New Delhi 110 044

India

SAGE Publications Asia-Pacific Pte. Ltd.

3 Church Street

#10-04 Samsung Hub

Singapore 049483

Program Director: Dan Alpert

Senior Associate Editor: Kimberly Greenberg

Senior Editorial Assistant: Katie Crilley

Production Editor: Amy Schroller

Copy Editor: Jared Leighton

Typesetter: C&M Digitals (P) Ltd.

Proofreader: Dennis W. Webb

Indexer: Sheila Bodell

Cover Designer: Anupama Krishnan

Marketing Manager: Maura Sullivan

Copyright © 2017 by Corwin

Printed in the United States of America

ISBN 978-1-5063-5277-0

This book is printed on acid-free paper.

21 22 23 24 25 26 20 19 18 17 16 15 14

Contents

Chapter 8: Supporting ELs' Reading for Multiple Purposes Through Using Scaffolded Text-Dependent Questions   203

Foreword

Last spring, while working on a video project highlighting how collaboration can benefit English learners (ELs), I had the opportunity to visit Mason Crest Elementary School in the Washington, DC, suburb of Annandale, Virginia. Mason Crest is home to a diverse student body, nearly half of whom are ELs. The school leaders and staff are champions of collaboration, whether in the classroom, in professional development, or parent engagement, and on my visit, I was able to see lots of collaborative partnerships—and the opportunities made possible by collaboration—in action.

One project was particularly exciting to see in person: the Super Secret Science Club. Created by fifth-grade specialist in English for speakers of other languages (ESOL), Katy Padilla, the idea was based on research about the strategy of preteaching minilessons with ELs and special education students in small groups before students encountered new content in the classroom with their peers. Katy learned that the strategy could increase student participation in the larger class setting and decided to give it a try. Based on her work with the fifth-grade team of classroom teachers, special educators, and other resource teachers, she knew that science was an area where kids needed lots of extra support in learning vocabulary and background knowledge. She came up with the idea of an optional club that would meet at lunchtime on Mondays, where ELs would have a chance to learn about different words or concepts in an informal setting. The name was chosen to generate excitement and interest, and Katy explained to the students that they would be the experts in their class because they had already started learning the new material.

Katy chose her target content for the lessons based on her collaboration with her fifth-grade team, which met during regularly scheduled periods throughout the week to discuss lessons and plan instruction. These meetings were made possible by a school-wide commitment to embed time for collaboration into everyone's schedule. On the day we visited, kids were learning about vascular and nonvascular plants. As I sat in the back of the room while the club met, about eight ELs ate their lunch, and Katy went through a presentation filled with visuals of different kinds of plants and parts of plants. She also included images of objects the students would recognize, such as pipes and—because they were at lunch—straws. It was brilliant. The kids practiced saying and using the words, laughing and picking up their straws to take a closer look at them with new appreciation.

Later, when the science lesson was delivered, it was clear that the preparation had worked—the ELs spoke up confidently, raising their hands and using the new words. They also had opportunities to practice new language with the related sentence starters that Katy had prepared for all of the fifth-grade teachers, a tool that provided some extra scaffolding for the ELs but helped other students in the class develop their academic language as well.

This kind of creativity and strategic support embodies the spirit in which Diane Staehr Fenner and Sydney Snyder have written their new book: The question is not *if* English learners (ELs) can succeed in classrooms that are using more rigorous standards but *how*. This book is all about the *how*. It provides a toolbox of concrete strategies, examples, templates, activities, and reflection questions in a one-stop shop that can be used by K–12 teachers in grade-level and content classrooms across the country, as well as by ESOL specialists, to help ELs meet more demanding standards.

The book evolved from the work Diane and Sydney have done on a blog they write for Colorín Colorado, the nation's leading website serving educators and families of ELs. The blog, which was created with the support of the American Federation of Teachers (AFT) Innovation Fund, initially focused on the early implementation of the Common Core State Standards and then expanded to broader questions of how to help ELs meet more challenging standards, such as the Next Generation Science Standards and the other college- and career-readiness standards that states have adopted in recent years.

The most popular posts were those that focused on practical strategies and skills that could be applied in the classroom, such as choosing what kinds of background knowledge to teach, writing text-dependent questions, and teaching ELs how to do a close reading of a grade-level text. Educators were hungry for guidance and ideas on how to help ELs meet these new standards successfully, and the blog posts that Diane and Sydney wrote helped address that need as the standards were making their way into classrooms around the country.

We all saw firsthand that what teachers of ELs were being asked to do as the new standards were being rolled out was daunting in the best of circumstances—and most teachers of ELs were not working in the best of circumstances. I sat in on teacher discussions guided by Dr. Diane August, who was leading some of the earliest efforts to provide teachers with tools to help ELs meet newer, more demanding content and language standards. These conversations often started with a straightforward question, such as, "How can my ELs read grade-level text if they are two grade levels behind in their reading?"

The strategies that Diane and Sydney posted on the blog were informed by conversations like these from their visits to schools nationwide as they heard from teachers who were uncertain of how to proceed. At the same time, they began collaborating with Dr. August to expand the resources she was developing that would help teachers create lessons that were scaffolded for ELs and aligned with new standards, many of which are referenced in the following pages. Together, they created a variety of tools that would help make those leaps possible, planting many of the seeds for this book.

The approaches described in the book represent some shifts in how we think about ELs. Three in particular are worth highlighting:

1. ELs are everyone's kids.

2. Collaboration is essential for ELs' success.

3. Focusing on ELs' assets will set them up for success.

As Diane and Sydney suggest, the term *teachers of ELs* no longer applies only to teachers who have an ESOL certification. Diane and Sydney have written their book with that reality and a number of different educator perspectives in mind, including those of classroom and content area teachers who might be new to working with ELs and new to collaboration with ESOL specialists. Chapter by chapter, these educators will learn more about what ELs need and the challenges of learning content in a new language. For example, a geometry problem written in German included in the book will be a great tool for experiencing what it is like to try to solve a word problem in another language! Classroom and content area educators will also learn how to draw upon their own expertise in collaboration with ESOL colleagues and develop a better understanding of what kinds of expertise ESOL colleagues have to offer.

At the same time, ESOL specialists will discover innovative ideas and suggestions for collaborating and advocating on behalf of ELs in their particular setting, no matter what the current level of collaboration looks like. They will also find lots of tips for building collaborative relationships from their position and leading professional development for colleagues. Diane's prior work on the topic of advocacy, highlighted in her book *Advocating for English Learners: A Guide for Educators* (Staehr Fenner, 2014), informs the approach presented in the book and encourages all teachers to look beyond the nuts and bolts of the lesson plan to broader questions of equity and access.

Finally, Diane and Sydney take an assets-based approach—in other words, they focus on what ELs bring to the classroom, rather than on skills students have not yet developed. They encourage educators to invest time in learning more about students' strengths, experiences, interests, cultures, and home languages and to look at these resources as assets rather than deficits. Once educators make that shift, they can think about how to harness those resources in order to build upon an existing foundation, rather than start from scratch.

Readers will see that the book is written in a clear, accessible format with lots of hands-on examples across different ages and tools that make it a rich resource for any educator in any role. Ideas are also included for differentiating strategies for English learners at varying language proficiency levels. Teachers will be able to jump right in and try these ideas immediately, learning about the purpose and research base of particular strategies, as well as ways those strategies may help other students in the classroom. The strategies highlighted in the book, along with the featured templates and tools, will be easy to share among colleagues when coplanning or leading professional development.

Be prepared to take lots of notes as you read. Each chapter is sure to spark ideas as you think about how to apply the suggestions to your situation. And a final piece of advice is this: Don't hesitate to start small, even if you are working alone. Small steps, like Katy Padilla's science lunch club, can yield big results, and with these small steps, you will be on your way to unlocking your students' potential as they progress on their path to success.

Lydia Breiseth
Manager, Colorín Colorado

Reference

Staehr Fenner, D. (2014). *Advocating for English learners: A guide for educators.* Thousand Oaks, CA: Corwin.

Acknowledgments

When we initially decided to write this book, we figured it would be a pretty straightforward process. After all, we thought we had already developed a lot of the book's content through our Colorín Colorado blog posts, as well as the professional development we designed based on the content and our work with Diane August. Also, we had been working and writing together for years. However, the process that seemed to be initially straightforward soon grew in complexity as we explored the depths of our material and pushed ourselves to challenge our assumptions, all in the spirit of better serving the English learner (EL) students we love and the educators who interact with them every day. With that collaborative spirit in mind, we greatly benefited from the expertise many other colleagues provided to help shape this book. The process of writing became more and more of a team effort beyond the two of us working together, and as a result, there are quite a few people we'd like to acknowledge, as well as offer a heartfelt thank you.

We would first like to deeply thank two colleagues who provided ongoing expertise and support with the research cited in this book, as well as the flow of the chapters' content: Laura Kuti and Jill Kester. Their thoughtful comments, contributions, and initial reviews of the book's chapters helped strengthen each and every chapter of the book. We value their expertise and attention to detail nearly as much as we value their friendship. We would also like to recognize Maria Konkel for her help with the book in its earlier stages and for her much appreciated moral support in general. In addition to Laura, Jill, and Maria, we'd like to thank Maureen McCormick, ESOL teacher at Laurel Ridge Elementary School in Fairfax, Virginia. Maureen secured the beautifully written English learner writing sample you will see in Chapter 9. We would also like to thank Susan Hafler, Jennifer Rawlings, and Tina Vasquez for contributing authentic examples of classroom vignettes. We greatly appreciate the insight these educators shared.

The other critical part of our team effort was made up of multiple Corwin colleagues who each contributed specific expertise. We are especially appreciative of Corwin senior acquisitions editor Dan Alpert for immediately embracing the need for this book and helping us craft our vision and our message in the name of equity for ELs. Dan has been our supporter and source of inspiration for several years now through many projects, and we treasure his belief in us. In addition, we would like to give a special shout out to Maura Sullivan, marketing strategist, who tirelessly shared ideas and put those ideas into action to expand the book's reach and get it in the hands of those who could truly benefit from it. Also, we say thank you to Kim Greenberg, senior associate editor, Katie Crilley, editorial assistant, and Amy Schroller, production editor, for their tireless support during the publication process, as well as Jared Leighton for carefully editing the book.

Last but not least, we'd like to thank our families for their encouragement of us while we were writing and revising the book. Diane thanks her husband, David, and children, Zoe, Maya, and Carson. Sydney thanks her husband, Gus, and children, Sylvia and Iris. We are especially encouraged to see our own children learning about the book-publishing process through witnessing it firsthand and are hopeful our kids appreciate that their moms wear multiple hats.

Publisher's Acknowledgment

Corwin gratefully acknowledges the contributions of the following reviewer:

Odalys Igneri
Director of Science/STEM
New York City Department of Education,
Division of English Language Learners
New York, NY

About the Authors

Diane Staehr Fenner, PhD, is the president of SupportEd, LLC, a woman-owned small business that provides educators of ELs the skills and resources they need to champion ELs' success within and beyond students' classrooms. At SupportEd, Diane serves as project lead for the team's work, providing professional development, programmatic support, and research to school districts, states, organizations, and the U.S. Department of Education. Diane is an author of four books, a blogger for the Colorín Colorado website, and a frequent keynote presenter on EL education at conferences across North America. Diane was a research associate at George Washington University's Center for Equity and Excellence in Education; spent a decade as an ESOL teacher, dual-language assessment teacher, and ESOL assessment specialist in Fairfax County Public Schools, Virginia; and taught English in Veracruz, Mexico, and Berlin, Germany. These experiences showed her how crucial educators' collaboration, advocacy, and leadership are in supporting ELs, in addition to providing high-quality instruction. Diane earned her PhD in multilingual/multicultural education, with an emphasis in literacy, at George Mason University. She received her MAT in TESOL at the School for International Training and her master's in German at Penn State University. You can connect with her via e-mail at Diane@GetSupportEd.net or on Twitter at @DStaehrFenner.

Sydney Snyder, PhD, is a principal associate at SupportEd. In this role, Sydney has had significant experience in developing and conducting interactive professional development for teachers of ELs. She also has expertise in program management, curriculum development, research, and technical writing. Sydney has contributed to a series of blog posts on the Colorín Colorado website on strategies to support ELs. Sydney has extensive instructional experience, having taught ESOL/English as a foreign language for over fifteen years. She started her teaching career as a Peace Corps volunteer in Guinea, West Africa. This experience taught her the extent to which effective strategies can support students' language acquisition, even when resources are limited. She taught most recently in Falls Church, Virginia, where she was the K–12 ESOL curriculum and instruction resource teacher for the district. Sydney also served as an English teaching fellow at Gadja Mada University in Yogyakarta, Indonesia. Sydney earned her PhD in multilingual/multicultural education at George Mason University and her MAT in TESOL at the School for International Training. You can connect with her on e-mail at Sydney@GetSupportEd.net or on Twitter at @SydneySupportEd.

This book is dedicated to all teachers of English learners.
May you find the joy and passion that working with these students can bring.

We also dedicate this book to our families,
David, Zoe, Maya, and Carson Fenner and
Gus, Sylvia, and Iris Fahey, for the boundless love and support they offer.

Introduction

Have you noticed something different lately? Huge changes are taking place that affect all teachers' work with English learners (ELs). In today's educational climate, ELs are expected to develop a deep level of challenging content knowledge, engage with increasingly complex texts, and interact with their peers in more sophisticated ways than in the past, all while developing proficiency in English. The level of rigor has increased for all students, and ELs must meet the same challenging content standards as their English-proficient peers. As a result, all teachers of ELs must have the specialized skills and resources to be able to support their students in these practices. The phrase *teachers of ELs* no longer points directly to the ESOL teacher as the educator primarily responsible for supporting ELs' language development, as well as acclimation to the school setting. Rather, every teacher who works with at least one student acquiring English is now a *teacher of ELs*.

With the increasing number of ELs in today's classrooms, it is essential that *all* teachers understand and use strategies that effectively support ELs and can also model how to implement those strategies. In addition to all teachers of ELs being responsible for facilitating ELs' acquisition of English, all teachers of ELs also play an important role in helping students recognize that they are welcome members of the school and larger community and have linguistic and cultural resources to offer their classrooms and communities. During these times of great change, both in classroom expectations for ELs and nationwide, where EL students' place in the fabric of our society is facing increased scrutiny, the charge all teachers of ELs face has grown infinitely more crucial.

We recognize, however, that the realities of teacher preparation often fall short in preparing all teachers of ELs to meet these challenges. We know that many teachers of ELs were not provided with training to approach their work with ELs with a toolbox full of ready-to-go, research-based strategies to reach their learners. In addition to being able to use effective strategies to support ELs of different proficiency levels, all teachers of ELs are increasingly called upon to do even more in areas that are sometimes overlooked and undervalued. All teachers of ELs must now collaborate, advocate, and serve as leaders at their schools to unlock their ELs' potential in the classroom and also have a long-term positive effect in preparing them for college and careers. This book helps educators develop their own interpersonal, advocacy, and leadership skills that are essential to fully support their ELs and for educators to engage with other professionals as leaders.

As we wrote this book, we imagined all of the different types of current and future educators who might use the book and took steps to adapt the content, as well as structure of the book, to reach a wide audience. First, we were sure to frame the book around solid research that grounds the EL strategies you will encounter and apply. Next, we structured the book in a way that provides the background that teachers with less training in working with ELs will need to understand the support from research, the rationale, and the use of particular strategies. At the same time, we also included ample modeling and examples, application activities, and reflection questions that can support even an experienced teacher of ELs in deepening his or her understanding and use of the selected research-based strategies, weaving in scenarios that span grade levels and content areas. We are confident that anyone from kindergarten dual-language teachers to high school mathematics teachers can find useful strategies that they can apply to their context and can voice the rationale for using such strategies to support ELs by using this book. We are also sure that preservice teachers in teacher education programs will greatly benefit from reading and applying this book.

We have structured the book so that you can use it independently, as part of a course, or within a professional learning community (PLC), where ideally, ESOL teachers and content teachers can discuss and interact with the material together. The book is organized so that the first three chapters introduce our organizational framework and provide overarching strategies for ELs that are meant to be implemented in combination with other strategies shared in Chapters 4–9 of the book. Chapters 4–9 then each introduce a very specific strategy in a multilayered fashion that you can incorporate into your instruction. Each chapter includes scenarios that allow you to reflect on how the strategy might be applied to a particular classroom setting and tools to help you implement the strategies in your own setting. If you are reading this book as part of a PLC or in a coteaching partnership, you could select any of Chapters 2–9 to read, discuss, and implement in your classroom.

Even though integrating research-based strategies is crucial to ELs' success, educators must also constantly monitor and strengthen their professional skills with other educators to most effectively serve ELs. Our approach to work with ELs is unique, and so is this book. Because we believe the principles of collaboration, equity, advocacy, and leadership are fundamental to supporting ELs, we have woven these ideas into each chapter. As a result, we have included two sections at the end of each chapter that identify the role collaboration can have in relation to each specific strategy and also how equity, advocacy, and leadership can play out in the facilitation of each strategy. This book offers you a space in which you can hit the pause button, reflect on your own practice and your relationship with your colleagues, and recharge your batteries to better support ELs. We encourage you, as you implement the different strategies recommended in this book, to examine how you can strengthen your collaboration with your colleagues in service of equitable education for ELs. We also hope you will reflect on how you can bolster your advocacy and leadership skills to share the new considerations, approaches, and strategies that you are implementing with other educators as a result of your learning in this book. This book will provide you with the opportunities to begin conversations not only around strategies that all teachers can use to support their ELs but also around ways in which teachers can continue to enhance their own professional development and grow as leaders and advocates for ELs. So getting back to our original question, "Have you noticed something different lately?" We hope you have, and we know you will lead positive changes to better serve the ELs you work with.

A summary of each chapter follows.

Chapter 1: Why You Need This Book to Support ELs

Chapter 1 identifies the urgent need to provide ELs with the type of instructional support that they require to succeed academically and recognize they are equal members of any classroom. The chapter provides an overview of the current educational context, demographics, research, and climate within which ELs are being educated. We also introduce the five guiding principles that define our work with ELs and their educators. These principles provide an easily accessible theoretical framework that forms the foundation for the remaining chapters in the book.

Chapter 2: Using a Culturally Responsive Framework to Meet the Needs of ELs

Chapter 2 provides an understanding of the role culture plays in the education of ELs. The chapter includes working definitions of culture and culturally responsive teaching, a description of the characteristics of culture, and strategies to support culturally responsive teaching. It also provides opportunities for you to reflect on your own culture and how it shapes your instruction, classroom expectations, and interactions with ELs.

Chapter 3: Scaffolding Instruction for ELs

Chapter 3 shares an overview of what scaffolds are and why they are essential to incorporate into lessons for ELs. The chapter's deeper focus is on research-based strategies for selecting and developing scaffolds based on such factors as the academic task at hand and ELs' proficiency levels, as well as other background factors. The chapter includes examples of a variety of different types of scaffolds, checklists, and practical tools for you to plan and implement scaffolded lessons for ELs in your context.

Chapter 4: Academic Conversations: A Tool for Fostering ELs' Oral Language Development

Chapter 4 begins with a discussion of the importance of integrating academic conversations in the content-based instruction of ELs framed around relevant research. It introduces and provides examples of four student practices that will foster ELs' engagement in academic discussions in order to support their oral language development and their understanding of challenging content. The chapter also includes tools that you can use when planning and incorporating oral language activities into your instruction and offers recommendations for different types of oral language activities.

Chapter 5: Teaching Academic Language to ELs

Chapter 5 defines what academic language is and shares why it is critical for ELs to acquire academic language in order to access challenging content standards and be fully integrated into content classrooms. It also includes practical examples of how to analyze a text's academic language and how to teach the linguistic forms and functions necessary for ELs to interact with challenging grade-level texts and topics. The chapter gives you guidance on how to leverage different types of teachers' strengths in order to effectively collaborate, thereby weaving together academic language and content instruction.

Chapter 6: Vocabulary Instruction and ELs

Chapter 6 describes why focused teaching of academic vocabulary is critical to ELs' academic achievement. Recognizing that teachers must select vocabulary for ELs carefully and judiciously, the chapter includes research-based guidelines on selecting what vocabulary to teach that will have the most benefit for ELs, as well as strategies for teaching and reinforcing those new words. The chapter also offers a tool for planning lessons focused on content-specific vocabulary.

Chapter 7: Teaching ELs Background Knowledge

Chapter 7 presents research on the role of background knowledge in ELs' reading comprehension and addresses the need to develop a new approach to the teaching of background knowledge to ELs within a focus of close reading. It presents a new four-step framework for deciding which types of background knowledge to teach ELs and ways to activate and teach background knowledge concisely. The chapter models several activities that you can use in your own planning and instruction to help you put the EL background knowledge framework into practice.

Chapter 8: Supporting ELs' Reading for Multiple Purposes Through the Use of Scaffolded Text-Dependent Questions

Chapter 8 synthesizes relevant research, discusses what it means for ELs to read for multiple purposes, and provides a framework that allows ELs to unlock the meaning of complex text. The chapter describes what text-dependent questions (TDQs) are and how they can be a tool to support ELs' reading for multiple purposes. It also includes recommendations, tools, and practical tips for you to develop and scaffold TDQs to effectively support ELs of varying proficiency levels as they engage with challenging text on multiple levels.

Chapter 9: Formative Assessment for ELs

Chapter 9 highlights the necessity of creating formative assessments that assess ELs' acquisition of academic language and content. The chapter includes a definition of formative assessment and provides a summary of relevant research on the practice of formative assessment for ELs. It also includes guidance on creating appropriate classroom assessments for ELs based on ELs' proficiency levels and offers you the opportunity to apply what you've learned to your own formative assessment of ELs.

Why You Need This Book to Support ELs

How many of you are language teachers?

When we recently facilitated a professional-development session, we asked a group of approximately sixty content and English for speakers of other languages (ESOL) teachers that same question. Only the thirty or so ESOL teachers in the room raised their hands. We then shared with the group that everyone should be raising their hands, which led to some teachers' surprised looks. Both groups of teachers discussed that many changes had taken place in their schools during the past few years, including (but not limited to) new content standards, new English language development (ELD) standards,[1] a new teacher evaluation system, and new state regulations aimed at more inclusive instruction of ELs. The content teachers, in particular, were exhausted and admittedly feeling even more "stretched" at now being expected to also serve as their English learners' (ELs') language teachers. Some of them wondered whether that wasn't supposed to be the ESOL teachers' job.

Times have changed. In the past, ESOL teachers tended to physically remove ELs from the content or grade-level teachers' classrooms, providing them ESOL instruction in a separate location. Now, more and more schools, districts, and even some states are moving to more inclusive instructional models in which ELs spend more of their time with their grade-level peers, and ESOL teachers provide support within content classrooms. The move by states to frame content instruction around challenging college- and

---

1. Some states might use the term English language proficiency (ELP) standards.

career-readiness standards (CCRS) solidifies that *all* teachers are to be teachers of academic language as well as content (Gottlieb, 2016; Walqui & van Lier, 2010). But many of you who are content teachers have not yet been trained in how to expand your repertoire to wear both hats—that of language teacher and that of content teacher—and will understandably need some guidance. Many of you who are ESOL teachers may not have received training in how to effectively collaborate with content teachers to learn from each other and work together to educate ELs and will need extra support in this area.

This chapter will provide a new framework for equitable EL education. It will first outline the sense of urgency in providing ELs the type of instructional support they need to be successful in today's challenging classrooms and also be respected and valued on a socioemotional level. It will include a brief synthesis of relevant current research and practice that underscores the dynamic educational landscape in which ELs are educated. It will also address shifts in content standards and subsequent teacher expertise that are necessary to effectively teach ELs. The bulk of the chapter will focus on the five guiding principles that frame the content of this book, as well as all of our work with ELs. For each guiding principle, we provide a brief research-based rationale for the principle, as well as practical tools for you to use to apply the principle to your own practice. The chapter ends with the opportunity for you to develop your own guiding principles, create a school or district vision for the equitable education of ELs, and craft your own "elevator speech" to define your role in supporting ELs.

What Is the Framework for Equitable and Excellent EL Education?

With increased rigor in standards come more challenging assessments, and the achievement gap between ELs and non-ELs is certainly not getting any narrower. Through our work with teachers and administrators who serve ELs, we recognize the need for a framework that identifies and addresses the need for all teachers to adjust their instruction to recognize ELs' strengths, as well as to support their needs. This framework for equitable and excellent EL education encompasses many areas related to instruction that are necessary for ELs to meaningfully engage in challenging content classes and develop their language skills. In addition, our framework is unique in that it also recognizes the need for all teachers of ELs to collaborate and operate within a context of equity, advocacy, and leadership to continually develop as professionals in order to best support ELs. The framework is driven by our five guiding principles, which we share in detail later in this chapter. Figure 1.1 provides a visual representation of the framework.

FIGURE 1.1 Framework for Equitable and Excellent EL Education

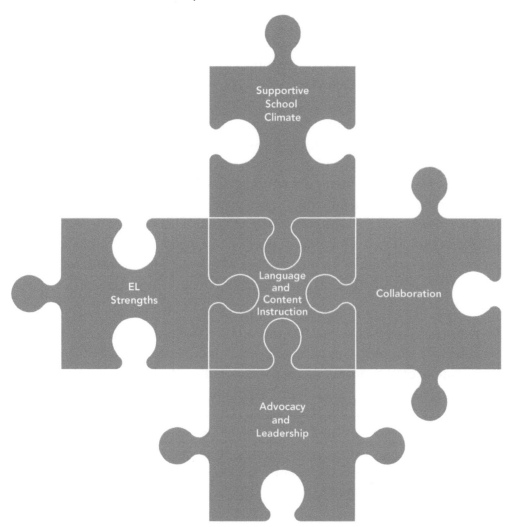

What Is the Sense of Urgency Around ELs' Equitable and Excellent Learning?

Our sense of urgency for this book stems from our synthesis of current research and practice, as well as our taking the pulse of ELs' education in our work with teachers and students across the country. Not only do we recognize the achievement gap that is not going away, but we are also concerned about ELs' and their families' sense of being welcomed and valued members of schools and communities (Ferguson, 2008; Henderson & Mapp, 2002; Staehr Fenner, 2014a). When ELs live in families that are struggling economically, as well as with learning English (Staehr Fenner, 2014a), their families' stressors can permeate all aspects of their education and provide an extra level of anxiety. As educators, it is our duty to promote not only equity but help our ELs reach their potential for excellence.

ELs' equity and excellence go beyond their success inside classroom walls, as assessed by such quantitative measures as test scores and attendance rates. EL equity and excellence extend to our moral obligation as educators to ensure that our ELs, who often navigate complex, conflicting cultural balances between home and school, are supported on a socioemotional, holistic level. ELs must sense that their teachers are providing a safe space in which they can learn and also trust their teachers enough to reach out to them if a personal factor is providing a barrier their learning. At a time in which issues such as immigration and poverty tend to influence ELs in a marked way, we must be especially vigilant and collaborate to provide a support network to embrace our ELs and encourage them to learn and thrive on many levels. While working toward ELs' equity, we must recognize EL students' inherent excellence and strive to unlock it.

As daunting as our charge as educators of ELs may seem on an academic and personal level, it often does not take heroic acts to help ELs feel welcome. One example of supporting ELs on a socioemotional level is an initiative to say ELs' names correctly. Called the "My Name, My Identity" campaign,[2] the National Association for Bilingual Education, the Santa Clara Office of Education, and McGraw-Hill Education have partnered to promote educators pronouncing diverse students' names correctly as a way to support their identities and integration into schools. As educators, we need to be aware of who our ELs are not just academically but also personally in order to develop a plan to recognize and build upon their strengths and meet their needs.

> *What are some ways that you or your school help make ELs and their families feel welcome? What other ideas do you have?*

How Are ELs' Demographics Changing?

Part of understanding who your ELs are begins with having a sense of the larger context for EL education. According to the National Center for Education Statistics, 9.3 percent of students in kindergarten through Grade 12 in the United States are ELs, or an estimated 4.4 million students. Between 2002 and 2003 and 2012 and 2013, thirty-nine states experienced an increase in the percentage of ELs in their public schools (U.S. Department of Education, 2015). Eighty-five percent of prekindergarten to fifth-grade ELs

---

2. Visit https://www.mynamemyidentity.org.

were born in the United States while 62 percent of sixth- to twelfth-grade ELs were born in the United States (Zong & Batalova, 2015).

Of that 9.3 percent, the top five languages spoken by ELs are Spanish (3,770,816), Arabic (109,170), Chinese (107,825), English (91,669), and Vietnamese (89,705). While it may seem surprising that English is on the list of the top-five languages, there are some cases where English would be reported as the home language. Examples of situations in which English might be reported as an English learner's home language include students who live in multilingual households and students adopted from other countries who speak English at home but also have been raised speaking another language. Although Spanish is the language most often spoken by ELs, five states (Alaska, Hawaii, Maine, Montana, and Vermont) have EL populations whose top language is a language other than Spanish (Migration Policy Institute, 2015).

> *Who are your ELs? What percentage of students in your school or district are ELs? What kind of growth has your school or district experienced over the last 10 years? What languages do your ELs speak?*

What Are ELs' Opportunity and Achievement Gaps?

ELs tend to experience significant opportunity and achievement gaps (NCELA, 2015a, 2015b, 2015c). For example, they frequently attend underfunded, under-resourced schools that experience regular teacher turnover. Those students who need the most stability due to the many changes they experience in their lives tend to be confronted with the least. In addition, ELs' achievement scores tend to be lower than those of non-ELs (NCELA, 2015b). Further, ELs experience a disproportionate representation in remedial, special, and gifted education programs. For example, 7 percent of non-ELs are enrolled in gifted and talented programs nationwide, compared with only 2 percent of ELs. (Donovan & Cross, 2002; Zehler et al., 2003). These gaps also extend to EL student retention rates. In Grades K–6, ELs represented 14 percent of students enrolled in public schools nationwide but 18 percent of students retained in 2011–2012. In Grades 9–12, ELs represented 5 percent of students enrolled in public schools nationwide but 11 percent of students held back in 2011–2012 (NCELA, 2015c). Further, wide disparities exist between graduation rates between ELs and non-ELs. Nationwide, 79 percent of all students graduate from high school, compared with 57 percent of ELs, based on data from the 2010–2011 school year, according to the National Center for Education Statistics (Stetser & Stillwell, 2014). There is great variance between and among states in their EL graduation rates. We strongly encourage you to analyze your school or district data to determine what opportunity and achievement gaps exist between your non-ELs and ELs.

What Shifts Have Occurred in Content Standards, and How Do These Affect ELs?

Now that we have situated our work to support ELs within a larger context, we will focus on a major change that has recently occurred that affects ELs' education. States have adopted college and career readiness standards (CCRS), which are rigorous standards in English language arts and mathematics whose goal is preparing all students for college and careers by the time they graduate from high school (U.S. Department of Education, n.d.). Under the umbrella of CCRS are the Common Core State Standards (CCSS).

Over the past few years, many voices of EL teachers, researchers, policy makers, and practitioners have been heard in the discussion of what we should keep in mind when implementing CCRS with ELs. When thinking of what is important when implementing CCRS with ELs at a very high level, we like to ground our thoughts in the three shifts in the CCSS for English language arts and literacy, as defined by Achieve the Core,[3] and adapt those shifts to encompass what *all* teachers must do to support ELs. While we recognize that ELs also take part in CCRS-aligned mathematics instruction, we believe a close examination of how to address the ELA and literacy shifts is a good place to start. In addition, the components of the shifts are transferable to other subject areas. Figure 1.2 provides an overview of the three shifts and what all teachers of ELs must to do support ELs.

What Are the Guiding Principles That We Use to Frame Our Work With ELs and This Book?

In our work supporting ELs and their teachers, we often analyze complex educational issues and try to make sense of them as they apply to ELs (such as the three shifts we detailed earlier), phrasing our findings and recommendations in a way that resonates with educators in different roles. Along those lines, we have developed a set of five guiding principles that synthesize our beliefs, grounded in research and practice, about the education of ELs. You will see these guiding principles exemplified in our recommendations and strategies throughout the chapters of this book. In this chapter, for each guiding principle, we provide an explanation of what

---

3. See http://achievethecore.org/page/277/the-common-core-shifts-at-a-glance

FIGURE 1.2 Three Shifts and Teachers of ELs

CCRS for ELA and Literacy Shift	To address this shift, all teachers of ELs must be able to . . .	Strategies That Cut Across All Shifts
1. Regular practice with complex text and its academic language	• Analyze complex texts for academic language that might impede ELs' comprehension • Explicitly teach the academic language necessary to comprehend complex texts so that ELs can draw on these texts to speak and write across content areas • Choose and adapt supplementary texts in English and/or ELs' home language(s) based on ELs' reading level, English language proficiency level, background, and culture • Teach ELs strategies to determine the meaning of unfamiliar vocabulary words (e.g., cognates, prefixes, roots, and suffixes) • Teach the meanings of words with multiple definitions, idiomatic expressions, and technical terms	• Collaborate with ESOL teachers to share expertise, plan instruction and assessment, deliver instruction, and revise lesson plans on an ongoing basis • Use English language proficiency and CCRS standards to plan instruction • Scaffold and support instruction for ELs at different proficiency levels • Design appropriate classroom assessments so that ELs can demonstrate what they know and can do
2. Reading, writing, and speaking grounded in evidence from both literary and informational text	• Know students' backgrounds and cultures, and integrate their backgrounds and cultures into instruction • Provide scaffolds and structures so that ELs can cite evidence from different types of text at different levels of complexity and/or in their home language(s) • Create text-dependent questions that are scaffolded for students at different levels of English language proficiency • Teach ELs the academic language necessary so that they can use evidence from literary and informational text in reading, writing, speaking, and listening • Provide ELs with linguistic structures and supports so that they can cite sources, avoid plagiarism, synthesize information from grade-level complex text, and create argumentative and/or persuasive speech and writing	
3. Building knowledge through content-rich nonfiction	• Activate and/or provide an appropriate amount of ELs' background knowledge about the content and structure of nonfiction text • Integrate ELs' background knowledge and culture into instruction to support their comprehension of nonfiction • Teach ELs differences between the structure of informational text and literary text • Draw from ELs' home language reading literacy skills as a support as appropriate • Adapt and/or supplement grade-level complex texts for ELs at lower levels of English language proficiency while also giving them access to scaffolded grade-level text	

Source: Adapted with permission by TESOL International Association. Copyright 2013. All rights reserved.

that principle means to us, we briefly share the research on which it is based, and we also leave you with reflection questions and practical tools that you can use to support your understanding of the principles as they apply to your context. Our guiding principles are as follows:

1. ELs bring many strengths to the classroom.

2. ELs learn best when they are taught in a welcoming and supportive school climate.

3. ELs should be taught language and content simultaneously.

4. ELs benefit when their teachers collaborate to share their expertise.

5. ELs excel when their teachers leverage advocacy and leadership skills.

Guiding Principle 1: ELs bring many strengths to the classroom.

ELs enter the classroom with a rich background of cultural and linguistic experiences that are often overlooked or underappreciated by their schools and teachers. Teachers and administrators who are not trained in ESOL or bilingual education are more likely to hold "deficit" perceptions of ELs (Baecher, Knoll, & Patti, 2013; Gándara, Maxwell-Jolly, & Driscoll, 2005; Reeves, 2006). In order to effectively educate ELs, it is important to first recognize the set of knowledge and skills that they already have. Moll, Amanti, Neff, and Gonzalez (1992) refer to these accumulated bodies of knowledge and skills as *funds of knowledge*. ELs' funds of knowledge should be incorporated into instruction, so as to give value to the life experiences of the students and to support their academic learning. For example, a refugee student may enter the U.S. education system with gaps in his or her education due to interrupted schooling, low-level literacy skills, and beginner-level English language proficiency. However, that same student might bring with him or her a strong oral tradition of sharing knowledge, persistence in overcoming obstacles, and creative problem-solving skills. A teacher educating this student should look for ways to build on these strengths as a tool for instruction, such as having oral language activities linked to writing tasks.

Providing ELs opportunities to share their backgrounds, experiences, and ideas benefits other students as well. Listening to and responding to diverse perspectives helps prepare all students to live in a multicultural society and interact with individuals from different backgrounds (Gorski, 2010). In addition, with more states recognizing the value of bilingualism and biliteracy,[4] ELs can serve as valuable language models for non-ELs studying world languages and in dual-language settings. The growing popularity of dual-language programs, often driven by non-EL parent interest, across the United States has been well documented (U.S. Department of Education, 2015). In such programs, ELs serve as linguistic models for non-ELs who are learning the target language. In addition, ELs can also share cultural and linguistic insights in less formal ways during content instruction. For example, in a discussion on U.S. elections, ELs who were born in countries outside the United States might share what the election process looks like in their home countries. Such straightforward ways to include ELs and highlight their perspectives can go a long way in creating an environment conducive to building their trust and facilitating deeper learning.

> *What linguistic and cultural strengths do the ELs that you work with bring to your classroom? How do you learn about and build upon these strengths?*

Guiding Principle 2: ELs learn best when they are taught in a welcoming and supportive school climate.

A school culture that supports equitable and excellent educational opportunities for ELs includes school-wide beliefs about the potential of ELs, interest in and appreciation for ELs' culture, and the desire to foster positive relationships with the families of ELs. As the leaders of the school, the principals influence this culture in terms of their commitment to the academic success of ELs, how they speak to and about ELs and their families, the types of professional development they offer staff, and how they evaluate teachers' work with ELs (Alford & Niño, 2011; Leithwood, Louis, Anderson, & Wahlstrom, 2004). Unfortunately, many school administrators have received insufficient training in how to create a school climate that fully embraces ELs as part of the school community and effectively supports their language and content learning (Staehr Fenner, 2014a). Administrators who are well versed in EL-oriented strengths and dispositions tend to be rare. Most administrators' educational experiences are far removed from ESOL instruction (Shumate, Muñoz, & Winter, 2005). However, in no way do we blame principals for this pervasive lack of training when it comes to ELs.

The principal's role is critical in developing a positive school culture, which includes the values, beliefs, and norms that characterize the school (Deal & Peterson, 2009). In building a school culture that supports high achievement for all ELs, shared beliefs at the school level should include recognition of the benefits of multilingualism, an appreciation of ELs' culture, and the need to overcome stereotypes and a deficit paradigm. The principal influences this culture in serving as a key spokesperson for the school, as an evaluator

---

4. State Laws Regarding the Seal of Biliteracy: http://sealofbiliteracy.org.

of practices, and as a model of commitment to student success (Alford & Niño, 2011). While the principal may set the tone in terms of school climate, the teaching staff play a large role in creating a welcoming school culture conducive to supporting ELs and their families. Application Activity 1.1 provides you with an opportunity to reflect on your school climate and whether or not your school uses strategies to help ELs and their families feel welcome.

APPLICATION ACTIVITY 1.1

Action Steps to Create a Welcoming Environment

First, review each of the following strategies found in Figure 1.3 to decide if you are currently making ELs and their families feel welcome in these ways. Then, prioritize three action steps, so you can create a more welcoming environment for ELs and their families.

FIGURE 1.3   EL and Family Welcoming Checklist

EL and Family Welcome Strategy At our school, do we . . .	Yes	No
Display student work on the walls (including work in home languages)?		
Have visible signs in students' home languages?		
Communicate with families in a variety of ways (e.g., information sent home in home language, phone calls, and home visits)?		
Display maps and flags of students' home countries?		
Have a bilingual staff or bilingual volunteers who can meet with families as needed?		
Provide staff opportunities to learn some common phrases in families' home languages and key information about families' cultures?		
Invite EL families to volunteer in the school (e.g., helping in a classroom or being a resource for other families)?		
Provide services that remove barriers that prevent EL families from attending school events (e.g., childcare, interpreters, and transportation)?		
Have bilingual books in students' home languages in the school library and classrooms?		
Connect new families with a contact person who speaks their home language and offer tours of the schools in home languages?		
Host events specifically for EL families (e.g., back-to-school events and international picnics)?		
Have a parent room with bilingual magazines, school information, and a computer for families to use?		

Source: Adapted from Breiseth, L., Robertson, K., & Lafond, S. (2011). *A guide for engaging ELL families: 20 strategies for school leaders.* Washington, DC: Colorín Colorado. Retrieved from http://www.colorincolorado.org/sites/default/files/Engaging_ELL_Families_FINAL.pdf

Action Steps: To make a more welcoming environment for ELs and families of ELs, we will . . .

1.

2.

3.

Guiding Principle 3: ELs should be taught language and content simultaneously.

As we stated earlier in this chapter, the CCRS identify specific language practices that students must engage in as they grapple with new content. In order to assist ELs in meeting challenging content standards, they will need language instruction that closely corresponds to the content they are learning. For example, direct instruction in academic language and language skills that provide a bridge to content standards will bolster ELs' achievement in specific content areas. In addition, language is acquired most effectively when it is taught through meaningful content and includes opportunities for students to practice all four modalities of language learning (i.e., speaking, listening, reading, and writing) using authentic texts and tasks wherever possible. Also, as more districts move toward collaborative, inclusive models of ESOL instruction in which ELs receive language support as part of their content classes, all teachers must learn how to teach language and content in an integrated way. Finally, with teachers' limited time and increasing demands placed on ELs, it is beneficial to maximize instructional time to teach language, as well as content. If you teach both academic language and content, you may find that students who are not ELs may also benefit from your focus on language.

The strategies presented in this book are intended to facilitate the teaching of language and content in tandem by ESOL as well as content teachers. We recognize it can be a challenge to step outside your area of expertise, especially when you may not have received adequate resources or training on teaching ELs. However, we hope that as you work through the chapters and try out the strategies used in this book (ideally, together with a colleague or two), you will gain increasing confidence in how to better support your ELs as they acquire language and content. Since the CCRS call for all teachers to teach academic language and challenging content simultaneously, all teachers must be skilled with new strategies that they can use with their ELs (as well as with their other students) under this new paradigm. Figure 1.4 outlines some—but not all—ways a content and an ESOL teacher can plan and prepare for, teach, and assess lessons that incorporate academic-language instruction along with content instruction.

FIGURE 1.4 Possible Roles of Teachers in Teaching Language and Content

Components of Instruction	Content Teacher	ESOL Teacher	Both
Planning and preparing for the lesson	• Select content • Identify content objectives • Identify content-specific vocabulary and language needed for students to meet content objectives	• Analyze language demands of lesson and texts • Identify language objectives • Develop supporting materials for ELs	• Reach consensus on language objectives • Determine key vocabulary • Decide on strategies for teaching and practicing academic language at sentence and discourse levels
Teaching the lesson	• Incorporate additional opportunities to practice academic language into lesson • Coteach large group of students, embedding scaffolds for ELs	• Work with small groups of ELs as needed to support language development • Coteach large group of students, embedding scaffolds for ELs	• Teach academic vocabulary and language • Teach language-focused minilessons (e.g., compound sentence structure or connecting ideas at discourse level)
Assessing student learning	• Develop assessment of content objectives • Determine scoring mechanism (e.g., rubric or checklist)	• Add assessment of language to assessment of content for ELs • Scaffold assessment as needed for ELs (e.g., word banks, bilingual glossaries, or visuals)	• Determine how ELs will be assessed • Reflect on ELs' assessment results, and determine how to adjust instruction of content and language • Work with ELs needing additional support

Guiding Principle 4: ELs benefit when their teachers collaborate to share their expertise.

The new demands of standards-based instruction call for increased collaboration between ESOL and content teachers (Honigsfeld & Dove, 2010, 2014; TESOL, 2016; Valdés, Kibler, & Walqui, 2014). Not only must the quantity of collaboration increase but also we must pay attention to the quality of the collaboration. In order to strengthen the quality of the collaborative experience, we offer a unique perspective by drawing from Edwards's (2011) framework of distributed expertise. This framework underscores that "building and using common knowledge is an important feature of the relational expertise required for working across the practice boundaries on complex tasks" (p. 33). When teachers successfully collaborate, they are able to leverage their specific expertise in the complex task of supporting of ELs' acquisition of language and content knowledge.

In addition, they can draw on each other's strengths to provide the kind of socioemotional support that is crucial to ELs so that students realize they are welcome and valued members of the classroom and school community.

ESOL teachers can share their knowledge of second language acquisition and language pedagogy and can model strategies that will support content teachers in becoming teachers of language, in addition to teachers of content (Maxwell, 2013; Valdés et al., 2014). Similarly, content teachers can share with ESOL teachers the skills and knowledge that all students, including ELs, will need to be successful in a particular content area. Both types of teachers can support each other in ensuring that ELs' individual personal characteristics (e.g., motivation and learning preferences), as well as their backgrounds (e.g., literacy in the home language and amount and/or quality of previous schooling), are part of the schooling equation.

In order to foster such high-quality collaboration, schools must have a structure in place so that teachers can work together in a systematic and ongoing way and share their expertise with one another. During this time of increased rigor and expectations for ELs, administrators must build time into schedules for collaboration to occur, make it a priority for the entire staff, and ensure it is occurring. If planning time provided by administrators is still insufficient, we recommend that teachers take it upon themselves to creatively look for ways to informally collaborate. In addition, administrators should create structures in which the quality of the collaboration is realized. In this way, all teachers should see themselves as experts in their area of expertise in service of ELs. Application Activity 1.2 provides options to consider when the quantity of coplanning time is limited.

APPLICATION ACTIVITY 1.2

Collaborating With Limited Planning Time

Review each of the options for ESOL and content teacher collaboration when time is limited in Figure 1.5. For each option, determine whether the recommendation is possible to use in your context and what steps you would need to implement it. Add any additional suggestions in the space provided. Then, answer the reflection questions that follow.

FIGURE 1.5 Options for ESOL and Content Teacher Collaboration When Time Is Limited

Option	Consider This Option? (Y/N)	Plan to Implement it
1. Plan online.		
2. Look for informal ways to check in (e.g., during lunch or after school).		
3. Carve out time to plan (begin monthly), and divide the workload.		
4. Identify specific and shared tasks for the ESOL teacher and content teacher to support ELs.		
5. Observe each other teaching, and discuss what you saw.		
6. My/our new idea:		

Discussion Questions

1. Why did you choose the collaboration model or strategy that you did?

2. When and how might you use this model or strategy?

3. What steps do you need to take in order to implement it successfully in your context (i.e., scheduling, planning time, or resources)?

Guiding Principle 5: ELs excel when their teachers leverage advocacy and leadership skills.

Being aware of and using strategies that support ELs' access to content and language is a wonderful start that requires expertise and energy, but it's not enough in order for ELs to experience what it means to have an equitable and excellent education. Because many inequities and injustices still exist for ELs, it's up to educators like you to speak on behalf of those ELs and their families who have not yet developed a strong voice of their own due to their acquisition of English and/or knowledge of the U.S. education system (Staehr Fenner, 2014a). To that end, in each chapter of the book, we include a section on ways in which to draw from your leadership skills to advocate for ELs' equitable education.

Advocating for ELs can sometimes be a daunting task. In order to begin advocating for ELs, it's often helpful to get a sense of what the larger advocacy issues may be to decide which direction your advocacy should take. Figure 1.6 provides an equity audit, which can help you reflect on your context at the school level. Working through this equity audit can support you in deciding which areas of advocacy for ELs present the highest needs. You simply can't take on each injustice simultaneously, and prioritizing the top advocacy issues will help you determine your path forward.

FIGURE 1.6 EL Advocacy Equity Audit

Potential EL Advocacy Issue	Questions to Ask: To What Degree . . .	Response	Action Items
Role of ESOL teacher	Are ESOL teachers working as experts and consultants and collaborating with general-education teachers?	Not at all Somewhat Extensively	
Instructional materials and curriculum	Are instructional materials and curriculum appropriate for ELs?	Not at all Somewhat Extensively	
Professional development	Does professional development focus on preparing *all* teachers to teach academic language and content to ELs?	Not at all Somewhat Extensively	
Assessment	Are teachers aware of demands of content assessments for ELs? Are they using effective formative assessments with ELs?	Not at all Somewhat Extensively	
EL family outreach	Are EL parents and families aware of the school's expectations of all students and supports available to them?	Not at all Somewhat Extensively	
Teacher evaluation and coaching	Is teacher evaluation and coaching for all teachers supporting teachers so that their ELs can access challenging content?	Not at all Somewhat Extensively	

Note: The concept is adapted from Betty J. Alford and Mary Catherine Niño's *equity audit,* which appears in *Leading Academic Achievement for English Language Learners: A Guide for Principals* (Corwin, 2011).

After you have taken the steps to determine which areas of advocacy you might like to prioritize at the school or district level, it's time to consider how you will approach your advocacy. In Figure 1.7, we offer the following EL advocacy steps and implementation suggestions for each step to collaborate and advocate on behalf of ELs.

While it's always beneficial to reflect on your advocacy priorities and steps, in order to effectively advocate for ELs' equitable and excellent learning, you will also need to draw from and, in some cases, develop the necessary leadership skills to do so. With the new roles ESOL and content teachers are taking on in order for their ELs to successfully engage with the CCRS, teachers will also need to leverage a wider range of leadership skills. While many definitions exist, leadership, in general, can be defined as "the process of influencing . . . the behavior of others in order to reach a shared goal" (Northouse, 2007; Stogdill, 1950). To advocate for ELs and support their equitable and excellent education, you have to first increase your awareness of your own leadership skills and build upon those skills to make

FIGURE 1.7 Steps for EL Advocacy and Implementation Suggestions

EL Advocacy Step	Implementation Suggestions for Each Step
1. Begin thoughtfully	Consider all of the areas in which you can advocate for ELs and collaborate to benefit them. Choose one or two areas to focus on in which you have the agency to enact changes, and plan out what your action steps will look like.
2. Build alliances first with those who seem open	Begin by carefully considering colleagues who seem open to working with ELs and supporting them. Approach those colleagues first to ascertain whether they would like to collaborate with you.
3. Demonstrate empathy first	When collaborating with content teachers or administrators, show your empathy for their challenges and frustrations related to working with ELs. Acknowledge those areas they find to be most challenging, such as their comprehension of grade-level texts.
4. Respect educators' expertise	Voice your understanding of their content area expertise so you can leverage it together. Operating within a strengths perspective when it comes to your colleagues (as well as your students) will go a long way.
5. Operate from a strengths-based perspective of ELs	While you acknowledge the challenges ELs may present content teachers and administrators, you may be the lone voice who embodies a strengths-based perspective of ELs. Aim to highlight ELs' contributions to classrooms, such as their home language, culture, and/or families' commitment to education.
6. Showcase EL achievement	Underscore the ways in which ELs make progress, be it academic or social. Often, ELs' progress may not be as apparent or obvious as it is with non-ELs.
7. Offer support and time for collaboration	Suggest concrete ways in which you can offer guidance to other teachers and/or administrators so that they can better serve ELs. Some supports include an ESOL teacher sharing a graphic organizer for ELs with a content teacher or a content teacher sharing a content lesson plan ahead of time with an ESOL teacher.

changes occur. As this is an area that teachers are typically not trained in, administrators need to use their own leadership skills and help develop these skills in their teachers. In our work with ELs, we have seen many educators rise up as leaders who successfully advocate for ELs, serve as allies to ELs, and bring about much-needed changes. It's truly inspiring to witness teachers serve ELs on multiple levels to impact change.

In order to leverage these leadership skills to advocate for ELs, it takes a strong foundation of interpersonal skills, many of which we are not explicitly taught or are not even mentioned in our preparation as educators. These interpersonal skills are increasingly important in today's educational landscape, which relies on more collaboration in order to lead and support ELs' equitable education. Figure 1.8 provides a self-awareness checklist[5] and discussion questions about a sampling of crucial leadership skills that you may need to draw from to advocate for ELs and strengthen your voice as a leader.

---

5. Adapted from Riggio and Tan (2014).

FIGURE 1.8 Leadership Skills Self-Awareness Checklist

Leadership Skill or Attribute	Description	My Rating: Low (1) to High (5)
Character	The moral self that reflects the principles and ideals of the collective to which the leader belongs, including trustworthiness and credibility	1 2 3 4 5
Political skills	Social astuteness, networking ability, sincerity, integrity, honesty, charisma, and not being seen as manipulative	1 2 3 4 5
Nonverbal communication	Sensitivity to colleagues; use of accepted behaviors, such as nodding; body openness	1 2 3 4 5
Conflict resolution	Managing one's own and others' emotional experiences, establishing norms and rules, and refocusing on tasks at hand	1 2 3 4 5
Interpersonal skills	Relationship development, trust, intercultural sensitivity, providing feedback, motivating and persuading others, empathy, and support	1 2 3 4 5
Interpersonal communication skills	Skill in sending and receiving nonverbal and emotional messages, listening and speaking skills, and effectively engaging others in conversation	1 2 3 4 5

Source: Adapted from Riggio, R. & Tan, S. (2014). *Leader interpersonal and influence skills: The soft skills of leadership.* New York: Routledge.

1. What area(s) am I strongest in?
2. What area(s) am I weakest in?
3. What is one example of how each leadership skill affects my work with ELs?
4. What implications are there for my leadership in advocating for and supporting ELs?

How Do I Get Started Using All Five Guiding Principles?

The following three-step application activity will support you to analyze our five guiding principles, draw from them to create your own guiding principles, create a vision for your school or district's equitable and excellent instruction of ELs, and culminate the process by developing an elevator speech for your role in ensuring ELs' equitable education. We find in our work that we have very precious little time to reflect on where we are in order to plan for where we'd like to go. This application activity will give you the gift of space for reflection. First, you will compare our guiding principles with your own. If you don't already approach your work with ELs from a set of guiding principles, this application activity will allow you the time and place for reflection in order to develop your own guiding principles. Then, you will use your vision to create a succinct elevator speech to define your role and accountability in the process. By doing so, you will use this chapter's contents to create an aligned framework to support your work with ELs that will guide you as you work through the subsequent chapters.

Step 1. Using Figure 1.9, review the book's five guiding principles, compare them with your own, and add any comments you have.

FIGURE 1.9 Comparison of Guiding Principles

Book's Guiding Principle	My/Our Guiding Principle	Comments
1. ELs bring many strengths to the classroom.		
2. ELs learn best when they are taught in a welcoming and supportive school climate.		
3. ELs should be taught language and content simultaneously.		
4. ELs benefit when their teachers collaborate to leverage their expertise.		
5. In order for ELs to have an equitable education, teachers need to develop advocacy and leadership skills.		

Step 2. Drawing from your own guiding principles, create a vision for educating ELs in your school.

Your school or district needs to have a vision so that all stakeholders can share a common direction and destination in order to align their improvement efforts (Gabriel & Farmer, 2009). We suggest convening a group of educators committed to ELs' equitable and excellent education to develop a shared vision statement for your school or district. You may need to meet several times to revise and refine the vision statement, but your work will certainly pay off. For example, the Fairfax County (Virginia) Public Schools' ESOL Department vision reads:

ESOL services prepares students to be college and career ready by developing proficiency in the English language. ESOL services help students achieve academic success, develop critical thinking skills, and solve problems.[6]

To create your vision, consider these questions:

1. Which aspects of your guiding principles from Figure 1.9 resonate the most with you?

---

6. See https://www.fcps.edu/academics/academic-overview/english-speakers-other-languages-esol.

2. What content from your guiding principles can you synthesize into succinct key ideas, values, and beliefs regarding equitably educating ELs?

Step 3. Referring to your vision for equitably educating ELs, outline a brief elevator speech that defines your role in the process.

One way for ESOL and content teachers to reflect upon their roles and effectively explain them to others is to develop an *elevator speech*, which is a concise summary of a topic—so concise that it can be delivered during a short elevator ride (Staehr Fenner, 2014b). We recommend limiting your elevator speech to about thirty seconds. ESOL and content teachers can also use it as a tool to clearly define the expertise they bring in serving ELs in their school within their school vision and explain it to administrators. The elevator speech you develop corresponds to your guiding principles and school or district vision for educating ELs. It should outline how you see your role shifting and the unique skills you leverage in supporting your ELs' equitable and excellent education. To develop your elevator speech, consider these questions:

1. What aspects of your school or district's vision resonate the most with you?

2. In which aspects can you take a lead role to equitably educate ELs so that they excel?

Once your elevator speech draft is complete, compare yours with that of your colleagues to ensure you're creating a framework of distributed expertise to support ELs. You may need to revise your elevator speech periodically as your skills with working with ELs evolve.

Conclusion

In this chapter, we shared why it is crucial to equitably instruct ELs so that their potential for excellence is unlocked. We began with a brief review of EL demographics and shared relevant information on the EL opportunity and achievement gaps. Next, we detailed the implications for all teachers of ELs due to the shifts in the CCRS. The bulk of the chapter was devoted to our five guiding principles. For each principle, we described relevant research, as well as provided practical tools for you to use to apply the principles. Finally, we gave you the opportunity to draw from our five principles to create your own guiding principles, a school or district vision, and develop your own personalized elevator speech, which outlines your crucial role in supporting ELs. In the next chapter, we focus on learning about and incorporating ELs' home languages and cultures into instruction.

Reflection Questions

1. Which guiding principles resonated the most with you? Why?

2. What are your three takeaways from this chapter? Why?

References

Alford, B. J., & Niño, M. C. (2011). *Leading academic achievement for English language learners: A guide for principals*. Thousand Oaks, CA: Corwin.

Baecher, L., Knoll, M., & Patti, J. (2013). Addressing English language learners in the school leadership curriculum: Mapping the terrain. *Journal of Research on Leadership Education, 8*(3), 280–303.

Deal, T. E., & Peterson, K. D. (2009). *Shaping school culture* (2nd ed.). San Francisco, CA: Jossey-Bass.

Donovan, S., & Cross, C. (2002). *Minority students in gifted and special education*. Washington, DC: National Academy Press.

Edwards, A. (2011). Building common knowledge at the boundaries between professional practices: Relational agency and relational expertise in systems of distributed expertise. *International Journal of Educational Research, 50*(1), 33–39. doi:10.1016/j.ijer.2011.04.007

Ferguson, C. (2008). *The school–family connection: Looking at the larger picture*. Austin, TX: National Center for Community and Family Connections with Schools.

Gabriel, J. G., & Farmer, P. C. (2009). *How to help your school thrive without breaking the bank*. Alexandria, VA: ASCD.

Gándara, P., Maxwell-Jolly, J., & Driscoll, A. (2005). *Listening to teachers of English language learners: A survey of California teachers' challenges, experiences, and professional development needs*. Santa Cruz, CA: Center for the Future of Teaching and Learning.

Gorski, P. C. (2010, April 14). The challenge of defining "multicultural education." Retrieved from http://www.edchange.org/multicultural/initial.html

Gottlieb, M. (2016). *Assessing English language learners: Bridges to educational equity: Connecting academic language proficiency to student achievement*. Thousand Oaks, CA: Corwin.

Henderson, A., & Mapp, K. (2002). *A new wave of evidence: The impact of school, family, and community connections on student achievement*. Austin, TX: National Center for Family and Community Connections With Schools, Southwest Educational Development Lab.

Honigsfeld, A., & Dove, M. G. (2010). *Collaboration and co-teaching: Strategies for English learners*. Thousand Oaks, CA: Corwin.

Honigsfeld, A., & Dove, M. G. (2014). *Collaboration and co-teaching: Strategies for English learners. A leader's guide*. Thousand Oaks, CA: Corwin.

Leithwood, K., Louis, K., Anderson, S., & Wahlstrom, K. (2004). *How leadership influences student learning*. New York, NY: Wallace Foundation.

Maxwell, L. (2013, October 28). ESL and classroom teachers team up to teach Common Core. *Education Week*. Retrieved from http://www.edweek.org/ew/articles/2013/10/30/10cc-eslteachers.h33.htm

Migration Policy Institute. (2015). Top languages spoken by English language learners nationally and by state. Retrieved from http://www.migrationpolicy.org/research/top-languages-spoken-english-language-learners-nationally-and-state

Moll, L., Amanti, C., Neff, D., & Gonzalez, N. (1992). Funds of knowledge for teaching: Using a qualitative approach to connect homes and classrooms. *Theory Into Practice, 2*, 132–141.

National Clearinghouse for English Language Acquisition (NCELA), Office of English Language Acquisition (OELA). (2015a). Fast facts: English learners (ELs) and NAEP. Retrieved from http://www.ncela.us/files/fast_facts/OELA_FastFacts_ELsandNAEP.pdf

National Clearinghouse for English Language Acquisition (NCELA), Office of English Language Acquisition (OELA). (2015b). Fast facts: Profiles of English learners (ELs). Retrieved from http://www.ncela.us/files/fast_facts/OELA_FastFacts_ProfilesOfELs.pdf

National Clearinghouse for English Language Acquisition (NCELA), Office of English Language Acquisition (OELA). (2015c). Fast facts: Retention and suspension of English learners (ELs). Retrieved from http://www.ncela.us/files/fast_facts/OELA_FastFacts_ELsandCRDC_RetentionandSuspension.pdf

Northouse, G. (2007). *Leadership theory and practice* (4th ed.). Thousand Oaks, CA: Sage.

Reeves, J. R. (2006). Secondary teacher attitudes toward including English-language learners in mainstream classrooms. *Journal of Educational Research, 99*(3), 131–142.

Riggio, R. E., & Tan, S. J. (Eds.). (2014). *Leader interpersonal and influence skills: The soft skills of leadership*. New York: Routledge/Psychology Press.

Shumate, T., Muñoz, M. A., & Winter, P. A. (2005). Evaluating teacher-leaders for careers as administrators: Effects of job attributes, teacher leader role, and teaching assignment area. *Journal of Personnel Evaluation in Education, 18*(1), 21–38.

Staehr Fenner, D. (2014a). *Advocating for English learners: A guide for educators*. Thousand Oaks, CA: Corwin.

Staehr Fenner, D. (2014b). What's your "elevator speech" about your expertise with the Common Core for ELLs? [Web log post]. Retrieved from http://www.colorincolorado.org/blog/whats-your-elevator-speech-about-your-expertise-common-core-ells

Stetser, M., & Stillwell, R. (2014). *Public high school four-year on-time graduation rates and event dropout rates: School years 2010–11 and 2011–12*. Washington, DC: National Center for Education Statistics. Retrieved from http://nces.ed.gov/pubsearch

Stogdill, R. M. (1950). Leadership, membership and organization. *Psychological Bulletin, 47*(1), 1–14. doi:10.1037/h0053857

TESOL International Association. (2013, March). Overview of the Common Core State Standards Initiatives for ELLs. Alexandria, VA: Author.

U.S. Department of Education. (n.d.). College- and career-ready standards. Retrieved from http://www.ed.gov/k-12reforms/standards

U.S. Department of Education, Office of English Language Acquisition. (2015). *Dual language education programs: Current state policies and practices.* Washington, DC: Author.

Valdés, G., Kibler, A., & Walqui, A. (2014). *Changes in the expertise of ESL professionals: Knowledge and action in an era of new standards.* Alexandria, VA: TESOL International Association.

Walqui, A., & van Lier, L. (2010). *Scaffolding the academic success of adolescent English language learners: A pedagogy of promise.* San Francisco, CA: WestEd.

Zehler, A. M., Fleischman, H. L., Hopstock, P. J., Stephenson, T. G., Pendzick, M. L., & Sapru, S. (2003). *Descriptive study of services to LEP students and LEP students with disabilities.* Washington, DC: U.S. Department of Education, Office of English Language Acquisition, Language Enhancement, and Academic Achievement of Limited English Proficient Students.

Zong, J., & Batalova, J. (2015). *The limited English proficient population in the United States.* Washington, DC: Migration Policy Institute. Retrieved from http://www.migrationpolicy.org/article/limited-english-proficient-population-united-states#Age,%20Race,%20and%20Ethnicity

Using a Culturally Responsive Framework to Meet the Needs of ELs

Ms. Kay, an elementary ESOL teacher, receives a new student from Saudi Arabia. Ameena, a beginner English learner, is reserved and quiet. Ms. Kay is happy when she is contacted by Mrs. Khouri, Ameena's mother, who requests a time to meet to discuss how she could support Ameena at home. Mrs. Khouri is literate in English and speaks English with intermediate fluency. She never communicates with her daughter in English, but now that their family has relocated to the United States, her mother wants to work with her daughter at home to help support what she is working on in school. Ms. Kay thinks that this kind of parent involvement is very exciting to see and will help Ameena on her language development path.

During the parent–teacher meeting, Mrs. Khouri asks if Ms. Kay could gather some materials that she could use at home to work with Ameena. Ms. Kay promises to collect materials for her and send them home the next day. The following day, Ms. Kay sends home several workbooks to build literacy skills, a few books of short stories, and a list of websites. On the following Monday after the meeting, Mrs. Khouri returns the completed workbooks, along with printouts from the practice websites showing Ameena's progress on practice games and activities. Ms. Kay is surprised, as she never anticipated that Mrs. Khouri would have Ameena complete all of the work in a week.

She thought the materials would be used over the course of the marking period. Ameena is clearly overtaxed by such focused practice and no longer wants to participate in activities with Ms. Kay's small group.

As the opening scenario shows, culture can have a profound role in expectations for teaching and learning. Ms. Kay didn't understand that she was seen by Mrs. Khouri as the master and scholar. In addition, Ameena's mother and her teacher had different understandings of the pace at which the practice work should be completed. Because of the significant impact that culture can have in the work you do with ELs, we have decided to position our discussion of strategies within a framework of culturally responsive instruction. It is our intention that as you work though Chapters 3–9 in this book, you will refer back to this chapter and consider the cultural implications for your instruction, assessment, and general interactions with ELs and their families. We recognize that those of you who are choosing to read this book may be more informed and more passionate about the instruction of ELs than others that you work with. It is our hope that this chapter will also provide you with some strategies and talking points that you can use to strengthen your role as an EL advocate.

> How might culture have impacted Mrs. Khouri and Ms. Kay's expectations in this scenario? What steps might Ms. Kay take next?

In this chapter, we will define *culture* and characteristics of culture, discuss the importance of cultural understanding for your work with ELs, and provide strategies to support culturally responsive teaching. We will also ask you to step outside your comfort zone and think critically about your own culture and how it shapes your instruction, your classroom expectations, and your interactions with students.

What Is Culture?

While there are many, varied definitions of culture, it is generally understood that culture is "a system of shared beliefs, values, customs, behaviors, and artifacts that the members of society use to interact with their world and with one another" (Zion & Kozleski, 2005, p. 3). To frame our discussion of culture and culturally responsive instruction, we would like to highlight a few key ideas in regard to culture.

> How do you define culture? Why is an understanding of culture important for your work with ELs?

- **Culture is complex and dynamic** (Saifer, Edwards, Ellis, Ko, & Stuczynski, 2011). Understanding culture can be a challenge because culture is always changing, because it can manifest itself in different ways, and because many aspects of culture are invisible. Due to historical, political, or pop-culture shifts, as well as generational changes in attitudes, values, and behaviors, culture is ever evolving.

- **We are each members of different cultural groups, but there is no way of evaluating that the ways of one cultural group are better**

than the ways of another (Erickson, 2007). In addition, our connection to specific cultures and how the culture manifests itself in our ideas and behaviors can change throughout our lives. For example, when we are young, we may align ourselves closely with the culture of our parents, but as we are exposed to new ideas and experiences, our cultural identity can change.

- **There is great variability of cultures within social groups** (Erickson, 2007). For example, Bolivian culture in Bolivia is different from Bolivian culture as it appears in a Bolivian community in Virginia.[1] Even members of the same family can be culturally diverse. This is an important idea in connection to the ELs whom you work with because their culture(s) may be different from their parents' culture(s). This concept may be particularly true for ELs who were born in the United States. Second-generation immigrants are often pulled between the culture of their families and the culture that they learn at school or in the community (Stroink & Lalonde, 2009). Accordingly, it is important to avoid overgeneralizing aspects of culture (e.g., "Mexicans like to . . .") or asking one student to speak on behalf of his or her culture or nationality.

- **There are three different levels of culture**. An analogy is often made between these three levels and an iceberg (Hall, 1976). The elements of culture that are (1) visible (at the surface level), such as food, clothing, and language, are understood to carry a low emotional load. At this surface-level of culture, people expect that there will be cultural differences, and these differences are less likely to cause conflict or misunderstandings between people or groups of people (Hammond, 2015). However, the invisible elements of culture that include both (2) shallow and (3) deep culture are much more likely to carry an emotional weight. Figure 2.1 provides an overview of these three levels of culture, along with a definition and examples of each.

> As you look at Figure 2.1, think of a time when a difference in shallow or deep culture caused a conflict between you and someone else. How did you resolve the conflict?

FIGURE 2.1 Three Levels of Culture

Level of Culture	Definition	Examples
Surface	Comprises concrete elements of culture that can be seen; carries low emotional load	Food, clothing, celebrations, music, literature, and dance
Shallow	Comprises the cultural rules for everyday communication and behavior; carries strong emotional charge, and differences can lead to misunderstandings and disagreements	Beliefs about time, concepts of personal space, nonverbal communication patterns, and relationship to authority
Deep culture	Comprises the unspoken knowledge and unconscious understandings in how we relate to others and the world; carries substantial emotional charge, and differences at this level can lead to culture shock	Ideas about cooperation and collaboration, notions of justice, and concepts of self

Source: Adapted from Hammond, Z. (2015). Culture tree (p. 24).

---

1. There are also variations of Bolivian culture within Bolivia.

My Multicultural Self[2]

In order to think more about your own culture, answer Questions 1–4 that follow.

1. Make a list of all of the cultural groups that you belong to (e.g., Mexican American, female, Jewish, gay). Then, consider which ones you identify with most, and put a star next to those.

2. Describe a time that you felt proud to be a member of one of these cultural groups.

3. Describe a time that you found it challenging to be a member of one of these cultural groups.

---

2. Adapted from Gorski, P. (2015). Circles of my multicultural self. Retrieved from http://www.edchange.org/multicultural/activities/circlesofself.html

_____

_____

4. What made the difference between the two times?

_____

_____

_____

_____

_____

In this activity, we hope you recognized the complexity and emotional charge that can come with being a member of a specific cultural group, especially when confronted with the norms, values, and beliefs of a different cultural group. Saifer et al. (2011) explain that the coming together of diverse cultures creates what they call a *cross-cultural zone*, which includes such elements and emotions as acculturation, cultural privilege, historical mistrust and guilt, fear, anger, and curiosity (p. 10). How we are able to navigate in such cross-cultural zones will shape our relationships with individuals from other cultures.

Why Does Culture Matter for ELs' Teaching and Learning?

APPLICATION ACTIVITY 2.2

Ms. Montrose's Classroom

Read the scenario that follows, and then, answer the discussion questions.

Scenario: Ms. Montrose is a sixth-grade language arts teacher in a rural school with few ELs. The ELs in her class are from Guinea, India, and South Korea. She regularly includes discussion activities in her lessons and expects students to be active participants in these discussions. She selects discussion prompts that she hopes will encourage debate, as well as close analysis of the texts that the class is reading. Ms. Montrose has worked with the ESOL teacher to develop the *language scaffolding that her ELs may need to participate, including vocabulary instruction, sentence stems, and word banks. However, she has been frustrated by her ELs' participation in these discussions. Some of her ELs contribute very little, and in general, they tend to avoid controversial topics. Ms. Montrose thinks that several of her ELs aren't very motivated to be successful in her class, and she is at a loss for what more she can do to encourage these students to be more active in the discussions.*

Discussion Questions

1. What impact might culture have on ELs' participation in classroom discussions?

2. What might be preventing Ms. Montrose's ELs from being more active participants in the class discussions?

3. What might Ms. Montrose do to support greater participation on the part of her ELs? Consider linguistic supports, student groupings, and other types of support she could offer.

Culture impacts students' and teachers' beliefs about education and learning. It can impact ELs' ways of communicating, their classroom participation and behavior, and their expectations for the role of the teacher (Zion & Kozleski, 2005). Similarly, culture has an effect on educators' expectations for students, their ways of communicating with students, and their classroom management. This means that the expectations for student behavior and communication at home could be significantly different than the expectations for a student behavior and communication at school (Delpit, 1995; Ogbu, 2003). A home–school mismatch may arise when students come to school with learning styles, discourse behaviors, or values of education that are different from their teachers (Cooper, Jackson, Azmitia, Lopez, & Dunbar, 1994). Such a mismatch can be detrimental to student learning and also the relationship between the student and the teacher. Accordingly, teachers need to recognize this mismatch and support students in learning the expectations of the teacher and the school (Delpit, 1995). Students also need support in learning how to function within and across cultures, so as to emphasize that no one culture is better than another.

For example, in the scenario discussed earlier, Ms. Montrose had specific expectations for what student engagement and participation looked like, and when her ELs did not meet those expectations, she questioned their motivation. There are several things that might be standing in the way of student participation from a linguistic perspective, including students having sufficient understanding of the content and the structure of the discussion activities. However, Ms. Montrose should also explore cultural differences that may be preventing some ELs from participating and should be explicit with her students about expectations for academic discussions in her classroom. For example, she could engage in a discussion with her students about how norms for discussions and debate vary from culture to culture and even within cultures. She should also provide models of academic discussions that students can use to inform their understanding of her expectations. It would be important for Ms. Montrose to make sure that she does not call out, stigmatize, or make ELs feel unwelcome during these discussions. One possibility might be to use video clips to highlight cultural differences.

How Can I Begin to Understand How My Cultural Expectations May Differ From Those of My ELs and the Impact This Will Have in the Classroom?

Becoming aware of how your cultural expectations may differ from those of your ELs is a two-part process that will lead you to becoming a more culturally competent educator. The first part of the process is to reflect on the cultural values and beliefs that shape your expectations in the classroom. The second part of the process is learning more about the ELs you work with and recognizing how their values and beliefs may be different from your own. In order to think more about your own cultural values connected to education, complete the following application activity.

Reflecting on My Cultural Beliefs and Expectations

APPLICATION ACTIVITY 2.3

Reflecting on My Cultural Beliefs and Expectations

For each of the topics listed in Figure 2.2, write down your beliefs or expectations for your students associated with the topic. When you are finished, compare your responses with the information in Figure 2.3 that follows, and answer the discussion questions. As we have already mentioned in this chapter, it is important to recognize that these ideas are generalizations and will not apply to all students from a particular culture.

FIGURE 2.2   Reflecting on My Cultural Beliefs and Expectations

Topic	Your Beliefs and/or Expectations
Punctuality (How do you feel about students arriving on time for class or families arriving on time for school events?)	
Role of teacher in class (What do you think is the teacher's role in terms of managing a class, interacting with students, and supporting student learning?)	
Student participation in discussions (What are your expectations for what student participation looks like during a class discussion?)	
Student nonverbal communication (What are your expectations for how students should communicate nonverbally with you and with other students?)	
Student interactions with teacher (What are your expectations in terms of how [or if] a student should address a teacher, ask questions, or disagree with a teacher?)	
Independent versus collaborative learning (What are your expectations for when students should work independently? What are your expectations for when and how they should work collaboratively?)	
Plagiarism (What do you expect students to understand about what it means to plagiarize and how to avoid plagiarism?)	

FIGURE 2.3   Reflecting on My Cultural Beliefs and Expectations

Topic	Cultural Considerations
Punctuality	*Chronemics* refers to individuals' perceptions of time and whether the timing of things is seen as precise or more fluid. From culture to culture, the importance of punctuality can vary greatly (Steinberg, 2007). In the United States, arriving more than several minutes late to a function can be considered rude. However, in other cultures (e.g., African, Middle Eastern, and Latin American), arriving late is not considered impolite.
Role of teacher in class	The role of the teacher may vary between collectivist and individualist cultures. Collectivist cultures are those in which group goals and needs are generally placed above individual needs. In contrast, individualist cultures tend to value individual goals, individual rights, and independence. Students from collectivist cultures (e.g., Mexican, Korean, and Somali) may have been taught that they should show respect for teachers at all times by carefully listening to their teacher and not asking questions or disagreeing (Rothstein-Fisch & Trumbull, 2008). Group harmony is considered most important. In contrast, students from individualist cultures (e.g., Australian, German, or U.S.) recognize that they will be valued for sharing their unique ideas and opinions. They also tend to expect a more student-centered approach to teaching and learning.
Student participation in discussions	Whether ELs are from high-context cultures or low-context cultures may impact how they participate in discussions. In high-context cultures (e.g., Afghanistani, El Salvadoran, or Thai), it is expected that individuals will gain meaning from the context or situation, and some ideas may be assumed rather than stated. In contrast, members of low-context cultures (e.g., Swiss, Israeli, or U.S.) are less likely to rely on the situation and other contextual elements (e.g., body language or tone of voice) and tend to communicate information more directly. As a result,

Topic	Cultural Considerations
	students from high-context cultures may participate in discussions differently than students from low-context cultures. For example, both students and teachers from a high-context culture tend to be more indirect—that is to say, more implicit and vague—when asked a question or discussing a particular issue in the classroom (Al-Issa, 2005; Hall, 1976). On the other hand, students and teachers from low-context cultures are more straightforward and explicit in their communication style. In addition, students from a collectivist culture may believe that the survival and success of the group ensures the well-being of the individual, so that by considering the needs and feelings of others, one protects oneself. Harmony and interdependence of group members are stressed and valued. These values may make it difficult for a student from a collectivist culture to disagree with another student (Rothstein-Fisch & Trumbull, 2008).
Student nonverbal communication (including gestures, distance when speaking to someone, and eye contact)	Nonverbal communication patterns can vary greatly from culture to culture, and the rules regarding these behaviors are often unspoken (Steinberg, 2007). ELs may need explicit guidance in cultural expectations in this area. For example, the personal distance that two speakers are expected to maintain when speaking may vary between cultures. In the United States, it is considered strange to stand extremely close to someone you are conversing with. Eye contact is another example. Some ELs may come from cultures where it is considered impolite to look an adult in the eye, or direct eye contact may be a perceived challenge (e.g., Asian, African, and Latino cultures). Eye contact between opposite sexes is often seen as inappropriate in Middle Eastern cultures.
Student interactions with teacher (e.g., how to address teacher, asking questions, or disagreeing)	In some cultures, there is greater *power distance* between leaders and followers than in other cultures. Power distance refers to how people from a specific culture view power relationships. For example, in high-power-distance cultures (e.g., Guatemalan, Malaysian, and Saudi Arabian), the relationship between a teacher and a student would be very formal and respectful. In these cultures, there tends to be more focus on titles, formality, and authority. Students from these cultures may not feel comfortable talking to teachers, and parents may take the teacher's word without question (Hofstede, 2003). In contrast, in cultures where there is less power distance (e.g., Dutch, Norwegian, or U.S.), relationships are usually more informal. Parents may work together with teachers for the student's best interest, and the teacher may provide a more student-centered classroom, giving choice and autonomy to students.
Independent versus collaborative learning	Students from collectivist cultures (e.g., Japanese, Brazilian, and Indian) may value working together interdependently rather than working alone independently. Contributing to a group's well-being is valued more than one's individual achievement (Rothstein-Fisch & Trumbull, 2008). In contrast, students from individualist cultures (e.g., Greek, New Zealand, or U.S.) may see greater value in working independently towards individual goals and achievement.
Plagiarism	The concept of plagiarism is built on the understanding that ideas can be owned and that individuals have rights to intellectual property (Pennycook, 1996). These ideas may seem strange to students who have different cultural views about the nature of information and public discourse (Adiningrum & Kutieleh, 2011). Plagiarism tends to be culturally conditioned and may be understood differently in various cultures (Pennycook, 1996; Sowden, 2005). For example, in some Asian and Middle Eastern cultures, students are permitted to quote or paraphrase political and religious authorities without citing them specifically because it is understood that the reader will know the original source of the information (Howard, 1999). Additionally, ELs with lower levels of English proficiency may struggle to paraphrase challenging texts and will need significant support to do so.

Source: Adapted from Hiatt, J. E., Jones-Vo, S., Staehr Fenner, D., & Snyder, S. (2017). Understanding how culture impacts your expectations for your students handout.

Discussion Questions

1. What did you notice about how your cultural beliefs and expectations may differ from those of your ELs?

2. How might you address these differences in your classroom?

Learning About My ELs

In addition to reflecting on the impact culture has on your teaching and your expectations for students, you also need to take steps to learn about your ELs. We have included some suggestions for how to do this in the list that follows. Figure 2.4 provides a tool that you can complete as you learn more about each EL you work with.

- Look for opportunities for students to share about themselves, their families, and their backgrounds and experiences. You can build activities into instruction that ask students to describe their families, their home, their responsibilities, how they spend their time outside of school, and their literacy practices (e.g., the types of things they read, watch, and listen to outside of school) (Staehr Fenner, 2014). When you are asking students to describe their backgrounds and experiences, it is important to be clear that you are not asking students to speak for an entire cultural group.

FIGURE 2.4 What I Know About My EL

Name:	Country of birth:
Home language:	English proficiency level:
Can student read and write in home language?	English language proficiency scores
_____ Fluently	Composite (the combined score):
_____ Somewhat	Speaking:
_____ No	Reading
	Listening:
	Writing:
Educational experiences (e.g., amount of time in U.S. schools, educational experience in home country, or any interrupted schooling):	
Family background (e.g., who student lives with or family separation or reunification):	
Student interests:	
Student plans and/or goals:	

- Take opportunities to talk with students informally (e.g., at lunch, after school, or on field trips), and get to know more about them.

- Collaborate with other educators to find out relevant background information on ELs (e.g., home language or educational experiences).

- Attend school and community events that your ELs and their families attend.

- Conduct home visits with ELs and their families (as appropriate). It can be effective to visit in the beginning of the year as a get-to-know-each-other activity and limit discussions about behavior and academic progress.

- Research general information about your ELs' home cultures and important features of their home languages (Staehr Fenner, 2014).

APPLICATION ACTIVITY 2.4

Mr. Gerard's Classroom

Read the scenario, and answer the discussion questions that follow.

Scenario: *Mr. Gerard, an elementary school music teacher, has a new student in his class from Indonesia. He looks at her name on the attendance list, and then he asks her what her name is. She responds, "Cinta Hartono." Mr. Gerard immediately feels uncomfortable with this unfamiliar name and asks, "Can I call you Cindy?" Cinta agrees that would be fine.*

Discussion Questions

1. What is the underlying message that Mr. Gerard is sending to Cinta about her home language and culture?

2. What steps could Mr. Gerard take to become more comfortable learning and using the names of students that might be unfamiliar to him?

What Is Culturally Responsive Pedagogy?

Once you have begun to recognize how culture impacts who you are as an educator, as well as learned more about the backgrounds and experiences of your ELs, you can apply this new or more nuanced understanding to your teaching. Culturally responsive educators draw on the cultural knowledge, backgrounds, and experiences of their students in order to make the learning more meaningful. Ladson-Billings (1994) developed the term *culturally relevant teaching* to describe "a pedagogy that empowers students intellectually, socially, emotionally, and politically by using cultural referents to impart knowledge, skills, and attitudes" (p. 18).

In order to have a clearer understanding of what culturally responsive pedagogy is, it may be helpful to first understand what it is not. Nieto (2016) explains that "culturally responsive pedagogy is not

- A predetermined curriculum
- A specific set of strategies
- A watering down of the curriculum
- A 'feel-good' approach
- Only for students of particular backgrounds" (p. 1).

Instead, Nieto (2016) describes culturally responsive pedagogy as a mindset that respects and builds on students' backgrounds and experiences through the use of materials and specific teaching approaches. Culturally responsive educators strive to learn what makes each student unique in order to appreciate the diverse perspectives and insights they can bring to their classroom. Culturally responsive educators are also able to confront their own biases.

What Are the Guidelines of Culturally Responsive Teaching?

While educators and researchers describe varying characteristics of culturally responsive teaching, we have attempted to synthesize these ideas into four overarching guidelines. As can be seen in Figure 2.5, the guidelines overlap with one another. The guidelines are as follows:

- Guideline 1: Culturally responsive teaching is assets-based.
- Guideline 2: Culturally responsive teaching places students at the center of learning.
- Guideline 3: Culturally responsive teaching values students' languages, cultures, and backgrounds.
- Guideline 4: Culturally responsive teaching simultaneously challenges and supports students.

We will provide an explanation of each, its relationship to ELs, and some classroom "look-fors" that indicate these criteria are at work in the classroom in the sections that follow.

FIGURE 2.5   The Guidelines of Culturally Responsive Teaching

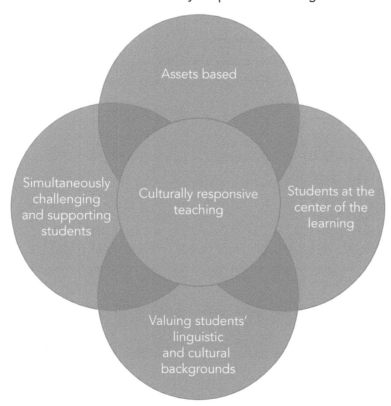

Guideline 1: Culturally responsive teaching is assets based.

When we consider the obstacles that ELs must surmount in order to acquire a new language while, at the same time, learning academic content, it can be easy to approach our work with ELs from a deficit perspective. A deficit perspective is one in which we focus on ELs' challenges and frame our interactions with them in terms of these challenges. Using a deficit lens, educators tend to view ELs' home language(s) and culture(s) as hindrances to overcome. In addition, they may attribute poor performance or achievement to ELs' linguistic abilities in English, motivation, lack of parental involvement, or other such factors (González, 2005; Valencia, 1997; Valenzuela, 1999). In contrast, an assets-based perspective is one that values students' home languages and cultures and sees them as foundations for future learning (González, 2005; Valencia, 1997; Valenzuela, 1999). Similarly, an assets-based perspective recognizes that parents of ELs are involved in their children's education and support their children in varied and perhaps unrecognized ways (Staehr Fenner, 2014). An additional benefit of using an assets-based perspective is that it provides opportunities to honor students' cultural and linguistic backgrounds and incorporate what students already know into their teaching.

In order to envision how an assets-based perspective plays out in the classroom, review the classroom look-fors in Figure 2.6.

FIGURE 2.6 Guideline 1 Classroom Look-Fors

✓ Teacher pronounces students' names correctly.

✓ Teacher shows interest in ELs' home languages by learning at least a few words or phrases.

✓ Teacher incorporates cultural, historic, and linguistic information about the target culture into instruction.

✓ Teacher uses instruction of home language cognates to reinforce vocabulary comprehension.

✓ Teacher is aware of each student's interests and challenges outside of the classroom.

✓ Teacher uses multiple means of communicating with EL families (e.g., translated notes, telephone calls, and use of an interpreter).

✓ Teacher puts supports in place to help students overcome obstacles that may get in the way of their learning (e.g., snacks for students who may not have had breakfast, system for catching up on missed work, and written agenda for ELs to follow).

APPLICATION ACTIVITY 2.5

Shifting to an Assets-Based Perspective

Consider the following reflection questions to help you better understand your perspective when working with ELs. For each question, answer *yes*, *sometimes*, or *no*. For any question that you answer with a *sometimes* or a *no*, write down a question or idea that you have about how to shift toward an assets-based perspective in this area.

Reflection Question	Yes	Sometimes	No	Question or Idea for a Shift to an Assets-Based Perspective
1. Do I view students' cultural and linguistic backgrounds as a valuable source of knowledge and skills that I can build on in my lessons?				
2. Do I view diverse perspectives as a beneficial resource for all students and look for ways to incorporate these diverse perspectives into my teaching?				

Reflection Question	Yes	Sometimes	No	Question or Idea for a Shift to an Assets-Based Perspective
3. Do I recognize and appreciate that EL families may contribute to their children's educations in varied and sometimes unseen ways?				
4. Do I hold my ELs to the same high standards as other students?				
5. Do I recognize that ELs who are struggling in my class may be doing so because they need additional forms of support to acquire language and content knowledge that they are not currently receiving?				

An assets-based perspective requires that you approach the work you do with ELs with respect and empathy. Respect and empathy will grow when you try to put yourself in the shoes of ELs and their families and imagine what it is like to assimilate into an unfamiliar culture, learn a new language, and figure out a new school system (Staehr Fenner, 2014). As an example of how you can build empathy into your teaching, Saifer et al. (2011) describe a teacher who recognized that one challenge her students faced was missing class or coming to class late because of personal factors. Rather than setting up an uncomfortable or punitive situation for these students in her class that may have increased their likelihood of missing more class, this teacher set up a system so that when a student arrived to class, he or she could jump right in. The day's agenda and class handouts were readily available, and each class had an appointed student who was the go-to person for directions and class notes (p. 33).

Respect and empathy are also needed when you are confronted with a situation where you find yourself using a deficit perspective to understand what happened. For example, if you happen to catch yourself blaming ELs or their families, try to "shake up" your thinking so that you start by assuming the best about the student or the family members involved and consider their perspective, as well as challenges or obstacles that they might be facing. Application Activity 2.6 provides you with an opportunity to think about how you might reframe a deficit perspective into actions that come from a place of respect and empathy for ELs and their families.

Assets-Based Perspective Scenarios

We present three scenarios in Figure 2.7.

1. Read the first scenario. Also, read the second and third columns, which present another way of understanding the scenario.

2. For the second and third scenarios, complete the second two columns yourself. First, approach the ELs and their families in each scenario from a respectful and empathetic perspective, and then determine what steps the teacher(s) in the scenarios might take to change his or her deficit perspective.

3. In the final row, write a scenario that is relevant to your context.

FIGURE 2.7 Assets-Based Perspective Scenarios

Scenario	Respectful and empathetic perspective	Steps you might take to support ELs and their families
The members of an elementary school parent teacher association (PTA) are complaining that despite there being a significant number of ELs in the school, none of the EL parents attend the PTA meetings. They feel that families of ELs are not interested in supporting the school.	There are many reasons why the families of ELs may not be involved in the PTA. For starters, EL families may come from countries where parent associations do not exist or information about the PTA meeting may not be clearly shared with families in a language they can understand. Additionally, family members may have such constraints as having to work, not having childcare, or not having transportation.	<ul><li>Make sure meeting information is clear and delivered in families' home languages.</li><li>Reach out to families and explain what the PTA does and how their participation would benefit the group.</li><li>Offer childcare during PTA meetings.</li><li>Offer support with transportation if needed.</li></ul>
A sixth-grade science teacher has students work in groups on various assignments. He has three ELs in his class who are at a low-to-intermediate proficiency level, and he has tried to group them with ELs at higher proficiency levels. However, he finds that when they are grouped together, they like to speak Spanish. He feels uncomfortable because he doesn't know what they are saying, and he is worried that they are off task or talking about him.		

Scenario	Respectful and empathetic perspective	Steps you might take to support ELs and their families
During parent–teacher conference time, four elementary teachers are eating lunch together. They begin to complain about how many of the parents of their ELs show up late for conferences, attend the conference with a younger child in tow, and/or do not actively participate in the conference. They decide they will share their frustrations with the ESOL teacher.		
Scenario from my context:		

Guideline 2: Culturally responsive teaching places students at the center of the learning.

Student-centered learning is not new in the field of education, and there are a variety of approaches that fit within this model (e.g., collaborative learning, inquiry-based learning, or project-based learning). Student-centered learning can be defined as an instructional approach in which the students in the classroom shape the content, instructional activities, materials, assessment, and/or pace of the learning. Student-centered learning also focuses on the idea that students are provided with opportunities to learn from one another rather than solely from the teacher.

In order to incorporate student-centered learning practices in your classroom, review the classroom look-fors in Figure 2.8.

One step toward student-centered learning is making sure that the learning goals are explained in student-friendly language so that students can participate in setting goals for their learning and assessing their learning (Stiggins, Arter, Chappuis, & Chappius, 2004). For ELs, this could be an unfamiliar experience. Deconstructing the standards that you are working

FIGURE 2.8 Guideline 2 Classroom Look-Fors

✓ Student-friendly learning objectives (content and language) are posted in the classroom.

✓ ELs are provided clear visual and oral instructions for activities.

✓ All new activities are modeled for ELs.

✓ ELs are given choice in their learning.

✓ ELs are given opportunities to speak and write about their lives and people and events that are important to them.

✓ ELs are involved in goal setting and assessment through the use of student goal sheets, checklists, peer-editing activities, and teacher–student or student–student conferencing.

✓ EL student work is displayed in the classroom.

✓ Lessons include activities that foster relationship building (e.g., think-pair-share discussions and collaborative tasks).

✓ Lessons include intentional groupings of students to support student learning and to allow for grouping that considers language backgrounds.

✓ Group work is intentionally structured so that all students have specific roles or ways to meaningfully contribute.

> *How might you adapt Figure 2.10 for your own context?*

on in order to present them in student-friendly terms can be a challenge. Figure 2.9 provides an example of how to rephrase content standards so as to present them in terms of what students will be able to do. This is an example of a content objective, but you can use the same approach for developing student-friendly language objectives.

Figure 2.10 is a document that you could use for helping students set goals for their learning.

FIGURE 2.9 Example of Student-Friendly Learning Objectives

Common Core State Standard: RL.9-10.1 Cite strong and thorough textual evidence to support analysis of what the text says explicitly as well as inferences drawn from the text.

Student content objective: I will be able to answer questions about the text by using information that is stated in the text (explicit information) and by drawing inferences from the text (coming up with answers that are not stated or written in the text).

Source: August, D., Staehr Fenner, D., Snyder, S., & Pook, D. (2014, June). *Secondary curricular units for New York City Department of Education.* Washington, DC: American Institutes for Research, Center for English Language Learners. Reprinted with permission of American Institutes for Research. Retrieved from http://schools.nyc.gov/NR/rdonlyres/68300610-4F11-433E-8D0C-6DE718752989/0/SecondaryUnits.pdf

FIGURE 2.10 Student Goal Setting for an Academic Conversation

Name _____   Date _____

During today's discussion, I want to focus on the following:

_____ Using appropriate eye contact and body language for a discussion

_____ Making connections between my ideas and what someone else said

_____ Using evidence from the text to support my answer

_____ Using this unit's academic vocabulary when speaking

Something that I might need to help me accomplish this goal is _____

(e.g., sentence frames, a word bank of unit vocabulary, or a reminder from the teacher).

Student-Centered Classroom Environments

There are also several ways to create an environment that is student centered. Saifer et al. (2011) make the following recommendations:

- Display pictures of your students engaged in learning activities.

- Display student work (including examples of bilingual work).

- Post student quotes.

- Display signs in other languages, or label classroom objectives in students' home languages.

- Have a multicultural classroom library, including supporting resources in students' home languages.

Guideline 3: Culturally responsive teaching values students' languages, cultures, and backgrounds.

The third guideline focuses on ways that teaching and learning can give value to students' home language, cultures, and experiences. Figure 2.11 offers some suggestions for what you would expect to see in a culturally responsive classroom. The "Additional Resources" section of this chapter on pages 57–58 provides some recommended resources for materials and lesson ideas.

FIGURE 2.11   Guideline 3 Classroom Look-Fors

✓ Lessons include multicultural materials and resources.

✓ Lessons and units include perspectives of individuals that come from ELs' home cultures (e.g., literature written by non-U.S. American authors).

✓ Lessons include activities that draw on ELs' backgrounds and experiences.

✓ Lessons include opportunities for ELs to use bilingual resources (e.g., dictionaries, books, or glossaries) and home languages.

✓ EL families and communities are included in the learning (e.g., community members are invited to speak in class).

APPLICATION ACTIVITY 2.7

Mr. Washburn's Classroom

Read the scenario that follows, and consider how Mr. Washburn might make his unit on immigration more culturally responsive to the ELs whom he is teaching. Answer the discussion questions that follow.

Scenario: Mr. Washburn is a middle school social studies teacher at an urban middle school with a large population of ELs from Mexico and Central America. He has seven ELs in one of his social studies classes. Three of the ELs have been in the country for less than a year. The other ELs have been in the U.S. for two to six years. Mr. Washburn is currently teaching a unit on U.S. immigration, focusing on the experiences of immigrants that came to the United States in the early 1900s. As part of this unit, students will take a virtual tour of Ellis Island, read excerpts from Island of Hope: The Story of Ellis Island and the Journey to America *(Sandler, 2004), and give an oral report on one aspect of the immigrant experience during this time (e.g., travel to the United States or life in the tenements).*

Discussion Questions

1. In what ways is the unit plan relevant to the lives of the students in the class? In what ways could the unit be made more relevant to their lives?

2. What steps could the teacher take to build on the backgrounds and experiences of the ELs in the class?

3. What additional recommendations do you have for activities that would strengthen students' engagement with the unit and bring in diverse perspectives?

As you probably concluded, a unit on immigration is most likely very relevant to the lives of ELs. However, rather than focusing only on immigration in the early 1900s, the teacher could also discuss current immigration. There are many young adult novels that address issues of immigration (e.g., *Day of the Pelican* [Paterson, 2010], *Inside Out & Back Again* [Lai, 2013], *How Many Days to America?* [Bunting, 1990], *Star in the Forest* [Resau, 2012], and *Shooting Kabul* [Senzai, 2011]). Students could also read and discuss editorials about current immigration from a social justice lens. They could make connections between why immigrants came to the United States in the early 1900s and why they come now. There are many great resources for teaching about immigration that support a multicultural perspective on the topic, such as *Teaching Tolerance*'s "The Human Face of Immigration" (Costello, 2011). You can also find text sets on a particular topic, such as immigration, that offer resources at varied reading levels. As you plan lessons, even on those topics that may seem far removed from the lives of the ELs you work with, look for opportunities to make meaningful connections to their own experiences.

What About Home Language Use?

A common misconception in regard to the teaching of ELs is that they should be discouraged from speaking their home language with their families and peers and that home language use should not be incorporated into instruction. However, research indicates that ELs can draw from their home language when acquiring knowledge and skills in English (Dressler, 2006). Furthermore, instruction that incorporates and builds on ELs' home language will support them in developing literacy in English (August, Branum-Martin, Cardenas-Hagan, & Francis, 2009; Carlo et al., 2004; Liang, Peterson, & Graves, 2005; Restrepo et al., 2010). In addition, by providing ELs opportunities to use their home language, you are validating their cultural and linguistic background and recognizing the benefits of being multilingual.

There are many different ways to incorporate home language into instruction, even if you do not speak students' home languages. One excellent way to support home language development is to use home language resources. School librarians are often wonderful resources for finding translated or home language texts to support the content you are working on (e.g., a translated copy of a graphic novel about Paul Revere). You can also provide students with opportunities to do bilingual work on their assignments (e.g., use a bilingual glossary, write a story in both English and their home language, or have them interview a family or community member in their home language). When providing students opportunities to work in their home language or use home language resources, it is essential that you have a clear understanding of their literacy skills in that language.

Students who do not have strong home language literacy skills may not benefit from such written resources, and they might also be embarrassed if they do not feel comfortable reading and writing in their home language.

Another strategy for supporting home language development is intentionally grouping students to allow opportunities for them to use their home language during group work (as appropriate). It is understandable that if you don't speak the home language, you may be uncomfortable with this strategy because you don't know what is being discussed in the group. However, if you set up concrete tasks for the group, you will be able to identify whether or not students are engaged in the activity. You can also have students record their discussions and seek support from a colleague who speaks the home language to interpret the conversation for you.

Guideline 4: Culturally responsive teaching simultaneously challenges and supports students.

This final guideline is based on the importance of having high expectations for the ELs in your classes while at the same time giving them the support that they need to achieve. ELs should have access to the same grade-level content and texts as their non-EL peers, but they should be given sufficient instructional support for this work.

This guideline is also framed around the idea that within our society, certain cultural groups have privileges that are not granted to individuals outside these groups. Culturally responsive teachers develop lessons that include the history and experiences of diverse groups and explicit instruction about structures that reinforce power, privilege, and discriminatory practices in society. In addition, culturally responsive teaching provides opportunities for students and educators to think critically about institutionalized inequity, how inequity and injustice impact their lives, and steps needed to address this inequity (National Center for Culturally Responsive Educational Systems, 2008).

Figure 2.12 offers some suggestions for how to apply this guideline in your classroom.

An example of what Guideline 4 might look like in practice is a unit that is taught at a diverse urban high school in California. The ninth-grade English teachers at the Nelson Mandela Academy have developed a unit called "Linguistic Biographies" in which students reflect on their own experiences of using language in different contexts and engage in collaborative academic tasks designed to foster students' appreciation for linguistic diversity and strategies for responding to negative comments about their home language(s) and/or dialects (California Department of Education, 2015). During this unit, students take part in a variety of collaborative activities, including reflecting on their own multilingual or multidialectal experiences, analyzing poetry and contemporary music to understand the connections

FIGURE 2.12 Guideline 4 Classroom Look-Fors

✓ ELs are taught grade-level content and texts. Instructional texts include a balance of grade-level texts and texts at students' reading levels.

✓ Instruction and materials are appropriately scaffolded so ELs are able to access and engage with grade-level content and texts.[3]

✓ The classroom contains visual supports for ELs (e.g., word wall with visual and/or home language translations).

✓ Instruction includes regular, structured small-group and pair work.

✓ Instruction includes activities that foster critical thinking and reflection (e.g., open-ended discussion prompts and student monitoring of their learning).

✓ Instruction includes activities that require students to make connections with their prior learning.

✓ Instruction includes activities that require students to consider alternative ways of understanding information and are open to diverse perspectives (e.g., analyzing the change that some states have made from celebrating Columbus Day to celebrating Indigenous People's Day).

between language choices and cultural values and identity, and producing writing and multimedia pieces that examine the connection between language, culture, and society.

What Is the Role of Collaboration in Developing a Culturally Responsive Classroom?

Collaboration is at the heart of a culturally responsive classroom. The task of learning more about the cultures of others while, at the same time, reflecting on your own culture requires risk-taking, openness, flexibility, and occasional feelings of discomfort. There will be times that you will make mistakes, and there will be times that you may feel angry or frustrated. However, the relationships that you build and the knowledge that you gain can be incredibly rewarding. We make the following recommendations for collaboration with colleagues and EL families.

• Collaborate with colleagues to learn more about the backgrounds, experiences, and cultures of ELs and their families. You can share what you know about specific instructional strategies that have worked well with certain students and strategies for building on students' linguistic and cultural backgrounds. You can also share ways that you have for communicating with and engaging EL families. ESOL teachers and classroom teachers may want to participate in home visits together.

---

3. For more on scaffolded instruction strategies, see Chapter 3.

- Collaborate with colleagues to share resources. Building a multicultural library and/or developing online file sharing can be effective ways to support culturally responsive teaching. A multicultural library can include resources related to particular themes (e.g., peace building or civil rights movement), books written by authors from a variety of cultures, books that share perspectives that may be traditionally overlooked, bilingual books, and more. Your school librarian might be an excellent person to collaborate with on this work. Online file sharing can be a way to share resources or online tools connected to a particular unit or theme. It can also be a way to share information about student backgrounds, goals, and achievement.

- Collaborate with families of ELs to support ELs' engagement and achievement. School programs that foster family involvement in student learning at home and in school activities result in greater student achievement and improved student attitudes about school (Mexican American Legal Defense Fund and National Education Association, 2010). In order to build parental engagement, you should begin by looking for effective and varied ways to communicate with families (e.g., using an interpreter, same home language phone chain, or a communication tool such as ClassDojo that translates text messages into multiple languages). Be flexible about the times you are available to meet with families, and look for ways your school can address potential challenges to parent participation at school events (e.g., transportation, childcare, language barriers, work, and family obligations) (Staehr Fenner, 2014). In addition, look for opportunities to invite families to volunteer in the classroom to share their culture and language and also to help build their familiarity and level of comfort with the school.

What Is the Role of Equity, Advocacy, and Leadership in Developing a Culturally Responsive Classroom?

Having a culturally responsive classroom that builds on the strengths of your students, encourages the sharing of diverse perspectives and experiences, and ultimately supports each EL in acquiring language proficiency and mastering content knowledge is the very definition of equity and advocacy for ELs. However, a climate of cultural awareness and inclusiveness is something that must be cultivated not only in your classroom but throughout the entire school. If your school currently does not offer a welcoming environment for ELs and their families or if you feel interactions with ELs are often framed from a deficit perspective, you can take on a leadership role in order to advocate for these students. We suggest that you prioritize an area you have the greatest opportunity to make an impact in, rather than focusing on an area in which there is little chance for change. Then, find an ally or two who can help you promote an assets-based perspective of ELs. Next, plan out some steps you will take to make positive changes and advocate for equity for ELs.

APPLICATION ACTIVITY 2.8

Ms. Monahan's Classroom

Read the scenario, and answer the discussion questions that follow.

Scenario: Ms. Monahan is an ESOL teacher at a suburban high school with a growing number of ELs. She felt that the school administration, in general, and the assistant principal, Mr. Sheridan, in particular, did not have a strong understanding of the needs of the ELs in the school or respect for these students and their families. At one point, when advocating for more professional development for the teachers at the school working with ELs, Mr. Sheridan commented to her that the students didn't seem to be making much progress and that he found them hard to understand. Ms. Monahan decided to invite Mr. Sheridan into her class as a guest. She had her students prepare short presentations on some of their favorite things about the high school (e.g., particular classes, friendships they had, and school activities), and she also encouraged them to speak about some of the challenges that they had (e.g., navigating the lunch room, understanding some of their teachers, and making new friends). Ms. Monahan also asked Mr. Sheridan to prepare some questions that he could ask the students in order to learn more about their interests, goals, and challenges.

Discussion Questions

1. What do you think was Ms. Monahan's goal in inviting the assistant principal into her classroom?

2. What else might Ms. Monohan do to advocate for the ELs in her school?

This scenario and the teacher's response demonstrate the need for teachers to take a lead in advocating for better understanding of ELs at all levels within the school. In some situations, complex planning and collaboration will be necessary.[4]

---

4. In *Advocating for English Learners: A Guide for Educators* (2014), Staehr Fenner provides useful tools and ideas for advocating for ELs in your context.

Next Steps

We have provided a lot of information in this chapter, and we will explore many of these topics in greater depth throughout the remaining chapters of the book. However, in order to start down the path of culturally responsive teaching, use the template in Figure 2.13 to reflect on a unit that you will be teaching in the upcoming month. As you think about the unit, consider the four guidelines that we have outlined in this chapter, and decide on one strategy for each guideline that you would like to try out in your classroom. You can also think about what support you may need to help you incorporate these strategies into your teaching (e.g., knowledge about ELs or bilingual resources) and who might be able to help you (e.g., ESOL teacher or school librarian).

FIGURE 2.13   Culturally Responsive Teaching Goal-Setting Template

Guidelines	To Incorporate This Guideline, I Will . . .
1. Culturally responsive teaching is assets based.	
2. Culturally responsive teaching places students at the center of the learning.	
3. Culturally responsive teaching values students' languages, cultures, and backgrounds.	
4. Culturally responsive teaching simultaneously challenges and supports students.	
Some support I may need: Possible resources:	

Conclusion

In this chapter, we have provided you with an opportunity to reflect on your own culture and how it impacts your beliefs about teaching and learning. We have also provided you with some insight into how ELs who come from different cultural backgrounds may have varying beliefs about and approaches to education. Finally, we presented four guidelines for culturally responsive teaching, along with some tools for using these guidelines in your classroom. In the next chapter, we will provide some strategies for scaffolding instruction to recognize the strengths and meet the needs of ELs of varying proficiency levels. Chapter 3 correlates directly with Guideline 4: Culturally responsive teaching simultaneously challenges and supports students.

Reflection Questions

1. What new understandings do you have about how your own culture shapes who you are as a teacher?

2. What are two ideas that you have for drawing on students' cultural backgrounds and experiences to make connections to content in your classroom?

References

Adiningrum, T., & Kutieleh, S. (2011). How different are we? Understanding and managing plagiarism between East and West. *Journal of Academic Language and Learning, 5*(2), A88–A98.

Al-Issa, A. (2005). When the west teaches the east: Analyzing intercultural conflict in the classroom. *Intercultural Communication Studies, 14*(4), 149–168.

August, A., Branum-Martin, L., Cardenas-Hagan, E., & Francis, D. J. (2009). The impact of an instructional intervention on the science and language learning of middle grade English language learners. *Journal of Research on Educational Effectiveness, 2*(4), 345–376. doi:10.1080/19345740903217623

Bunting, E. (1990). *How many days to America? A Thanksgiving story.* New York, NY: Clarion Books.

California Department of Education. (2015). English language arts/English language development framework: Snapshot 7.1: Investigating language, culture, and society: Linguistic autobiographies (pp. 726–727). Retrieved from http://www.cde.ca.gov/ci/rl/cf/documents/elaeldfwchapter7.pdf

Carlo, M. S., August, D., McLaughlin, B., Snow, C. E., Dressler, C., Lippman, D. N., & White, C. E. (2004). Closing the gap: Addressing the vocabulary needs for English language learners in bilingual and mainstream classrooms. *Reading Research Quarterly, 39*(2), 188–215. doi:10.1598/RRQ.39.2.3

Cooper, C. R., Jackson, J. F., Azmitia, M., Lopez, E. M., & Dunbar, N. (1994). *Multiple selves, multiple worlds survey: Qualitative and quantitative versions.* Santa Cruz: University of California at Santa Cruz.

Costello, M. (2011, Spring). The human face of immigration. *Teaching Tolerance.* Retrieved from http://www.tolerance.org/magazine/number-39-spring-2011/feature/human-face- immigration

Delpit, L. (1995). *Other people's children: Cultural conflict in the classroom.* New York, NY: New Press.

Dressler, C. (2006). First- and second-language literacy. With M. L. Kamil. In D. August & T. Shanahan (Eds.), *Developing literacy in second-language learners: Report of the National Literacy Panel on Language Minority Children and Youth* (pp. 197–238). Mahwah, NJ: Lawrence Erlbaum.

Erickson, F. (2007). Culture in society and educational practices. In J. Banks & C. A. Banks (Eds.), *Multicultural education: Issues and perspectives* (6th ed.) (pp. 33–61). Hoboken, NJ: John Wiley & Sons.

González, N. (2005). Beyond culture: The hybridity of funds of knowledge. In N. González, L. C. Moll, & C. Amanti (Eds.), *Funds of knowledge* (pp. 29–46). Mahwah, NJ: Erlbaum.

Gorski, P. (2015). Circles of my multicultural self. Retrieved from http://www .edchange.org/multicultural/activities/circlesofself_handout.html

Hall, E. T. (1976). *Beyond culture.* New York, NY: Doubleday.

Hammond, Z. (2015). *Culturally responsive teaching and the brain.* Thousand Oaks, CA: Corwin.

Hiatt, J. E., Jones-Vo, S., Staehr Fenner, D., & Snyder, S. (2017). *Foundational background for educators of ELs* [EL professional development modules]. Johnston, IA: Heartland Area Education Agency.

Hofstede, G. (2003). *Culture's consequences: Comparing values, behaviors, institutions, and organizations across nations* (2nd ed.). Thousand Oaks, CA: Sage.

Howard, R. M. (1999). *Standing in the shadow of giants: Plagiarists, authors, collaborators.* Stamford, CT: Ablex Publishing.

Ladson-Billings, G. (1994). *The dreamkeepers: Successful teaching for African-American students.* San Francisco, CA: Jossey-Bass.

Lai, T. (2013). *Inside out & back again.* New York, NY: Harper.

Liang, L. A., Peterson, C. A., & Graves, M. F. (2005). Investigating two approaches to fostering children's comprehension of literature. *Reading Psychology, 26*(4–5), 387–400.

Mexican American Legal Defense Fund and National Education Association. (2010). *Minority parent and community engagement: Best practices and policy recommendations for closing the gaps in student achievement.* Washington, DC: National Education Association.

National Center for Culturally Responsive Educational Systems (NCCREST). (2008). Module 6: Culturally responsive response to intervention. Tempe, AZ: Mary Lou Fulton College of Education. Retrieved from http://www.niusileadscape .org/docs/pl/culturally_responsive_response_to_intervention/activity1/ RTI%20Academy%201%20FacMan%20ver%201.1%20FINAL%20kak.pdf

Nieto, S. (2016). Culturally-responsive pedagogy: Some key features. Retrieved from http://www.sonianieto.com/wp-content/uploads/2016/02/Culturally-Responsive-Teaching.pdf

Ogbu, J. U. (2003). *Black American students in an affluent suburb: A study of academic disengagement.* Mahwah, NJ: Erlbaum.

Paterson, K. (2010). *The day of the pelican.* Boston, MA: Clarion Books.

Pennycook, A. (1996). Borrowing others' words: Text, ownership, memory and plagiarism. *TESOL Quarterly, 30*(2), 201–230.

Saifer, S., Edwards, K., Ellis, D., Ko, L., & Stuczynski, A. (2011). *Culturally responsive standards-based teaching: Classroom to community and back* (2nd ed.). Thousand Oaks, CA: Corwin & Education Northwest.

Resau, L. (2012). *Star in the forest*. New York, NY: Delacorte Press.

Restrepo, M. A., Castilla, A. P., Schwanenflugel, P. J., Neuharth-Pritchett, S., Hamilton, C. E., & Arboleda, A. (2010). Effects of a supplemental Spanish oral language program on sentence length, complexity, and grammaticality in Spanish-speaking children attending English-only preschools. *Language, Speech, and Hearing Services in Schools, 41*(1), 3–13.

Rothstein-Fisch, C., & Trumbull, E. (2008). *Managing diverse classrooms: How to build on students' cultural strengths*. Alexandria, VA: ASCD.

Sandler, M. W. (2004). *Island of hope: The story of Ellis Island and the journey to America*. New York, NY: Scholastic.

Senzai, N. H. (2011). *Shooting Kabul*. New York, NY: Simon & Schuster.

Sowden, C. (2005). Plagiarism and the culture of multilingual students in higher education abroad. *ELT Journal, 59*(3), 226–233.

Staehr Fenner, D. (2014). *Advocating for English learners: A guide for educators*. Thousand Oaks, CA: Corwin.

Steinberg, S. (2007). *An introduction to communication studies*. Cape Town, South Africa: Juta.

Stroink, M., & Lalonde, R. (2009). Bicultural identity conflict in second-generation Asian Canadians. *Journal of Social Psychology, 149*(1), 44–65.

Stiggins, R., Arter, J., Chappuis, J., & Chappuis, S. (2006). *Classroom assessment for student learning: Doing it right—using it well*. Upper Saddle River, NJ: Pearson Education.

Valencia, R. R. (1997). Conceptualizing the notion of deficit thinking. In R. R. Valencia (Ed.), *The evolution of deficit thinking: Educational thought and practice* (pp. 1–12). London, UK: Palmer Press.

Valenzuela, A. (1999). *Subtractive schooling: U.S.-Mexican youth and the politics of caring*. Albany: State University of New York Press.

Zion, S., & Kozleski, E. (2005). *Understanding culture*. Tempe, AZ: National Institute for Urban School Improvement. Retrieved from http://guide.swiftschools.org/sites/default/files/documents/Understanding_Culture_Part_1_.pdf

Additional Resources

Breiseth, L. (2016). Getting to know ELLs' families. *Educational Leadership, 73*(5), 46–50.

Ernst-Slavit, G., & Mason, M. (2015). Making your first ELL home visit: A guide for classroom teachers. *¡Colorín Colorado!* Retrieved from http://www.colorincolorado.org/article/making-your-first-ell-home-visit-guide-classroom-teachers

Genesee, F. (2015). The home language: An English language learner's most valuable resource. *¡Colorín Colorado!* Retrieved from http://www.colorincolorado.org/article/home-language-english-language-learners-most-valuable-resource

Gonzalez, A. (2015, December 1). Tips for connecting with non-English speaking parents. *Education Week*. Retrieved from http://www.edweek.org/tm/articles/2015/12/01/tips-for-connecting-with- non-english-speaking-parents.html

How to create a welcoming classroom environment. (2015). *¡Colorín Colorado!* Retrieved from http://www.colorincolorado.org/article/how-create-welcoming-classroom-environment

Mitchell, C. (2016, May 11). Mispronouncing students' names: A slight that can cut deep. *Education Week*. Retrieved from http://www.edweek.org/ew/articles/2016/05/11/mispronouncing-students-names-a-slight-that-can.html?qs=english+language+learners+inmeta:gsaentity_Source%2520URL%2520entities%3DEducation%2520Week%2520Articles

Scaffolding Instruction for ELs

During an end-of-unit assessment, students in Mr. Lee's seventh-grade math class work to solve word problems in which they compare decimals with fractions. As the students solve the problems, they are also expected to explain their thinking in writing. During the assessment, the principal, Ms. McNally, walks in to observe. She notices that the ELs in the classroom receive various types of scaffolds to support their work. For example, ELs of lower proficiency levels are given word banks and sentence frames and higher-level ELs use sentence stems to support their work.

During her postobservation discussion with Mr. Lee, Ms. McNally asks him about these supports and questions whether it is unfair to the non-ELs in the class. Mr. Lee explains that he is assessing students' skills in mathematics and mathematical thinking. The scaffolds, or temporary supports, that he provides ELs give them the language assistance needed in order for them to more accurately demonstrate what they know and can do. He also explains that as the students are given these types of scaffolds during instruction, it would be a significant disadvantage to them to remove the scaffolds during the assessment. He further explains that as the ELs in his class gain greater language proficiency (including the acquisition of mathematical vocabulary and expressions), he will remove the scaffolds, and the students will be able to complete the work independently.

As we describe in the prior scenario, in order for ELs to meet the challenging demands of content-based instruction and acquire the academic language required to do so, they need instructional supports in the form of scaffolds. Findings by the National Literacy Panel showed that the impact of general instructional practices (those practices used with both ELs and non-ELs, such as comprehension monitoring, question asking, and summarizing) is weaker for ELs than it is for their non-EL peers (August & Shanahan, 2006). These findings illustrate that effective instructional practices designed for English-proficient students may be insufficient to meet the learning needs of ELs. This means that ELs require additional types of supports in order to benefit from instruction to the same extent as their English-proficient peers (Goldenberg, 2008). Appropriate scaffolds, which correspond to ELs' strengths and challenges at their particular stage of English language development, can provide this additional support.

This chapter will provide a definition of scaffolds, categories and examples of scaffolds, and strategies for selecting and developing scaffolds based on the academic task and ELs' proficiency levels, as well as other EL background factors. You will also have an opportunity to think about how to select and use scaffolds in your own context. As the use of scaffolds is an essential step in supporting ELs' content and language development, each strategy presented in this book's subsequent chapters also incorporates the use of scaffolded instruction and materials. Throughout this chapter, we indicate specific chapters or pages in the book that you can refer to in order to find out more information on a particular strategy.

What Is a Scaffold?

A scaffold is a temporary support a teacher provides to a student that enables the student to perform a task he or she would not be able to perform alone (Gibbons, 2015; National Governors Association for Best Practices, CCSSO, 2010). This support could come from the materials and/or resources provided to the student, the instructional practices the teacher uses, or how students are grouped during instruction. Gibbons (2015) notes, "Scaffolding, however, is not simply another word for *help*" (p. 16). The ultimate goal of scaffolding is for the student to be able to perform the task independently and no longer require the scaffold.

> Take a minute to jot down a list of the scaffolds that you use in your classroom. Then, consider the following questions:
>
> 1. What factors do you take into consideration when selecting appropriate scaffolds for ELs (e.g., prior schooling and home language literacy), and why?
>
> 2. What are some scaffolds that work best for the ELs in your classroom?
>
> 3. How do you differentiate the scaffolding you provide in order to meet the needs of ELs of varying proficiency levels?

In order to select appropriate scaffolds, you must know your ELs' backgrounds, their strengths and needs, understand the linguistic demands of instructional tasks, and determine which scaffolds will best support your ELs in being able to successfully engage with and complete the academic task. Gibbons contends that instead of simplifying the tasks we give ELs, it is the nature of the scaffold that is critical for ELs' success (2015). It is also important for you to understand how to gradually remove scaffolds so that your ELs can learn to perform tasks independently.

What Are Different Types of Scaffolds?

As we described earlier, scaffolds can be grouped into three main categories: (1) materials and resources, (2) instruction, and (3) student grouping. Figure 3.1, "Categories of Scaffolds," provides examples of each type of scaffold. In determining which scaffolds to use for a particular instructional task, it can helpful to consider which scaffolds would be most effective in each category to support the needs of your ELs. Following the figure, we provide more information on the categories and examples of scaffolds.

FIGURE 3.1 Categories of Scaffolds

Categories of Scaffolds	Examples
Materials and resources	Graphic organizers
	English and/or bilingual glossaries
	English and/or bilingual dictionaries
	Home language materials
	Sentence frames, sentence stems, and paragraph frames
	Visuals
	Word banks or word walls
Instruction	Preidentified and pretaught vocabulary
	Concise instruction of background knowledge
	Reduced linguistic load, repetition, paraphrasing, and modeling
Student Grouping	Structured pair work
	Structured small-group work
	Teacher-led small-group work

Source: Adapted from WIDA Consortium. (n.d.). *WIDA support examples across levels.* Retrieved from https://lincwellell .wikispaces.com/file/view/WiDA+Support++Examples+Across+Levels.pdf

What Types of Materials and Resources Can I Use to Scaffold Instruction?

Materials and resources are the instructional tools that you can provide to ELs to support them in accessing content and sharing their understanding of content orally or in writing.

Graphic organizers can support ELs in a variety of ways, including helping them to organize new information and verbalize the relationships between concepts. You should select which graphic organizer to use based on the task students are being asked to complete. For example, you would use one type of graphic organizer to introduce a new topic (e.g., concept map) and another type of graphic organizer to support students in discussing the development of a story (e.g., story map). Graphic organizers most likely will need to be used in conjunction with other scaffolds, especially for ELs at lower proficiency levels. The graphic organizer in Figure 3.2 could be used as part of a vocabulary sorting activity to reinforce key vocabulary. Students could then use the scaffold to compare and contrast the experiences of colonists and Native Americans (e.g., both colonists and Native Americans grew corn).

English and/or bilingual glossaries can be an effective scaffold for ELs to support them in learning academic vocabulary and engaging with complex texts. In order to most effectively support ELs, glossaries should include student-friendly definitions of key terms and visual representations of each word, whenever possible. For more information on creating student-friendly definitions, see Chapter 6, page 154.

Bilingual glossaries can be beneficial for students who are literate in their home language. They can also provide opportunities for students to build

FIGURE 3.2 Graphic Organizer: Example of Venn Diagram

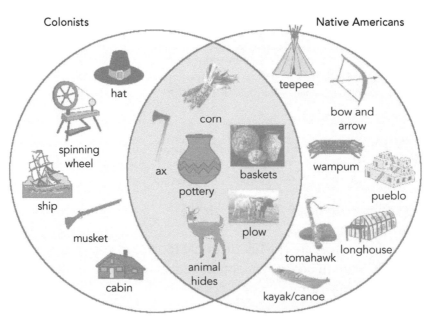

Colonist or Native American
Were these artifacts used by the colonists, Native Americans, or both?

Source: Venn diagram graphic organizer created using Kidspiration® reprinted with permission from Inspiration® Software, Inc. Retrieved from http://www.inspiration.com/Kidspiration-social-studies-examples

FIGURE 3.3 Bilingual Glossary Example

	Glossary			
Word and Translation	English Definition	Example From Text	Picture or Phrase to Represent the Word	Cognate (Yes or No)
bribe *soborno*	*money someone receives in return for help or favors*	*There had to be money for* **bribes**—*tea money, Uncle called it—at both ends of the ocean.*		
escort *acompañar*	*to take someone to a place*	*Father would probably have to go over after her and* **escort** *her across.*		

Source: Adapted from August, D., Staehr Fenner, D., & Snyder, S. (2014). *Scaffolding instruction for English language learners: Resource guide for ELA* (p. 70). Reprinted with permission of American Institutes for Research. Retrieved from https://www.engageny.org/resource/scaffolding-instruction-english-language-learners-resource-guides-english-language-arts-and; text source: Yep, L. (1975). Dragonwings. New York, NY: HarperCollins.

their knowledge of cognates, or words in different languages that have the same linguistic derivation (e.g., *membrane* and *membrana*). Figure 3.3 provides an example of a bilingual glossary. To use a bilingual glossary during instruction, students can be asked to add underlined words in a text to the glossary. The teacher can provide a student-friendly definition. The student can be asked to provide the example from the text, include a picture or phrase that will support their understanding, and note whether or not the word is a cognate in their home language.

Students can also benefit from the use of word family glossaries that not only provide a definition of new vocabulary but also provide students with opportunities to make connections to other words. Figure 3.4 is an example of a word family glossary.

FIGURE 3.4 Word Family Glossary Example

Word	Meaning	Inflectional Forms	Prefixes and Suffixes	Related Words
colony	*(n.) a place that is under the control of a faraway country*	*colonies (pl.)*	*colonize* *colonist* *colonial* *colonialism* *decolonize*	
structure	*(n.) a thing made up of parts that are connected in a certain way*	*structures (pl.)* *structure (v.)* *structuring* *structured*	*restructure* *structural*	*construct* *destruct* *instruct*

Source: Adapted from Strategic Education Research Partnership (2010), Harvard University. Retrieved from http://serpinstitute.org

English and/or bilingual dictionaries are appropriate resources for students who possess literacy skills either in their native language or in English. In fact, based on research conducted on the most useful assessment accommodations for ELs, English and bilingual dictionaries showed promise as effective support tools for ELs when used appropriately (Abedi, Hofstetter, & Lord, 2004; Kieffer, Lesaux, Rivera, & Francis, 2009). Use of an English dictionary is suitable for students who may not be literate in their native language but who have literacy skills in English. It is critical that ELs using an English or bilingual dictionary be provided explicit instruction and guided practice to use the dictionary.

Home language materials can be an effective scaffold for ELs who are literate in their home language. Instructional methods and materials that capitalize on ELs' home language knowledge and skills have been shown to support them in developing literacy and content knowledge in English (August, Branum-Martin, Cardenas-Hagan, & Francis, 2009; Francis, Lesaux, & August, 2006; Restrepo et al., 2010). Home language support can be provided in various ways, but you should have an understanding of ELs' home language literacy skills in order to determine how to best build on ELs' home language knowledge and skills. Examples of supporting materials in the home language include supplementary texts in the home language, home language translations, home language videos, and bilingual homework activities. For more information on home language use and resources, see Chapter 2.

Sentence stems, sentence frames, and paragraph frames can be useful for ELs at varying proficiency levels. Sentence frames (a complete sentence with spaces for students to fill in missing words) can be used with word banks to support ELs of lower proficiency levels in responding to content-based questions and participating in oral pair and group work. Sentence stems (the beginning few words of a sentence) can be used with intermediate ELs. Examples of sentence stems and sentence frames are provided in Figure 4.9 on page 100 in Chapter 4. Paragraph frames can be developed to support ELs of varying proficiency levels by providing the degree of support needed. Paragraph frames can be designed so as to provide greater support at the beginning of the writing task and gradually provide less support as students progress through the task (see Figure 3.5). Paragraph frames could also be used with graphic organizers, glossaries, and/or word banks, as appropriate.

The use of visuals to support the understanding of key ideas and vocabulary is another effective tool for ELs at all levels of proficiency. Visuals can be used when introducing or reinforcing new vocabulary, when providing background knowledge to support understanding of a text, and when learning about a new content topic. Examples of visuals include pictures, videos, and concrete objects (i.e., realia). Figure 3.2 demonstrates how visuals can accompany key vocabulary to support student understanding.

FIGURE 3.5 Paragraph Frame Example

Text Analysis Essay
In _____ a central theme was _____. The author developed the central theme through the use of _____ (insert literary device). _____ (literary device) is _____ (define literary device used).
For example, _____. (Include an example of the use of the literary device in the text). In this example, the author _____ _____. (Explain, in your own words, how the author used the device to support the theme).
Another example is when _____.
In conclusion, _____. (Restate your main argument about the central theme of the text and how the author developed the theme).

Word banks or word walls, like the example in Figure 3.6, can be an effective scaffold for ELs in variety of tasks. For example, ELs might use word banks or word walls when responding to content questions (orally or in writing). ELs might also refer to word walls or word banks when engaging in other content-based tasks, such as completing a graphic organizer on a particular topic, writing a summary of their understanding of a topic, or engaging in an academic conversation. Word banks and word walls can be developed to be used either with a specific task or in conjunction with a content-based unit. However, they should be developed in tandem with vocabulary instruction and practice. They should not be so lengthy as to overwhelm ELs and prevent their use. They can also be accompanied by visuals and home language translations, whenever possible. Figure 3.6 provides an example of word banks used during a math unit focused on multiplication and division.

FIGURE 3.6 Example of Mathematics Word Banks

Multiplication Words	Division Words
as much as	average
by	divide
equal groups	each
groups of	equal parts
multiply	evenly
multiplied by	out of
per	quotient
product of	ratio
times	shared equally

What Instructional Practices Can I Use as Scaffolding?

In addition to scaffolded materials, you can also scaffold your instruction by preteaching vocabulary, providing concise instruction of background knowledge, and using language with a reduced linguistic load, repetition, paraphrasing, and modeling.

The preidentification and preteaching of content-specific academic language and vocabulary is a component of effective instruction for ELs (National Reading Panel, 2000). Instruction that includes an intensive focus on a few key vocabulary words across several days and using varied instructional practices has been shown to be highly effective in supporting ELs' understanding of new content (Baker et al., 2014). Chapters 5 and 6 delve into what academic language is and suggest strategies for teaching and practicing academic language and vocabulary. As a scaffold, the preidentification and preteaching of vocabulary will support ELs in more successfully engaging with complex texts, participating in academic conversations, and gaining content knowledge.

The concise instruction of background knowledge can be an essential scaffold to support ELs in learning new content and engaging with complex texts. ELs may differ from their non-EL peers in terms of the type of content knowledge that they bring to the classroom. Teachers of ELs should determine what background knowledge is necessary for an academic task and how they can concisely teach the information needed or draw on students' previous learning and experiences to help set the context for the lesson. Chapter 7 provides in-depth guidance in determining which background knowledge is essential to teach, as well as concrete steps for concisely teaching background knowledge. For an example of how to concisely teach background knowledge, see Chapter 7.

The use of language with a reduced linguistic load, repetition of key ideas and instructions, paraphrasing key concepts, and modeling thought processes, language skills, and activities can also facilitate ELs in more effectively engaging with and completing academic tasks. With each activity students will be completing, it is important for you to provide straightforward directions and to be cognizant of vocabulary or language structures that may be confusing to ELs. It can be helpful to have the directions written somewhere so that students can refer to them as needed. It can also be helpful to have a student repeat the directions for the class to confirm understanding. However, it should not always be the same student doing this. In addition, it is essential that all activities be modeled so that ELs clearly understand what is expected of them. Activities can be modeled as a whole-group activity, by the teacher, or by a student. You should also check in with ELs as they work on the activity to ensure that they are on track to be successful. The vignette of Ms. Lawrence's ESOL classroom provides an example for how you might model a skill that students will then practice.

Ms. Lawrence's ESOL Classroom: Paragraph Writing

Ms. Lawrence teaches an ESOL class to beginner and intermediate ninth- and tenth-grade ELs. In her class, they have been studying community issues and working on developing claims and counterclaims in their writing. In order to help them prepare to write on a community issue of their choice, she has the class develop an idea web based on the problem of littering in local parks. She asks the students to explain why littering is an important issue and how the problem might be addressed by the community. She also asks students to provide challenges that the community could face in trying to address this issue. Once the class has collaboratively developed the idea web, Ms. Lawrence models for students how they can transition from a graphic organizer to writing a paragraph. She asks for students to identify the main idea from the web, and she also asks them to identify similar ideas in the web. As a class, they write a sample paragraph on the board. Then, Ms. Lawrence asks her students to work in pairs to complete a similar task about their own community issue.

In addition to modeling, you should also be cognizant of the language that you use when practicing key concepts or working with new texts and include repetition and paraphrasing in your instruction. Teachers of ELs need to adjust their vocabulary, rate of speech, and sentence complexity based on ELs' levels of proficiency (Goldenberg, 2008). ELs also benefit from having the opportunity to practice language and skills in multiple different settings and ways (Grabe, 1991; McLaughlin, 1987). For example, in learning about the water cycle, students might be asked to watch a video on the water cycle and answer questions, label a picture that illustrates the water cycle, discuss the water cycle in pairs, and write a short summary of the water cycle.

In addition, when reading new texts, the texts should be broken down into shorter sections, which could mean a few sentences to one to two paragraphs, depending on grade level (August, Staehr Fenner, & Snyder, 2014). Students should be provided opportunities to work closely with each segment of text, and you should help ELs build text knowledge by summarizing or having students summarize and paraphrase texts (Goldenberg, 2008). For more on strategies specific to reading and understanding texts, see Chapter 8.

What strategies do you use to model activities, academic strategies, or skills with your students?

How Can I Use Student Grouping to Scaffold Instruction?

In addition to materials and resources and instructional practices, student groupings can be an effective scaffold (Mackey & Gass, 2006). In order to ensure that student grouping is serving as an effective scaffold, students will need sufficient structure and guidance in engaging in the pair or group task. Also, they most likely will need other types of scaffolds to facilitate the task. Furthermore, it is essential that the teacher be mindful of the purpose of the grouping in the selection of the students (Brooks & Thurston, 2010). In this section, we provide guidelines for pair work and group work.

> What factors do you take into consideration when grouping students?

Pair work can be an effective scaffold when carefully structured. You should be intentional in pairing students. For example, you could pair ELs with the same home language to work together, thus bringing in home language support that you may not be able to provide. Alternatively, you may create mixed-ability or language proficiency pairings in which one student is providing additional support to the other. You might also pair an EL with a non-EL as a way to provide language modeling. It is important that you draw on students' strengths so that all students can have an opportunity to demonstrate what they can do. You will most likely want to mix up your pairings so that students have opportunities to work with different students, practice different skills, and get new perspectives.

Small-group work (either student led or teacher led) can also be an effective scaffold for ELs. In order for small groups to work effectively, ELs need structured activities, practice and preparation for working in groups, and intentional groupings. You can choose to group students in homogeneous groups in order to provide directed support to students with similar strengths and needs. For example, you could provide targeted minilessons (e.g., features of academic language or specific language functions) based on the needs of the group. You could also group students in heterogeneous groups in order to build on students' strengths and have non-ELs or ELs with higher levels of proficiency serve as language models for lower-level ELs. In order to effectively participate in a group, ELs will need to have the task modeled for them and practice with the language demands of the group task. Depending on their proficiency level, they may also need other types of scaffolds, such as sentence stems, graphic organizers, and/or word banks. Small-group work can also be a time to have students receive home language support through the materials provided, teacher-directed support, or the intentional grouping of students with the same home languages.

Planning a Scaffolded Lesson

Think about a lesson that you will soon teach or a lesson with which you are very familiar. Consider what scaffolds might be most appropriate in each of the three categories. Complete the "Scaffold Planning Template" in Figure 3.7.

FIGURE 3.7 Scaffolding Planning Template

Lesson:	
Background of ELs (e.g., home language literacy and ELP levels):	
Categories of Scaffolds	**Possible Scaffold**
Materials and resources	☐ Graphic organizers ☐ English and/or bilingual glossaries ☐ English and/or bilingual dictionaries ☐ Home language materials ☐ Sentence frames, sentence stems, and paragraph frames ☐ Visuals ☐ Word banks or word walls
Instruction	☐ Preidentified and pretaught vocabulary ☐ Concise instruction of background knowledge ☐ Reduced linguistic load, repetition, paraphrasing, and modeling
Student grouping	☐ Structured pair work ☐ Structured small-group work ☐ Teacher-led small-group work

What Steps Should I Take to Scaffold a Lesson?

Planning and preparing to teach differentiated scaffolded lessons that meet the needs of ELs of varying proficiency levels can seem like a daunting task. However, once you gain practice and familiarity with these steps, the process will become an intuitive part of lesson planning. Also, if the thought of differentiating a lesson for ELs of varying proficiency levels seems overwhelming, begin by trying one or two scaffolds that will support all of the ELs in your classroom on a particular task. As you experiment with different types of scaffolds, your ability to meet the varied needs of the ELs

FIGURE 3.8   Five Steps for Scaffolding a Lesson

that you work with will grow. Figure 3.8 lists the five steps we recommend when scaffolding a lesson. Figure 3.10 on page 74 offers a checklist that you can use when developing scaffolded lessons.

Steps for Developing Scaffolded Lesson Plans

1. **Know your ELs.** Before you begin scaffolding lessons for ELs, you have to have an understanding of their backgrounds, needs, and strengths. It may be helpful to keep an index card or use an online tool through your school to keep track of information on each student that will help you to appropriately scaffold instruction. You could also use the template provided in Chapter 2, Figure 2.4, "What I Know About My EL." In determining appropriate scaffolds, you will want to know the student's home language and level of literacy, educational background, and English language proficiency (ELP) level. You will also want to consider your student's

strengths and needs in order to best determine what supports to provide and when it is time to remove a specific support. You should give a preassessment to your students before beginning each unit in order to gauge your students' understanding of content, vocabulary, and language skills. Effective preassessments can help you determine specific scaffolds that you will need to support student understanding.

2. **Analyze the language demands of the lesson.** For each lesson that you will teach, it is essential that you analyze the academic-language demands of every task. In other words, what will ELs have to do during the lesson, and what challenges might they face? Chapter 5 provides specifics on how to analyze the language demands of a text. Once you understand the language demands of the lesson, you can begin to determine how you will support the ELs in your classroom.

As you consider how to scaffold a specific activity, think about the three categories of scaffolds that you may wish to include. It is also important to remember the specific needs of your ELs and recognize that their needs will vary depending the academic task that they are working on. For example, an EL may be testing at an intermediate level but may need the scaffolded support of a high beginner student when completing writing tasks because the student needs a greater degree of support in organizing his or her ideas.

There are no hard and fast rules for selecting appropriate scaffolds for ELs of varying proficiency levels. However, it is important to keep in mind that the goal of scaffolding is to gradually remove scaffolds after providing sufficient structure and support. Ultimately, your ELs should be able to complete academic tasks with the same instructional tools and practices provided to their non-EL peers. That is to say, some scaffolds might be developmentally appropriate for all students (e.g., graphic organizers or pair work) and may be used as supports for the whole class. It is also important to note that an EL's need for a particular scaffold will vary depending on the familiarity of the content and the complexity of the task. For example, a student may be able to draw comparisons between two sports teams the student is familiar with using only sentence stems as a scaffold. However, when asked to draw comparisons between two content-based, grade-level texts read in class, the student may need sentence stems, a word bank, and a graphic organizer in order to be able to successfully complete the task.

Figure 3.9, "Suggested Scaffolds at Each Proficiency Level," provides some general guidelines for selecting scaffolds for ELs at different language proficiency levels. However, it is always important to take into consideration the strengths and needs of your individual ELs when making decisions about scaffolding. The vignette of Ms. Olson's class on pages 72–73 describes the process one teacher used when determining appropriate scaffolds for the ELs in her social studies class.

Scaffolding at Varying Proficiency Levels

Review Figure 3.9, and answer the following questions:

1. Are there any recommendations that you disagree with? Why?

2. What additional scaffolds can you add to each level?

FIGURE 3.9 Suggested Scaffolds at Each Proficiency Level

ELP Level	Scaffolds for Instruction by Level	Scaffolds for All Levels
Beginning	• Access to text, video, and/or instructions in home language, as well as in English • Sentence frames to help ELs respond to text-dependent questions posed throughout the lesson • Word walls and word banks • Reduced linguistic load for language of instruction	• Concise background knowledge • Pretaught vocabulary • Graphic organizers • Glossaries • Dictionaries • Repetition, paraphrasing, and modeling • Pair and small-group work
Intermediate	• Access to text, video, and/or instructions in home language, as well as in English, as appropriate • Sentence stems • Word walls and banks	
Advanced	• See scaffolding for all levels	

Source: Adapted from August, D., Staehr Fenner, D., & Snyder, S. (2014). *Scaffolding instruction for English language learners: A resource guide for ELA.* Retrieved from https://www.engageny.org/resource/scaffolding-instruction-english-language-learners-resource-guides-english-language-arts-and

Ms. Olson's Class: Scaffolding a Unit on Immigration

Ms. Olson, a middle school ESOL teacher, teaches a sheltered social studies class. There are not many ELs in her school, and as a result, her class ranges from beginner to high intermediate students. She is teaching a unit on U.S. immigration. As part of this unit, her students are going to read a text on Ellis Island and answer text-dependent questions to determine the main idea and key details of the text.

In thinking about her students' strengths and needs, Ms. Olson realizes that all students will benefit from having the text chunked into short segments that they will read multiple times in order to answer text-dependent questions in pairs. She also plans to preteach key vocabulary and provide visuals for students. For her beginner students who are Spanish speakers, she plans to offer a supporting text and video in Spanish. She also plans to have bilingual glossaries for all students to complete as they are reading the text since she knows all of her students are literate in their home languages. In developing the text-dependent questions, she plans to provide her beginner ELs with sentence frames and a word bank of terms that they can use to complete the frames. For her low intermediate students, who need less support than her beginners, she plans to provide sentence stems and the glossary for students to use. She determines that two of her high intermediate students will be able to answer the questions without sentence frames using only the text and glossary. Once Ms. Olson has determined the specific scaffolds she will provide, she begins to develop the materials.

3. **Plan your lesson.** Once you have determined the academic-language demands of a lesson, you will need to account for these language demands when planning the lesson. Your lesson plan can include the following:

- Lesson objectives that include language objectives or language performance indicators. In addition to content objectives, include the specific language skills will you be working on in the lesson. In the "Additional Resources" section of this chapter, on page 83, we provide some resources for writing language objectives.

- A list of key vocabulary for preteaching and how you will teach and practice it, additional vocabulary that may also be explained during the course of the lesson, and any visuals or examples that can support students in understanding the unfamiliar words

- Instruction for specific aspects of oral and written language (e.g., understanding idioms, use of cognates, and breaking down complex sentence structures)

- What background knowledge to teach (if any) and how to teach it

- How you will group students during the lesson

- Opportunities for students to practice key concepts in varied ways using multiple modalities (i.e., reading, writing, speaking, and listening)

- How you will assess student learning

4. **Select and develop appropriate materials.** Once you have determined the specific aspects of your lesson, you will need to select

and/or develop the materials that will you will use. Such materials would include the following:

- Graphic organizers
- Home language supporting materials
- Scaffolded text-dependent questions (see Chapter 8)
- Sentence stems, sentence frames, and paragraph frames
- Visuals
- Word banks and word walls

5. **Teach the lesson, adapting scaffolds and materials as needed.** As is common in teaching, you may realize during the course of the lesson that you need to adjust your instruction and/or materials to better meet the needs of your students. Perhaps your students have mastered a key concept, and you need to spend less time on it than you thought, or perhaps some students are struggling with a particular aspect of the lesson, and you need to develop some additional opportunities for students to practice that skill

FIGURE 3.10   Scaffolded Lesson Planning Checklist

Checklist Statement	Yes	No
1. I know the strengths and needs of each EL in relation to the language demands of the lesson. I have set individual goals to help my ELs progress in their acquisition of English.		
2. I have analyzed the language demands of the lesson and identified areas that may be challenging for my ELs.		
3. I have developed a list of key vocabulary to preteach and determined how I will teach and provide opportunities to practice this vocabulary.		
4. I have determined specific aspects of language use that I will focus on during my lesson.		
5. I have determined what background knowledge to teach (if any) and how to teach it in a concise manner.		
6. I have determined how to effectively group students in order to most effectively support their learning of content and acquisition of English.		
7. I have included opportunities for students to practice key concepts in varied ways using multiple modalities.		
8. I have selected home language resources (as appropriate) that can support ELs in learning the new content and academic vocabulary.		
9. I have selected or developed scaffolded materials to support ELs of varying proficiency levels (e.g., graphic organizers, sentence stems and/or sentence frames, and visuals).		
10. I have determined how I will assess student learning and how I will scaffold the assessment for ELs of varying proficiency levels.		

or concept. Formative assessments can help guide your decision making in this area. See Chapter 9 for more information on designing formative assessments for ELs.

You will also need to consider how to scaffold any assessment that you give. For example, it is not reasonable to expect that an EL (particularly a beginner or intermediate EL) who has been completing tasks using scaffolds, such as sentence stems, word banks, and graphic organizers, will be able to successfully complete an assessment without these. After teaching the lesson, you will also need to reflect on its effectiveness with your ELs and revise it as necessary.

How Do I Select the Most Appropriate Scaffold for a Task for Each Modality of Language?

We have provided descriptions and examples and many different kinds of scaffolds. Depending on the language modality (i.e., listening, speaking, reading, and writing) being practiced, ELs will need different kinds of scaffolds. For example, although both speaking and writing require students to produce either oral or written text, the rate of production is usually much greater when speaking. Accordingly, students will need scaffolds that provide easily accessible forms of support, such as a graphic organizer, sentence stem, or word bank. In contrast, when producing written text, ELs have more time to think about their word choice. In addition to a graphic organizer, sentence stem, or word bank, students may also benefit from a glossary or paragraph frame. Figure 3.11 provides a list of the scaffolds that we have discussed in this chapter categorized by modality (listening, speaking, reading, or writing).

FIGURE 3.11 Scaffolding Guidelines by Language Modalities

| Language Modalities | Recommended Scaffolds | | |
	Materials and Resources	Instruction	Student Grouping
Listening	• English or bilingual glossaries • Guiding questions • Supporting materials in home language • Visuals • Word banks or word walls	• Concise background knowledge instruction • Modeling • Paraphrasing • Preidentified and pretaught vocabulary • Repetition	• Pair work • Small-group work

(Continued)

FIGURE 3.11 (Continued)

Language Modalities	Recommended Scaffolds		
	Materials and Resources	Instruction	Student Grouping
Speaking	• Graphic organizers • Sentence stems and sentence frames • Word banks or word walls	• Preidentified and pretaught vocabulary • Modeling	• Pair work • Small-group work
Reading	• English or bilingual glossaries • Guiding questions • Supporting materials in home language • Visuals • Word banks or word walls	• Concise background knowledge instruction • Modeling • Paraphrasing • Preidentified and pretaught vocabulary	• Pair work • Small-group work
Writing	• English or bilingual glossaries • Graphic organizers • Sentence stems, sentence frames, paragraph frames	• Preidentified and pretaught vocabulary • Modeling	• Pair work • Small-group work

APPLICATION ACTIVITY 3.3

Selecting Appropriate Scaffolds

Read the scenario. Then, complete the template to explain which scaffolds you would choose to use for the activity. Provide a reason for your selected scaffolds in the "Rationale" column. We have completed the materials scaffolds and rationale to get you started.

Scenario: A fourth-grade class is working on a unit on conservation. Students have read and discussed several texts that explained why conservation is necessary and offered strategies for conserving natural resources. The students have been asked to select one conservation strategy that they will present to the class. During today's lesson, students will be creating a poster that they will use the following week to present their strategy to the class. In the class, nine of the twenty-four students are ELs. They range in proficiency level from beginner to advanced. If you were the teacher of the class, which scaffolds would you use, and why? Refer to Figure 3.11 to guide your work.

Task:		
Proficiency Level	Selected Scaffolds	Rationale
Beginner	Materials: *Word bank with visuals* Instruction: Student grouping:	
Intermediate	Materials: Instruction: Student grouping:	
Advanced	Materials: Instruction: Student grouping:	

What Is the Role of Collaboration in Scaffolding Instruction for ELs?

As you begin scaffolding your instruction, look for other educators who can support you in this work. Content teachers can turn to the ESOL teachers in their school for resources and advice on how to scaffold a particular lesson. ESOL teachers, on the other hand, should work with content teachers to make sure they know the critical vocabulary and language structures that ELs need to master and the objectives and key understandings for each unit of instruction. For further discussion of collaboration strategies, see pages 138–140 in Chapter 5. The vignette of Ms. Ivanova and Mr. Barnes's science class provides an example of how an ESOL teacher and content teacher might collaborate to plan for a scaffolded lesson. In collaborating, you can leverage each other's leadership skills and areas of expertise to create lessons and scaffolds best suited to your ELs.

Ms. Ivanova and Mr. Barnes's Science Class: A Model for Collaboration

Ms. Ivanova is an EL specialist in a school with a large EL population. She coteaches a fifth-grade science class with Mr. Barnes, a science teacher. There are seven ELs in the class of varying proficiency levels and home languages. To plan a lesson on the basic characteristics of light, Ms. Ivanova and Mr. Barnes met to go over the lesson objectives and discuss the vocabulary that might present challenges. As there are many former ELs in the class, Ms. Ivanova and Mr. Barnes decided to provide scaffolding to the whole class for extra language support. They figured that many students in class who were native English speakers could also benefit from many of the same supports. Ms. Ivanova designed a bilingual concept sort for the key words—*transparent*, *translucent*, and *opaque*—and included definitions, pictures, and the three words in both English and Spanish. This sort will be glued in interactive notebooks and posted on the wall for additional support to those who need it. For the student who speaks Amharic at home, Ms. Ivanova tried to use an online Amharic dictionary but couldn't find a translation for the word *translucent*. She plans to contact a parent who might be able to help. Ms. Ivanova also planned a minilesson to introduce basic sentence stems to the three students at the beginner and low intermediate level that will provide them with the language to participate in the application activity. She plans to print the sentence stems on strips of paper for students to take with them during the activity to use when needed.

- I can see _____. (through it, light)

- I can't see _____. (through it, light)

- It is _____. (transparent, translucent, opaque)

Ms. Ivanova and Mr. Barnes discussed how they would model the conversations they expect to hear in the pair activity. Finally, they planned a quick reinforcement minilesson for any students who indicate in a thumbs up, down, or sideways understanding check that they aren't quite clear on the three terms yet.

What Is the Role of Equity, Advocacy, and Leadership in Developing Scaffolded Materials?

An essential component of advocacy for ELs is equitable educational opportunities and access to effective instruction (Staehr Fenner, 2014). In order for ELs to have access to content to the same extent as their non-EL peers and to minimize the achievement gap that exists between ELs and non-ELs, ELs need instructional practices and materials that are adapted to meet their specific needs (Goldenberg, 2008). Advocating for equity for ELs requires that educators go beyond providing high-quality instructional practices and think critically about what the specific ELs in their classroom will need to acquire language and master content.

APPLICATION ACTIVITY 3.4

Scaffolding a Text

In order to practice the strategies covered in this chapter, read the scenario and the excerpt from *The Great Fire* by Jim Murphy that follows. Then, complete Figure 3.12, "Application Task Template." We have provided a couple of examples to get you started. Once you have completed the task, compare your responses with the responses in Figure 3.13, "Completed Application Task Template," on page 81.

Scenario: An ESOL teacher and a content teacher are coteaching a seventh-grade social studies unit together on the Chicago Fire of 1871. As part of the unit, students will read a text or an excerpt from a text, answer questions about the key ideas of the text, and determine the main idea of the text. Students will be asked to provide evidence from the text to support their answers. There are eight ELs in the class out of a total of twenty-four students. They range in proficiency level from beginner to advanced.

Unit: Chicago Fire of 1871

Text excerpt: *The Great Fire* by Jim Murphy (pp. 18–19)

Chicago in 1871 was a city ready to burn. The city boasted having 59,500 buildings, many of them—such as the Courthouse and the Tribune Building—large and ornately decorated. The trouble was that about two-thirds of all these structures were made entirely of wood. Many of the remaining buildings (even the ones proclaimed to be "fireproof") looked solid, but were actually jerrybuilt affairs; the stone or brick exteriors hid wooden frames and floors, all topped with highly flammable tar or shingle roofs. It was also a common practice to disguise wood as another kind of building material. The fancy exterior decorations on just about every building were carved from wood, then painted to look like stone or marble. Most churches had steeples that appeared to be solid from the street, but a closer inspection would reveal a wooden framework covered with cleverly painted copper or tin.

The situation was worst in the middle-class and poorer districts. Lot sizes were small, and owners usually filled them up with cottages, barns, sheds, and outhouses—all made of fast-burning wood, naturally. . . . Interspersed in these residential areas were a variety of businesses—paint factories, lumberyards, distilleries, gasworks, mills, furniture manufacturers, warehouses, and coal distributors.

Wealthier districts were by no means free of fire hazards. Stately stone and brick homes had wood interiors, and stood side by side with smaller wood-frame houses. Wooden stables and other storage buildings were common, and trees lined the streets and filled the yards.

FIGURE 3.12 Application Task Template

ELP Level	Scaffolds
Beginning ELs	• Background knowledge on parts of a house (prior to reading; perhaps in home language) • Preidentified and pretaught vocabulary (prior to reading, in text-dependent questions, additional practice following lesson)
Intermediate ELs	
Advanced ELs	

Conclusion

In this chapter, we have provided descriptions and examples of different types of scaffolds, general recommendations for scaffolding instruction, and guidelines to use in determining which scaffolds to use in order to meet the needs of ELs of varying proficiency levels in your classrooms. Throughout the remainder of the book, we provide additional strategies for scaffolding materials and examples of scaffolded materials that correspond to each strategy. As you work through the exercises in the remaining chapters, it may be helpful to refer back to this chapter for scaffolding ideas and considerations. In the next chapter, you will learn more specifics on how to incorporate oral language activities into your instruction in order to support ELs' language development and understanding of new content.

Application Activity Responses

The following figure provides a list of possible responses for Application Task 3.4.

FIGURE 3.13 Completed Application Task Template

ELP Level	Scaffolds
Beginning ELs	• Background knowledge on parts of a house (prior to reading; perhaps in home language) • Preidentified and pretaught vocabulary (prior to reading, in text-dependent questions, additional practice following lesson) • Bilingual glossary (during reading) • Chunked text (during reading) • Text-dependent questions with sentence frames and word bank (during reading) • Pair work reading and answering text-dependent questions (during reading)
Intermediate ELs	• Background knowledge on parts of a house (prior to reading) • Preidentified and pretaught vocabulary (prior to reading, in text-dependent questions, additional practice following lesson) • Bilingual glossary (during reading) • Chunked text (during reading) • Text-dependent questions with sentence stems (during reading) • Pair work reading and answering text-dependent questions (during reading)
Advanced ELs	• Preidentified and pretaught vocabulary (prior to reading, in text-dependent questions, additional practice following lesson) • English glossary (during reading) • Chunked text (during reading) • Text-dependent questions (during reading) • Pair work reading and answering text-dependent questions (during reading)

Reflection Questions

1. If you are teaching in a collaborative setting, how might you divide the work to plan and prepare for teaching scaffolded lessons?

2. What steps will you take to get started scaffolding your upcoming lessons?

References

Abedi, J., Hofstetter, C., & Lord, C. (2004) Assessment accommodations for English language learners: Implications for policy based research. *Review of Educational Research, 74*(1), 1–28.

August, A., Branum-Martin, L., Cardenas-Hagan, E., & Francis, D. J. (2009). The impact of an instructional intervention on the science and language learning of middle grade English language learners. *Journal of Research on Educational Effectiveness, 2*(4), 345–376. doi:10.1080/19345740903217623

August, D., & Shanahan, T. (2006). *Developing literacy in second-language learners: Report of the National Literacy Panel on Language Minority Children and Youth.* Mahwah, NJ: Lawrence Erlbaum.

August, D., Staehr Fenner, D., & Snyder, S. (2014). *Scaffolding instruction for English language learners: A resource guide for ELA.* Retrieved from https://www .engageny.org/resource/scaffolding-instruction-english-language-learners-resource-guides-english-language-arts-and

Baker, S., Lesaux, N., Jayanthi, M., Dimino, J., Proctor, C. P., Morris, J., & Newman-Gonchar, R. (2014). *Teaching academic content and literacy to English learners in elementary and middle school* (NCEE 2014-4012). Washington, DC: National Center for Education Evaluation and Regional Assistance (NCEE), Institute of Education Sciences, U.S. Department of Education. Retrieved from http://ies.ed.gov/ncee/wwc/publications_reviews.aspx

Brooks, K., & Thurston, L. P. (2010). English language learner academic engagement and instructional grouping configurations. *American Secondary Education, 39*(1), 45–60.

Francis, D., Lesaux, N., & August, D. (2006). Language of instruction. In D. August & T. Shanahan (Eds.), *Developing literacy in second-language learners* (pp. 365–414). Mahwah, NJ: Lawrence Erlbaum.

Gibbons, P. (2015). *Scaffolding language, scaffolding learning: Teaching English language learners in the mainstream classroom* (2nd ed.). Portsmouth, NH: Heinemann.

Goldenberg, C. (2008, Summer). Teaching English language learners: What the research does—and does not—say. *American Educator.* Retrieved from http://www.aft.org/sites/default/files/periodicals/goldenberg.pdf

Grabe, W. (1991). Current developments in second language reading research. *TESOL Quarterly, 25*(3), 375–406.

Kieffer, M., Lesaux, N., Rivera, M., & Francis, D. J. (2009). Accommodations for English language learners taking large-scale assessments: A meta-analysis on effectiveness and validity. *Review of Educational Research, 79*(3), 1168–1201.

Mackey, A., & Gass, S. (2006). Introduction to special issue on new methods of studying L2 acquisition in interaction. *Studies in Second Language Acquisition, 28*(2), 169–178.

McLaughlin, B. (1987). *Theories of second language learning.* London, UK: Edward Arnold.

Murphy, J. (2010). *The great fire.* New York, NY: Scholastic.

National Governors Association for Best Practices, Council of Chief State School Officers (2010). Common Core State Standards for English language arts and literacy in history/social studies, science, and technical subjects. Appendix A: Research supporting key elements of the standards. Glossary of key terms. Retrieved from http://www.corestandards.org/assets/Appendix_A.pdf

National Reading Panel. (2000). *Report of the national reading panel: Teaching children to read: An evidence-based assessment of the scientific research literature on reading and its implications for reading instruction.* Washington, DC: National Institute of Child Health and Human Development.

Restrepo, M. A., Castilla, A. P., Schwanenflugel, P. J., Neuharth-Pritchett, S., Hamilton, C. E., & Arboleda, A. (2010). Effects of a supplemental Spanish oral language program on sentence length, complexity, and grammaticality in Spanish-speaking children attending English-only preschools. *Language, Speech, and Hearing Services in Schools, 41*(1), 3–13.

Staehr Fenner, D. (2014) *Advocating for English learners: A guide for educators.* Thousand Oaks, CA: Corwin.

Additional Resources

Himmel, J. (2013). Language objectives: The key to effective content area instruction. Retrieved from http://www.colorincolorado.org/article/language-objectives-key-effective-content- area-instruction-english-learners

Levine, L. N., Lukens, L., & Smallwood, B. A. (2013). *The GO TO strategies: Scaffolding options for teachers of English language learners, K–12.* Retrieved from http://www.cal.org/what-we-do/projects/project-excell/the-go-to-strategies

Sigueza, T. (n.d.). Using graphic organizers with ELLs. Retrieved from http://www .colorincolorado.org/article/using-graphic-organizers-ells

WIDA. (2012). WIDA focus on differentiation part 1. Retrieved from https://www .wida.us/get.aspx?id=526

Academic Conversations: A Tool for Fostering ELs' Oral Language Development

Mr. Hernandez's eighth-grade science class, which is about 20 percent ELs of varying proficiency levels, is working on a unit on the relationship among organisms within an ecosystem. They have learned key vocabulary, read a short text on the topic, and answered text-dependent questions about the text they are using. In order to reinforce the material before their next activity, Mr. Hernandez has prepared a set of discussion questions that require students to use the new vocabulary and provide evidence to support their thinking on the topic. Students are seated in groups of four with their desks facing each other.

Before beginning the activity, Mr. Hernandez reviews with students that the purpose of the lesson is for students to gain a deeper understanding of the topic but also to practice their discussion skills. He asks students what it looks like to actively listen to another student. A couple of students respond, saying that they should be facing and making eye contact with the speaker. Mr. Hernandez also refers students to the word bank of unit vocabulary that they have as a handout and sentence stems on the wall that they can use when having a discussion (e.g., I agree with _____ because _____). As the students engage in their discussion of the questions, Mr. Hernandez walks around the room with a checklist. He takes notes of the types of skills students are using in their discussions (e.g., supporting ideas with examples, clarifying, and building on one another's ideas), and he notes which skills the students need to work on. He also copies down some key ideas that students share. He will present these to the whole group as a way of reviewing important ideas and recognizing the contributions students have made during the discussion.

Mr. Hernandez knows that college- and career-readiness standards require that students be able to effectively participate in different types of conversations and with diverse partners. Students are expected to build on others' ideas and express their own ideas clearly and persuasively. Mr. Hernandez also knows that including academic conversations regularly in instruction can benefit both his ELs and non-ELs in terms of their academic language and literacy development, content understanding, and critical-thinking skills (Zwiers & Crawford, 2011). He recognizes that supporting ELs' oral language development will provide a foundation for their reading and writing (Roskos, Tabors, & Lenhart, 2009). However, in order to have ELs effectively participate in academic conversations, they need explicit preparation, scaffolded support, and instruction in what it means to participate, as well as an understanding of their teacher's expectations for participation.

In this chapter, we discuss the importance of including academic conversations in instruction, explain why oral language practice is important for ELs, and provide guidelines for developing effective oral language activities. We then highlight, in depth, four student practices that will foster ELs' engagement in academic discussions in order to support their oral language development and their engagement with challenging content material. We also include tools that you can use when planning and teaching oral language activities and give you some recommendations for different types of oral language activities to use with ELs.

Why Is It Important to Focus on ELs' Oral Language Development?

Most teachers understand that pair and group work provide excellent opportunities for ELs' oral language development because each student has more time to talk than in a large-group discussion, and students often feel more comfortable sharing their ideas in a small-group setting. However, if appropriately structured, pair and small-group discussions can also be highly beneficial to ELs for other reasons. Second language oral language development correlates importantly with second language literacy development, particularly in the area of comprehension (August & Shanahan, 2006). Oral discussions provide meaningful opportunities for ELs to hear and practice discipline-specific language and vocabulary (Zwiers & Crawford, 2011). In addition to supporting their language and literacy development, academic discussions are a powerful way for ELs to learn and remember content. However, despite these benefits, the inclusion of academic discussions in classrooms with culturally and linguistically diverse students is especially lacking (Zwiers & Crawford, 2011). Additionally, even in instances where a teacher includes oral language activities, ELs may find the work challenging if they do not understand their expected role in the task they are working on or if they do not feel confident in using the level of language required for the task.

How Do I Develop Effective Oral Language Activities for ELs?

A critical step in supporting EL engagement in academic conversations is developing oral language activities that will support their participation. To begin exploring this topic, read the following scenario, and then, answer the discussion questions that follow. You can find a discussion of this scenario on pages 88–89.

APPLICATION ACTIVITY 4.1

Ms. Michael Scenario Reflection

Scenario: Ms. Michael's fourth-grade class has been learning about the ways that Native Americans helped colonists in the New World. They have watched a short video on the topic and completed written questions about the video. Ms. Michael wants to build more academic conversations into her lessons, so before transitioning to a new topic, she asks students to *turn and talk*. She tells the students that each person in the pair should share one way Native Americans helped colonists. As the students talk, Ms. Michael walks around the room. She notices that many of her ELs, even those at intermediate and advanced levels of language proficiency, are saying very little or giving one- or two-word answers. She also notices that other pairs are off task, talking about what they want to do after school or what they did during music class. Ms. Michael feels frustrated and stops the activity after about three or four minutes.

1. What might Ms. Michael have done to have better prepared her ELs to participate in the pair discussion?

2. What recommendations would you make to Ms. Michael about how to improve the oral task she provided to her students?

The scenario described above is a cautionary tale. Just providing students opportunities to talk will not necessarily lead to the desired results. As we can see in this scenario, despite Ms. Michael's good intentions, her oral language activity did not meet her expectations, nor did it benefit students to the extent that it might have. Zwiers (2014) makes three recommendations for supporting the development of oral language skills. We have described these, along with our understanding of their importance for ELs.

1. **Adapt activities to include authentic talk.** This strategy requires that during oral language activities, students do not merely read a prepared sentence or two from a piece of paper. They must have opportunities to speak authentically about the topic. This can be a challenge for ELs who may not have the language skills or confidence to do so. For more on helping ELs prepare for opportunities for authentic talk, see Practice 1 on page 92. In developing oral language activities, think about how you might structure an activity in order to help prepare students to speak authentically. For example, you might have students discuss a question in small groups and write down their responses. Then, they could practice sharing their responses with each other (without their notes). After they have had this opportunity to practice, students could change groups and share their responses with someone new.

2. **Use activities that develop meaningful and robust language.** As was described in the example before, students need opportunities to practice, refine, and deepen their oral language responses. Such practice is especially beneficial to ELs, as they are able to hear and use key vocabulary and academic language several times. It also provides ELs, as well as other students, with opportunities to hear the content explained in varied ways and to think about the content from multiple perspectives. Language activities that allow ELs opportunities to practice expressing their ideas in clearer and more compelling ways will support their oral language development. Examples of these types of activities include an interview grid, 1-3-6, and debrief circles. For an explanation of these activities, see pages 98, 104, and 106.

3. **Use open-ended discussion prompts.** Zwiers (2014) recommends discussion prompts that support evaluation. If you ask students to rank,

prioritize, or choose something, it is likely to foster greater discussion and debate among students than if you ask them merely to identify. As we saw in the scenario in Application Activity 4.1, Ms. Michael's discussion prompt was insufficient to garner much student interest in the topic. Perhaps if she had asked students to identify the most important way Native Americans helped colonists and to support their answer with evidence, students might have had more to say.

The types of questions and prompts teachers develop are important for fostering student participation and engagement (Zwiers, 2010). Figure 4.1 provides examples of these types of prompts and questions that will encourage greater participation and student learning. Teachers can provide these types of prompts in a graphic organizer or a journal prompt prior to classroom discussions. We have adapted this table to include specific considerations for ELs.

In order to guide you in developing oral language activities that will support ELs' active participation, we have developed a checklist that you can refer to. Throughout this chapter, as we introduce new strategies and recommendations, we will add to the checklist. See Figure 4.2 for the first criteria of the checklist.

> *Think about an oral language activity that you included in a previous lesson that you taught. To what extent did you include authentic opportunities for ELs to speak, time for students to strengthen and deepen their responses, and engaging discussion prompts? What might you do to improve that activity if you were to teach it again?*

FIGURE 4.1   Types of Questions, Considerations for ELs, and Examples

Create questions that . . .	EL Consideration	Example Question
Focus students on key content concepts.	Ensure ELs have the proper scaffolding (e.g., visuals, glossaries, and home language support) to focus on key content concepts.	• What is the *Bill of Rights*, and why is it important? • Draw a picture of the water cycle, and explain how it works.
Allow for divergent and personalized responses, as long as they connect back to evidence in the material being studied.	Ensure that ELs' background experiences and cultures are valued and drawn from during instruction.	• How does our school manage waste? • If you were a soldier during this time, would you have . . . ? Why?
Emphasize one or more thinking skills being developed in the lesson and unit. Such skills include questioning, interpreting, classifying, persuading, evaluating, analyzing, comparing, and synthesizing.	Provide supports so that ELs can engage in these higher-order thinking skills (such as sentence stems and frames).	• What can you infer about the character's relationship with his grandmother based on his actions? • What do you think is the most significant effect of the Industrial Revolution? Why?
Deepen understandings and emphasize the essential objectives of the text, lesson, and/or unit.	Ensure that ELs understand the essential objectives and that instruction of academic language is intertwined with instruction of the content.	• What does this have to do with our goal of learning how plants get the materials they need to grow?

Source: Adapted from Think-pair-share tips. Retrieved from http://jeffzwiers.org/tools

FIGURE 4.2 Oral Language Activity Checklist

Criteria	Yes	No	Follow-Up Steps
1. Have I developed an oral language activity that will allow students authentic opportunities to speak, provides students time to strengthen and deepen their responses, and includes engaging discussion prompts?			

What Practices Can ELs Engage in to Support Their Participation and Engagement in Oral Language Activities?

In order to support ELs' participation and engagement in academic conversations, we have identified four practices for supporting this engagement, as well as instructional tools that can support these practices. These practices were synthesized and adapted from Zwiers and Crawford's (2011) work to account for the specific strengths and needs of ELs. The four practices are as follows:

1. Come to the discussion prepared.

2. Use appropriate body language.

3. Participate by taking turns.

4. Make connections.

We will be discussing each of these practices in depth, providing example scenarios to illustrate the practices and tools that can support the practices. In addition to focusing on these practices, it is also important for teachers to create a classroom climate that supports the sharing of diverse ideas, respectful listening, and active participation. Students need to understand that academic conversations are an opportunity for them to think more deeply and critically about a topic, and they will be able to do this deeper-level thinking when they take the opportunity to share their ideas and listen to the ideas of others.

Practice 1: Come to the discussion prepared.

In order for ELs to successfully participate in an academic discussion, they must have sufficient preparation in the content they will be discussing. It is unfair to expect ELs to engage in pair or small-group tasks in which they feel unprepared to contribute. For example, in the scenario on page 87, Ms. Michael provided no guidelines to students in terms of the types of language they should use. In addition, she did not scaffold the activity so as to support her ELs' participation and production of oral language.

In order to support ELs in being prepared for the academic conversation, you can draw on many of the strategies that we address in this book, including the following:

- Use of scaffolded materials (Chapter 3)

- Modeling (Chapter 3)

- Explicit vocabulary instruction (Chapter 6)

- Instruction of essential background knowledge (Chapter 7)

- Use of text-dependent questions for text analysis (Chapter 8)

This doesn't mean that oral language activities should only be used to summarize what students already know but rather that ELs should have sufficient content and language knowledge and support in order to be able to take their understanding of the content to a deeper level. For example, in the opening vignette about Mr. Hernandez's eighth-grade science class, prior to the discussion, students had learned key vocabulary, read a short text on the relationships among organisms in an ecosystem, and answered text-dependent questions about the text. Students were also given a word bank containing the list of vocabulary that they had been studying and sentence stems to support their participation in discussions.

In structuring group and pair discussions, it can be helpful for ELs to have written ideas or notes for reference. However, it is also important to help students transition to being able to speak without the use of notes so as to support more authentic conversations. For example, fifth-grade teacher Stacy Brewer has her students use sticky notes to write down ideas that they have that they want to share with the class as they are reading (Teaching Channel, 2012). In this way, students can remember their big ideas but not be overly dependent on written notes in a discussion.

Part of supporting ELs in being prepared is also helping them to build their confidence to participate in academic conversations. For example, you might first have students think about their responses to a text individually and take notes on their responses (as was described above with the use of sticky notes). Then, they can share their responses with a partner. This allows them to practice in a low anxiety-producing context. Finally, you can ask students to share their responses with the whole group. In addition to building confidence, this method also allows ELs to process the academic content and language from reading about it, writing notes about it, saying it to one person as a rehearsal, and then saying it confidently to the whole group as a polished product. It is important to note that some ELs (those with lower levels of language proficiency or those who are less confident speaking in front of a group) may need more time before they are ready to speak in front of the whole class.

In Figure 4.3, we have added to the checklist to account for Practice 1: Come to the discussion prepared. For the complete checklist, see Figure 4.10.

FIGURE 4.3   Oral Language Activity Checklist

Criteria	Yes	No	Follow-Up Steps
1. Have I developed an oral language activity that will allow students authentic opportunities to speak, provides students time to strengthen and deepen their responses, and includes engaging discussion prompts?			
2. Have my ELs had sufficient exposure to the content and academic language needed to participate in the activity? (Practice 1)			

Practice 2: Use appropriate body language.

In order to effectively participate in academic conversations, students must understand that there are certain cultural expectations for how you should conduct yourself when participating in a discussion. Zwiers and Crawford (2011) identify the following behaviors as those valued in an academic setting:

- Appropriate eye contact (which can mean not constantly staring at the other person but also not always looking down, away, or past the other person)

- Facing one another with the entire body

- Leaning toward the person speaking

- Showing understanding through head nodding

- Appropriate gesturing (not rolling eyes, sighing, or folding arms)

- Showing interest by laughing and smiling appropriately

- Using encouraging language to promote continued conversation (e.g., uh huh, hmm, interesting, yes, okay)

- Interrupting to ask for clarification if needed (pp. 41–42)

It is likely apparent from reviewing this list that these behaviors are the expectations of teachers from a common cultural background, and it is important to note that nonverbal communication may be incongruent across cultures.

ELs may need direct instruction in what is considered culturally appropriate body language for discussions. It is important to recognize that what is considered appropriate body language in U.S. culture may not be appropriate in other cultures, and you need to be careful in how you use nonverbal communication when interacting with students from diverse backgrounds. You can provide students some examples of how expectations of body language vary among cultures as a way of getting the discussion started, and you can also ask students to provide their own examples. For example, in the United States, making eye contact with a speaker shows that you are interested in what he or she has to say. However, in other cultures, eye contact may be perceived as a challenge, or extended eye contact between members of the opposite sex may be considered taboo. As you explain what is considered appropriate body language in U.S. culture, be sure to demonstrate respect for your ELs' cultures. We don't

> *How might the ELs in your classroom have different understandings or expectations for what a conversation looks like (e.g., both in terms of body language and communication patterns)?*

want ELs to abandon their cultural practices in the name of assimilation. You can also work with families to tailor teaching practices so they're appropriate for all of the students in your classrooms (Hansen, 2010).

Another strategy for teaching ELs about appropriate body language for conversations is to model inappropriate body language. You could either do a role-play with a coteacher (if you have one) or you could ask select students to role-play different behaviors (e.g., slouching, doodling, or laughing at what other people say) during a small-group conversation while the rest of the class observes. Then, you could discuss what behaviors the students observed and what alternative, appropriate body language should look like. You could also use this opportunity to discuss how cultural expectations for body language and appropriate behaviors vary among cultures (e.g., in some cultures, students stand up when the teacher enters the room).

In order to reinforce appropriate body language, you could use an observation checklist to monitor student behaviors (see Figure 4.4 as an example). You could also have students complete a self-evaluation in which they reflect on their own body language during discussions (see Figure 4.5 as an example). Ms. Nguyen, a sixth-grade English language arts teacher, uses what she calls a *participation protocol* with her students (Teaching Channel, 2014a). She includes the following criteria in her class's participation protocol:

- Look at your partner.
- Lean toward your partner.
- Lower your voice.
- Listen attentively.
- Use evidence and examples.

FIGURE 4.4 Discussion Checklist

Student Name	Scaffolds used with ELs	Uses appropriate body language			Makes connections to what others said			Asks clarifying questions			Supports ideas with evidence			Comments
		1	2	3	1	2	3	1	2	3	1	2	3	

FIGURE 4.5 Student Discussion Self-Assessment

Name _____   Date _____

Discussion Self-Assessment

During today's discussion, I . . .

_____ Made eye contact when speaking and listening

_____ Used appropriate gestures

_____ Showed interest by nodding and using encouraging language

_____ Asked for clarification when I didn't understand

Something I did well in the discussion was _____.

Something I want to work on during discussions is _____.

As students are having discussions, she uses a checklist to monitor how well they are meeting these criteria.

Figure 4.4 is an example of a discussion checklist that can be used when observing student discussions (of ELs as well as non-ELs). The criteria being evaluated can change based on what skills you are working on in the lesson. The numbers represent the following: (1) needs additional support in achieving expectations, (2) meets expectations, and (3) exceeds expectations. You can also include a space to write down the types of scaffolds you used with your ELs (e.g., sentence frames or word banks) and ideas you have about next steps (in the comments section).

Figure 4.5 is an example of a student self-assessment of participation in discussions that could be used with all students. For ELs, you would need to discuss and model each of the criteria in the self-assessment. You could change the criteria based on what skills you are working on in your class and the grade level, as well as students' levels of English proficiency.

In Figure 4.6, we have added to the checklist to account for Practice 2: Use appropriate body language.

FIGURE 4.6 Oral Language Activity Checklist

Criteria	Yes	No	Follow-Up Steps
1. Have I developed an oral language activity that will allow students authentic opportunities to speak, provides students time to strengthen and deepen their responses, and includes engaging discussion prompts?			

Criteria	Yes	No	Follow-Up Steps
2. Have my ELs had sufficient exposure to the content and academic language needed to participate in the activity? (Practice 1)			
3. Have my ELs been taught appropriate body language for academic discussions? Do I have a way of monitoring their body language? (Practice 2)			

Practice 3: Participate by taking turns.

It is important for students to take turns speaking. In pairs, it is likely that turn taking will occur naturally. However, in a small or large group, it can be challenging for ELs to have their turn. A tool such as a *talking rock* or *talking stick* (a rock or a stick that students hold to "give them the floor" to talk) can encourage all members of the group to take part in the discussion. Students can pass the talking rock or talking stick around in a circle, and the student who has the rock or stick can take the opportunity to say something or pass. The rock or stick can also be placed in the center of the group, and students can take it as they have something to say.

How you set up your activity and the supports you provide can also encourage greater participation by all students, including ELs. Some examples of visual tools that would support participation include graphic organizers (e.g., story map or Venn diagram), manipulatives, and objects connected to the unit. For example, you might have students complete a Venn diagram in which they compare and contrast two key concepts from the unit. Then, in small groups, they can be required to take turns sharing similarities and differences that they found between the two concepts and adding to their diagrams. In this example, both the structure of the activity and the tool (Venn diagram) would support participation by all members of the group. Similarly, you could have students work in pairs to use manipulatives to explain how they solved a particular math problem. They could discuss how they could take different approaches to solve the same problem or how they might use a similar approach to solve different problems.

Figure 4.7 provides an example of an activity that you can use to have students speak to several different students. Students will have short conversations with three to four students in the class and summarize each person's response, first orally and then in writing, in an interview grid. The teacher could ask the students to write down three names in the column under "Name" that the teacher assigns as interviewees to one student. The teacher may want to consider assigning interviewees who speak the same

FIGURE 4.7 Interview Grid for High School Biology Class

Name	Contrast the differences between prokaryotic and eukaryotic cells	Explain how mitochondria convert energy in cells	Argue why cells must be small in size
Marcelo			
Sofia			
Amadou			

native language as the interviewer or perhaps assigning a native English speaker who is supportive to a beginning EL.

You could also adapt this activity to develop an information gap activity. For example, you could have two different sets of one to two questions and assign each student to either Group A or Group B. Students from Group A would meet up with Group B members in order to ask their questions. At the end of the activity, the class could compile a list of possible responses. ELs of lower proficiency levels may need word banks or sentence stems as support for this activity.

An additional way to encourage turn taking is to teach and model strategies for inviting someone into the conversation (e.g., Manuel, what do you predict the girl in the story will do next?). You can model these strategies, and you can also teach students to use these strategies in their small group. ELs of lower proficiency levels or those who may feel particularly uncomfortable speaking in a group should be given nonthreatening opportunities to practice speaking in both small groups and whole groups. For example, this could mean asking students to read the learning objective for the day or directions that are written on the board. It might also mean wrapping up a whole-group discussion by asking a question that all students who haven't yet contributed to the conversation can answer (e.g., What was one big idea you found most interesting from today's discussion?). If you plan to do that, it is helpful to tell students that you will be doing that, so they know to expect it. These types of less threatening opportunities to speak will help build students' confidence in their abilities.

In Figure 4.8, we have added to the checklist to account for Practice 3: Participate by taking turns.

Practice 4: Make connections.

Not only do students need to be able to share their own opinions by using evidence from texts or content material being studied, they also need to interact with the ideas of others. Modeling and providing ELs with key phrases can support them in their efforts to build on the ideas of others. Some educators, as well as the Teaching Channel, use the term *talk moves*

FIGURE 4.8 Oral Language Activity Checklist

Criteria	Yes	No	Follow-up Steps
1. Have I developed an oral language activity that will allow students authentic opportunities to speak, provides students time to strengthen and deepen their responses, and includes engaging discussion prompts?			
2. Have my ELs had sufficient exposure to the content and academic language needed to participate in the activity? (Practice 1)			
3. Have my ELs been taught appropriate body language for academic discussions? Do I have a way of monitoring their body language? (Practice 2)			
4. Have I provided sufficient structure to the activity (including the use of supporting tools) so as to encourage all of my ELs to participate in the activity? (Practice 3)			

to describe the discourse behaviors that students need to practice in order to effectively engage in a discussion. Such behaviors include restating what was said, agreeing and disagreeing, asking clarifying questions, adding to or piggybacking on what someone has said, and making connections between ideas.

In Ms. Groves's eighth-grade English development classroom, she posts sentence stems that correspond to the various talk moves on the wall (Teaching Channel, 2014b). These sentence stems are available for students to use during discussion, and Ms. Groves asks students to use them as she walks around monitoring the small-group discussions. Another idea for supporting talk moves is for each student to have a handout or index card with sentence stems that they could use during discussions. Depending on the language abilities of your ELs, you could provide them with simpler or more complex language to use. Figure 4.9 provides some possible sentence stems for specific types of talk moves.

A game that you can play to help your ELs practice using different types of talk moves is Conversation Bingo. Each student receives a conversation bingo card with sentence starters on it. Over the course of a week, when a student uses one of the sentence starters, he or she gets to cross it off. Once a student has crossed off a complete horizontal, vertical, or diagonal line, he or she can use it to be a listener for another group, win a prize, or earn bonus points for getting bingo and using five different conversation starters (L. Kuti, personal communication, September 22, 2016).

FIGURE 4.9 Talk Moves Sentence Stems and Frames

Talk Move	Sentence Stem/Frame
Restating	• So you are saying . . . • What I understood you to say is . . .
Agreeing	• I agree with (Yuri) because . . . • (Emma's) point about . . . was important because . . .
Disagreeing	• I disagree because . . . • I see it differently because . . .
Asking a clarifying question	• Could you give an example of . . . ? • I'm confused when you say . . .
Adding to an idea	• I'd like to add to (Rosa's) point. I think that . . . • I agree with (Woo Jin) and furthermore I think that . . .
Making connections between ideas	• When (Albert) said . . . , it reminded me of . . . • I see a connection between what (Laura) said and what (Karolina) said. The connection is . . .

Source: Staehr Fenner, D., & Snyder, S. (2015). Using pair and group work to develop ELs' oral language skills [blog post]. Retrieved from http://www.colorincolorado.org/blog/using-pair-and-group-work-develop-ells%E2%80%99-orallanguage-skills

A conversation minilesson is a way for teachers to introduce a conversation skill to students and then have them practice it in a relatively short time period. Examples of possible minilessons could include asking each other for supporting examples, building on a partner's idea, and paraphrasing conversation themes. Minilessons should include opportunities for students to watch and analyze strong models of the conversation skill being focused on and opportunities to practice and build independent skills.

In Figure 4.10, we have added to the checklist to account for Practice 4: Make connections.

FIGURE 4.10 Oral Language Activity Checklist

Criteria	Yes	No	Follow-Up Steps
1. Have I developed an oral language activity that will allow students authentic opportunities to speak, provides students time to strengthen and deepen their responses, and includes engaging discussion prompts?			
2. Have my ELs had sufficient exposure to the content and academic language needed to participate in the activity? (Practice 1)			

Criteria	Yes	No	Follow-Up Steps
3. Have my ELs been taught appropriate body language for academic discussions? Do I have a way of monitoring their body language? (Practice 2)			
4. Have I provided sufficient structure to the activity (including the use of supporting tools) so as to encourage all of my ELs to participate in the activity? (Practice 3)			
5. Have I provided ELs sufficient practice and support in making connections to others' ideas before and during the oral language activity? (Practice 4)			

APPLICATION ACTIVITY 4.2

Ms. Rawlings Scenario Reflection

Before we move on to describe some different types of oral language activities, read the following vignette about Ms. Rawlings's elementary English language development class. As you read it, reflect on the following questions:

1. The class described in the vignette is composed of all ELs. How might you adapt some of the strategies that she uses during this lesson in a classroom of ELs and non-ELs?

2. How might you differentiate the instruction to meet the needs of ELs of varying proficiency levels?

Scenario: Ms. Rawlings is an ESOL teacher in a district with a small but growing EL population. She works with a group of third-grade ELs with the primary goal of ensuring that these students can access the grade-level curricula. The students are at low intermediate level of proficiency, which means they know and use some social and academic language with visual support.

Her students are learning about fairy tales in their grade-level classroom. Through communication with their classroom teachers, Ms. Rawlings knows that her students need to develop more background knowledge around key elements of fairy tales and the specific content vocabulary involved in discussing them. They are also working on getting more comfortable with speaking in class in general.

In previous sessions together, they established discussion norms that included the following:

- Listen carefully to others

- Explain my ideas

- Ask questions when I am confused

- Participate

- Connect my ideas to others' ideas

They also created a reference chart of key sentence frames for giving examples (e.g., *for example* and *An example of this is _____*), agreeing or disagreeing (e.g., *I agree with _____ because* and *I respectfully disagree*), and supporting claims with evidence (e.g., *I think _____ because _____*). Ms. Rawlings has modeled using the frames and has set up simple practice activities using social topics to get students more comfortable with using this academic discussion language in a more familiar context. For example, they have discussed whether or not they should be allowed to chew gum in school.

During this lesson, Ms. Rawlings and her students review their discussion norms and frames chart. Then, she reads her students a simple version of *The Three Little Pigs* and introduces key vocabulary for fairy tale elements. Each vocabulary word is accompanied by a visual and a sample sentence containing the new vocabulary items. Then, as a group, the students identify the elements in the fairy tale they just read on a graphic organizer. As they respond, Ms. Rawlings uses probes to encourage more language use. A phrase such as "Say more" elicits more language and encourages them to go into more detail in a nonthreatening way. It also communicates her interest in what they have to say. At times, she asks her students to clarify their thinking by rephrasing what they've said: "So are you saying _____?" This again communicates her desire to understand what they are trying to say and gives them the opportunity to better explain their ideas.

Ms. Rawlings continues, "Can you find an example of _____ in the book?" As she prompts students, she gestures toward their sentence frame chart to encourage their use of the academic discussion language they've been practicing in previous sessions. A student flips through the book and describes the example using the sentence frame she's been learning. Ms. Rawlings turns to one of her other students, "Can you rephrase or repeat what _____ just said?" This seemingly simple act encourages careful listening by all. She then follows up, "Do you agree with _____? Why, or why not? What's your evidence for _____?"

They continue discussing the different elements of a fairy tale. Their follow-up lesson later in the week is to read a new, unfamiliar fairy tale, record the elements together, and discuss it using their elements and language charts. Eventually, students read and analyze a fairy tale independently using a graphic organizer to record their responses. They then come together and have a discussion around what they have found. This application activity presents several ways to create opportunities for academic discussion. To support students in participating in academic discussion, some lower proficiency level ELs may need opportunities to get more comfortable speaking in class in general.

What Are Some Activities for Supporting ELs' Oral Language Development?

There are many different oral language activities that you can use in your classroom. As you are deciding what activity to use, reflect on your learning objectives for the activity and what type of activity will best help your students meet those objectives. Also, remember, the activity should accomplish the following goals:

- Provide students opportunities to hear and practice key academic language.

- Be structured in such a way so that all students will have an opportunity (and sufficient support) to share their ideas.

- Push student understanding of content to deeper levels.

We have described a few of our favorite activities to support ELs' oral language development here, beginning with a more in-depth description of Socratic circles. You can adapt these activities to meet the specific needs of the ELs in your classroom by providing various types of scaffolding, such as sentence frames, sentence stems, word banks, and strategic student grouping. You can also encourage (or require) students to use specific vocabulary in their conversations.

Socratic Circle

We would first like to explain an activity that may take a bit more preparation to use successfully with ELs but one that can be highly effective for all students once they are familiar with the process. It is most commonly used with middle and high school students. A Socratic circle, also known as Socratic seminar, is a teaching strategy used to support deep understanding of a specific piece of writing, music, or art. It is based on Socrates's belief in the importance of developing students' ability to think critically and independently through the use of dialogue. The focus of the Socratic method is on giving students questions rather than answers. By posing and responding to questions, students examine and reevaluate their beliefs on a particular topic. In addition to fostering critical thinking, Socratic circles are designed to support student collaboration, creativity, and intellectual curiosity.

Prior to the Socratic circle activity, students read, analyze, and take notes on a common "text"[1] (e.g., novel, poem, song, or painting). Students are then typically divided into two groups—an inner and an outer circle. The activity begins with the inner circle of students engaging in dialogue about the text and the outer circle observing. After a specified period of time, the outer circle provides feedback to the inner circle on their conversation, and the two groups of students switch roles. Throughout the activity, the teacher acts as a facilitator. The activity is not meant to result in a winning argument, as opposed to debates. Students are expected to use the text to support their ideas, ask questions, share their opinions, and build on the ideas of others.

Although they present great potential to engage students in discussions around complex text, Socratic circles can be especially challenging to ELs. First of all, the mere thought of having to speak about a nuanced topic in front of the entire class without linguistic support could be especially nerve racking for ELs who are at lower levels of proficiency (or shy students in general). In order to effectively participate in this type of discourse, ELs need to have a deep understanding of the text being discussed.

Also, the pace and language of the discussion may prove a challenge for some ELs who need time and support to "digest" what others are saying and frame their ideas before presenting them orally. In addition, without specific support, ELs may not have the academic language necessary to orally summarize, refute, or support the ideas of others. Figure 4.11 provides specific strategies to help ELs prepare for and participate in Socratic circles.

Eight additional activities for supporting ELs' oral language follow.

1-3-6

In this activity, students are given a discussion question or task that they work on individually. Then, they move to a group of three where they discuss their responses to the question. Finally, two groups of three combine to form a group of six. With the group of six, they finalize their answers

---

1. For a more nuanced description of what text is, see Chapter 7.

FIGURE 4.11 Helping ELs Prepare for a Socratic Circle

Strategy	Recommendations for ELs
Preparing for Socratic circles: ELs need deep understanding of the text.	• Be sure that students are adequately prepared for the activity by giving them sufficient scaffolding to understand the text (e.g., concise background knowledge, glossaries, and scaffolded text-dependent questions). • Provide students with graphic organizers to help them frame their thinking about the text in writing. • Give students practice and support in developing open-ended questions about a particular text. • Give students practice in anticipating the types of open-ended questions that other students might ask about a text.
Modeling: ELs need to know what high-quality responses and questions sound like.	• Model a successful Socratic circle by first practicing the following steps with a familiar text at a lower level of complexity. • Provide ELs with opportunities to practice questioning and responding in small groups before expecting them to participate in a whole-class discussion. • Provide sentence stems that students can use in asking and responding to questions, clarifying others' ideas, and commenting on the ideas of others. Give students practice in using these stems. • Highlight questions or responses that are particularly effective. Explain why those particular questions or responses are of high quality.
Balancing Participation: Help support ELs' participation in the discussion.	• If some students are dominating the discussion, limit all participants to a certain number of questions and responses. • Guide students to invite those who are less active to participate (e.g., "Marisol, what do you think about what Sam said?"). • As the facilitator, use the last few minutes of the discussion to invite those students who haven't asked a question to take part in the discussion. • Be comfortable with silence. The time will allow those who need more time to think more opportunities to participate.

Source: Staehr Fenner, D., & Snyder, S. (2015). Socratic circles and the Common Core: An introduction [blog post]. Retrieved from http://www.colorincolorado.org/blog/socatic-circles-and-common-core-introduction-part-i

to the question and present these to the large group. These three steps can provide ELs opportunities to practice and refine their language and deepen their thinking on the topic.[2]

---

2. In Mr. Sevin's ninth-grade Advanced Via Individual Determination (AVID) class, his students are asked to individually complete a graphic organizer in which they list the most important ideas from a chapter they have read. Then, students discuss their ideas in groups of three and four. Finally, two groups combine to further refine their answers and develop a short presentation of their responses that they present to the rest of the class (Teaching Channel, 2013).

Action Thermometer

For this activity, you should decide on a statement that students can have an opinion about that is connected to your lesson. Ask students who agree with the statement to go to one end of the classroom. Students who disagree should go to the other end. Students who are neutral or undecided can go to the center of the room. Ask the students to find a partner in their group and share why they went where they did. You can also ask students to find someone in a different group to discuss why they went where they did. Call on a couple of students from each of the three groups to share what their partners said. Ask if any students have changed their minds after hearing the discussion.

Carousel

To set up for this activity, write questions connected to the unit of study on poster paper and around the room. There should be one piece of poster paper per question. Divide students into small groups so that there is one question per group. Give each group of students a different color marker, and assign them a question to start with. Students discuss and write their responses on the poster paper. After three to five minutes, have the groups rotate to another question. You can have each group discuss each of the questions if you have sufficient time. You should encourage the groups to add on to and provide additional evidence to the responses that are written. Debrief each question as a whole class, providing appropriate scaffolds for your ELs.

Debrief Circles (Also Known as Reel Activity)

For this activity, give each student an index card, and ask him or her to answer two questions (one on each side of the card). Have students count off by twos. They should form two concentric circles, with one student facing another student (e.g., number ones in the inner circle and number twos in the outer circle). Have students share their responses to one of the questions with each other. Then, have students in the inner circle move one or two students to the left. Students can then share their responses to the second question. You can have students move multiple times, each time sharing their responses and hearing other students' responses. You can also have students put away their index cards as they gain increasing confidence in speaking about the topic. If you want to up the rigor on this activity (and if the students have a high enough English proficiency level to do so), the students can write their own questions. The teacher can preview and accept the questions or send them back for edits before the questions are used. As a wrap-up to the activity, you can ask students to compare how their responses differed from those of their peers or to share whether their responses changed based on listening to their peers.

Each One to Teach One

In pairs, students take on the roles of teacher and student. The "teacher" teaches the student a certain concept that she or he has been working on in the class using specific sentence starters and academic vocabulary. Then, the students switch roles, and the new "teacher" has to teach a different concept (L. Kuti, personal communication, September 22, 2016).

Role-Play

Sometimes, students can feel intimidated or strange using academic language to discuss an issue. Role-playing can be a good way to have students tackle these issues under the guise of someone else. For example, during a science unit focused on conservation, you might ask students to take on specific roles (e.g., a scientist and a businessperson) and discuss, in pairs, the pros and cons of renewable energy sources, such as wind or solar energy. Similarly, in a history course, you might ask students to take on the roles of historical figures in order to discuss a particular topic (e.g., a Patriot and a Loyalist during the American Revolution).

World Café

Put students in groups of three to four. Give each group a topic to discuss. One person should be the designated leader. That person should take notes on the discussion on a piece of poster paper. After a set period of time, all students, except for the leader, should move to another discussion group. Students do not have to stay in the same groups. The leader provides highlights of the previous discussion to the new group. A new leader is assigned. The new group discusses the same topic and adds to the notes. In order to debrief the activity, you can hang the posters in front of the class and have students share highlights from their discussion.

How Can I Collaborate Around ELs' Academic Conversations?

The inclusion of academic conversations in lessons is also an excellent opportunity for ESOL teachers and content teachers to collaborate. Figure 4.12 illustrates the different roles teachers might fill in preparing for and teaching lessons that incorporate academic conversations. Please note that these are recommendations and should be adapted to meet your and your students' needs.

FIGURE 4.12 Potential Roles for Teaching Academic Conversations in a Collaborative Setting

Content Teachers	ESOL Teachers	Both
• Develop academic-conversation activity and prompt to support student understanding of content. • Be explicit with students about why they are practicing oral language skills and what academic conversations include. • Develop checklists and other assessments to monitor student progress (including self-assessments for students).	• Determine supports needed for ELs to effectively participate in an oral language task. • Share cultural differences that may impact ELs' participation. • Develop scaffolds to support ELs' understanding of content and participation in activity (e.g., background knowledge instruction and sentence stems). • Work with small groups of ELs to provide targeted language instruction.	• Model appropriate and inappropriate behaviors for discussions. • Teach minilessons on skills used during discussions (e.g., agreeing, disagreeing, and adding on). • Model language for encouraging deeper thinking on a topic (e.g., Can you say more about that?). • Monitor student participation and language development.

What Is the Role of Equity, Advocacy, and Leadership in Supporting ELs' Oral Language Development?

The focus on oral English development that is included in most English language development programs is insufficient to meet the needs of ELs (August & Shanahan, 2006). By developing lessons that support ELs' participation and engagement in academic conversations, you are advocating for ELs' equal access to content, supporting high academic expectations for ELs, and providing ELs with opportunities to develop their academic identity. You are also creating a classroom climate that encourages the sharing of diverse perspectives and the development of critical-thinking skills. As students acquire the skills to take part in academic conversations, they learn the ways in which hearing diverse perspectives can broaden their own thinking. They also can recognize the feeling that comes from being really listened to and having your ideas valued. Thus, as you focus on the often overlooked area of oral language development, you are fostering ELs' equitable and excellent education and advocating for ELs' voices to be heard in their classrooms.

Next Steps

Oral Language Activity Planning

In order to help you get started thinking about how you might incorporate an oral language activity into your next lesson plan, we have developed a planning template (Figure 4.13) that uses the four-practices framework. For the final application activity of this chapter, think about an upcoming lesson you will teach, and consider how you will build opportunities for students' oral language development into that lesson.

FIGURE 4.13   Oral Language Activity-Planning Template

Lesson topic:	
Content objective(s):	
Language objective(s):	
Oral language task:	
Practice 1: Come to the discussion prepared. How will you help ELs prepare for the academic conversation? ©iStockphoto.com/bjdlzx	**Practice 2: Use appropriate body language.** How will you support ELs in using appropriate body language during the discussion? ©iStockphoto.com/Wavebreakmedia

(Continued)

FIGURE 4.13 (Continued)

Practice 3: Participate by taking turns.

How will you support ELs in taking turns during the discussion?

Practice 4: Make connections.

How will you support ELs in making connections to what others have said and what they have previously learned?

Conclusion

In this chapter, we have explained why pair and small-group academic discussions can be an excellent way to foster ELs' language development and understanding of new content. We have also highlighted that in order for ELs to get the most out of these types of discussions and actively contribute to them, they need adequate support and structure to prepare for and participate in each activity. We presented four student practices and strategies connected to each of the four student practices that can support ELs in benefiting from academic conversations and oral language activities. In the upcoming chapter, we offer insights and strategies to provide ELs with the support they need to develop the academic language that is necessary for them to access and meaningfully take part in challenging content instruction.

Reflection Questions

1. How do you plan to incorporate academic conversations for ELs into your instruction in more systematic and intentional ways?

2. What is one oral language activity that you would like to try next in your class? What steps will you take to ensure that your ELs are prepared to participate?

References

August, D., & Shanahan, T. (2006). *Developing literacy in second-language learners: Report of the National Literacy Panel on Language Minority Children and Youth.* Mahwah, NJ: Erlbaum.

Hansen, J. (2010). Teaching without talking. *Phi Delta Kappan, 92*(1).

Roskos, K. A., Tabors, P. O., & Lenhart, L. A. (2009). *Oral language and early literacy in preschool: Talking, reading, and writing.* Newark, DE: International Reading Association.

Teaching Channel. (2012). Post-its: Little notes for big discussions [video file]. Retrieved from https://www.teachingchannel.org/videos/enhance-student-note-taking

Teaching Channel. (2013). Collaborative group work with the 1-3-6 protocol [video file]. Retrieved from https://www.teachingchannel.org/videos/1-3-6-protocol

Teaching Channel. (2014a). Participation protocol for academic discussions [video file]. Retrieved from https://www.teachingchannel.org/videos/participation-protocol-ousd

Teaching Channel. (2014b). Talk moves in academic discussions [video file]. Retrieved from https://www.teachingchannel.org/videos/teaching-ells-to-participate-in-discussions-ousd

Zwiers, J. (2010). *Building reading comprehension habits in grades 6–12: A toolkit of activities* (2nd ed.). Newark, DE: International Reading Association.

Zwiers, J. (2014). Key strategies for developing oral language [blog post]. Retrieved from https://www.teachingchannel.org/blog/2014/10/29/strategies-for-developing-oral-language-ousd

Zwiers, J., & Crawford, M. (2011). *Academic conversations: Classroom talk that fosters critical thinking and content understandings.* Portland, ME: Stenhouse Publishers.

Teaching Academic Language to ELs

Ms. Armstrong is a third-grade teacher in an urban, primarily low-income school district. Although she has been teaching for seven years, she now finds herself in a new, challenging situation. Prior to this year, the twelve ELs in her class of twenty-five were pulled for ninety minutes of ESOL instruction during her daily English language arts block. However, this year, her district has moved to a new model of "inclusive" ESOL instruction in which her ELs and non-ELs are together the whole day. She is under pressure to prepare all of her students to take the English language arts content test at the end of the year and to only use grade-level texts during instruction. However, her ELs are mostly at the beginning and low intermediate level and speak Amharic, Tigrinya, and Karen.[1] She is struggling to integrate her ELs into her instruction based on challenging, grade-level informational text. Meanwhile, many of her native English speakers are also below grade level in reading and writing. In the past, she has focused her instruction on teaching vocabulary, but this year, she knows she needs to find a different approach.

This chapter provides teachers like Ms. Armstrong support so that they can begin crucial conversations and dialogues in service of ELs' acquisition of

---

1. Amharic is the official working language of the Federal Democratic Republic of Ethiopia. Tigrinya is a language spoken by the Tigrayans and Tigrinyas. Tigrinya speakers primarily live in or come from Eritrea or Ethiopia. The Karen languages are tonal languages primarily spoken by individuals who reside in the Karen State in southern and southeastern Myanmar.

language and content. The chapter begins with an introduction to what academic language is and why it is critical for ELs to acquire academic language in order to access challenging content standards and be fully integrated into content classrooms. The chapter will include practical examples of how to analyze a text's academic language and how to teach the linguistic forms and functions necessary for ELs to interact with grade-level texts and topics. The chapter provides guidance on how to leverage different types of teachers' strengths in order to effectively collaborate on the weaving together of academic language and content instruction. It concludes with a lesson-planning application and discussion questions.

> *How do you define academic language? What questions do you have about teaching academic language to ELs?*

What Is Academic Language?

Academic language is one key to ELs being able to access challenging content and fully engage with their classroom context and peers. Not only ELs but all students need to be proficient in academic language to function in their classroom, college, and/or career. Before you can begin to teach academic language to your students, you will need to have a working definition of what the construct is. Alison Bailey (2007), an expert on academic language, defines it as "language that stands in contrast to the everyday informal speech that students use outside the classroom environment" (p. 12). It is the language used to "access and engage with the school curriculum" and "the unique interaction between language and the personal linguistic experiences of each child" (Bailey & Heritage, 2008, pp. 12–13).

The academic-language register differs significantly from social language in terms of discourse complexity, grammatical structure, vocabulary usage, and sociocultural context (WIDA, 2012). Academic language is a more formal register, or style of language, that differs in vocabulary, grammatical structures, and organization of language according to the context in which it is used. Academic language tends to be more abstract, more complex, and less contextualized, and it contains more sophisticated forms and greater precision and nuance (Bailey, 2012). Zwiers (2005) defines academic language as "the set of words and phrases that describe content-area knowledge and procedures; language that expresses complex thinking processes and abstract concepts; and language that creates cohesion and clarity in written and oral discourse" (p. 60). In addition, Scarcella (2008) adds that academic language is the language of power. She contends that students who do not acquire academic language fail in academic settings.

How Is Academic Language Different From Social Language?

Social language tends to be the everyday registers used in interactions outside and also inside school (WIDA, 2012). More specifically, it is the day-to-day language needed to interact socially with other people. ELs employ social-language skills when they are in the cafeteria, at parties, playing sports, texting, and talking on the phone. Social interactions are usually context embedded. That is, they occur in a meaningful social context. Social interactions tend to not be very demanding cognitively, and the language required for social use is not usually as specialized. However, even though social language may seem to be less complex and important, as educators, we must recognize and honor the inherent complexities of social language. Acquisition of social language requires an understanding of many constructs, including cultural and social norms, as well as nonverbal cues.

Academic language is distinctly different from "playground English" or "social English," which ELs tend to pick up more quickly than academic language. It is precisely because they tend to learn these other forms of English with less effort than they do academic language that they may sound fluent in English when, in reality, they are not. Research has found that it generally takes ELs three to five years to develop oral or social proficiency in English (Cook & Zhao, 2011; Hakuta, Butler, & Witt, 2000). In contrast, it typically takes at least four to seven years for ELs to develop academic English (Cook & Zhao, 2011; Hakuta et al., 2000). Figure 5.1 describes social and academic language, compares how long it typically takes to acquire them, and offers examples of each.

FIGURE 5.1 Distinctions Between Social Language and Academic Language

	Social Language	Academic Language
Description	• Everyday use for interactions inside and outside school • Social interaction • Less specialized language • Less cognitive demand • Use in social contexts • Acquisition requires understanding of cultural and social norms, including nonverbal cues	• Academic setting—use in areas such as classroom discourse, texts, assessments, content standards, and classroom materials • Mainly used in the classroom for reading and writing • Acquisition requires specialized knowledge • More cognitive demand due to complex vocabulary and grammatical structures

(Continued)

FIGURE 5.1 (Continued)

	Social Language	Academic Language
Acquisition	• Proficiency can develop in three to five years	• Proficiency can develop in a minimum of four to seven years
Examples	• Listening to a coach review the soccer practice schedule • Having an informal, face-to-face conversation about weekend plans • Writing in a friend's yearbook • Reading a lunch menu • Writing a post on Facebook • Texting	• Describing a classic work of art • Defining a scientific term • Explaining how to solve a complex math problem • Comparing and contrasting two opposing parties in a historical dispute • Summarizing information in a research paper

How Is Academic Language Structured?

Now that we have compared academic and social language, we'll take a deeper look at what academic language is and how it's structured. According to Bailey (2012), academic language comprises linguistic forms and functions that are found in such areas as classroom discourse, texts, assessments, content standards, and classroom materials. Linguistic forms are identifiable by the linguistic domain (e.g., phonological, lexical, syntactic, discourse, or text). These forms range from letters and sounds (the phonological domain), words (lexical domain), and the combination of words into phrases (syntactic domain) to the particular choice of words and sentences and other factors the speaker makes in particular social settings (discourse). Academic-language functions capture the intent of the content's discourse or text and can serve multiple purposes, depending on the context. Some of the purposes include describing, defining, explaining, comparing and contrasting, and summarizing information. Students need to be able to use these actionable language functions for such purposes on a daily basis in the classroom across multiple content areas.

Academic language is distinguished from English in other settings on three key levels:

1. Word level

2. Sentence level

3. Discourse or text level

FIGURE 5.2 Features of Academic Language

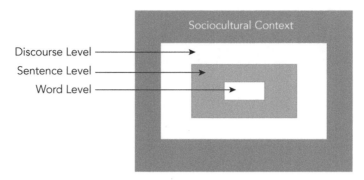

Source: Staehr Fenner (2014). Adapted from WIDA (2012).

When we ask educators their definition of academic language, many of them only mention vocabulary. While vocabulary is indeed one facet of academic language, vocabulary is found within the context of sentence structure, discourse, and the sociocultural context. Although it is important for ELs to learn vocabulary to access challenging content, they also need to master sentence- and discourse-level features of academic language in order to be positioned for academic success. While crucial, words alone will not allow ELs to access content and fully engage in classroom contexts. ELs need to know how to combine words to form sentences and how to combine sentences to create effective discourse in speaking and writing. They also need to be able to comprehend words within complex sentence and discourse structures when listening and reading. Further, teachers of ELs need to recognize the sociocultural context in which the acquisition of the different features of academic language takes place. Figure 5.2 illustrates the features of academic language, how they are nested within each other, and also framed within a unique sociocultural context.

What Is the Interplay Between Scaffolds, Errors, and Academic Language?

Figure 5.3 represents what happens in terms of ELs' expressive language (or spoken and written language) as they increase in proficiency. At the beginning level of proficiency, ELs require the most scaffolds but also produce the greatest number of errors. They also produce the least amount of academic language at the word, sentence, and discourse levels. However, as ELs gain proficiency, they require fewer scaffolds, produce fewer errors, and their academic language builds at the word, sentence, and discourse levels.

FIGURE 5.3 Relationship Between Scaffolds, Errors, and Features
of Academic Language

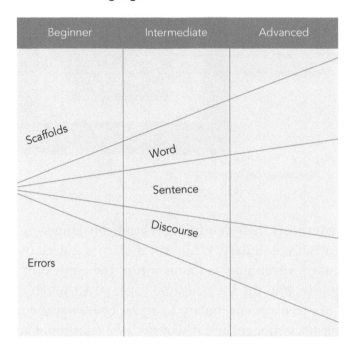

Finally, as ELs move into the advanced level of proficiency and beyond, they require the least number of scaffolds and produce the least number of errors. At this point, they produce the greatest amount of academic language at the word, sentence, and discourse levels.

What Is the Word Level?

Within the word level of academic vocabulary, there are several categories or "tiers" of different kinds of words (Beck, McKeown, & Kucan, 2002). All words are definitely not equal when it comes to learning and using academic vocabulary correctly on a consistent basis. There are three tiers of academic vocabulary. Tier 1 vocabulary, or familiar, concrete vocabulary, is the easiest for students to learn. Tier 1 words tend to be everyday vocabulary and words that students may acquire on their own. Tier 2 and Tier 3 words are more difficult for students to learn, but without them, students will have a significant challenge learning and demonstrating their understanding of new content.

We will present more information on Tier 1, 2, and 3 vocabulary here and follow with Figure 5.4, which summarizes this information and provides examples. Tier 1 is words that are easiest for students to acquire and are usually learned through social, informal conversations. Tier 2

FIGURE 5.4 Tiers of Academic Vocabulary, Definitions, and Examples

Tier	Definition	Examples
Tier 1	Words usually acquired through everyday speech	boy house run sleep
Tier 2	Academic words that appear across all types of text. These are often more complex, tend to be used across disciplines, and may have more than one meaning, depending on their use and context.	contrast obvious omit prediction
Tier 3	Domain-specific words that are tied to content. These are typically the types of vocabulary words that are included in glossaries, highlighted in textbooks, and addressed by teachers. They are considered difficult, precise words that are important to understanding content.	aristocracy hyperbole lava radius

words include vocabulary that shows up across content areas, such as *solve*, *establish*, and *verify*. In addition, some Tier 2 words are cross-content vocabulary with multiple meanings that depend on the context. These Tier 2 words require explicit instruction and attention. One example is the word *column*. In social studies, the word signifies an upright pillar (e.g., columns in Roman architecture). In language arts, the word could mean a regularly appearing newspaper article. And in mathematics, it can mean the vertical division of a table. Tier 3 words are specific, precise vocabulary words related to a topic within a given content area. For example, when discussing metamorphosis in science, the word *cocoon* would be a content-specific, or Tier 3, vocabulary word.

APPLICATION ACTIVITY 5.1

Words With Multiple Meanings

Identify at least one cross-content vocabulary word (other than *column*, from the example in this text), and provide the meanings for each content area. Share how you would teach, explain, or practice its different meanings with your students.

Cross-Content Vocabulary Word	Meaning in English Language Arts	Meaning in Mathematics	Meaning in Social Studies	Meaning in Science	How I Would Teach Its Meanings

What Is the Sentence Level?

As we shared earlier, teachers often tend to gravitate toward exploring word-level academic language or vocabulary when focusing on the challenges ELs face in accessing content. However, if you don't already, you will also need to expand your repertoire to focus on sentence-level academic language, which includes the grammar and syntax ELs need to acquire in order to access complex concepts and texts and engage with their peers and teachers. Many teachers were taught English grammar while they were in elementary or secondary school but may not feel comfortable with analyzing and teaching the grammatical structures in English.

What patterns or structures have you noticed your ELs struggling with? What resources can you use to make sense of the grammar—both for yourself and your students?

Some common academic grammatical features at the sentence level[2] that can challenge ELs include the following (National Research Council, 2014; Zhang, 2016):

- Conditionals (e.g., The children of the village would have been much worse off if not for the efforts of the educators.)

- Comparisons (e.g., Julia has more pencils than Boubacar.)

- Relative clauses (e.g., Sound waves are compression waves that move backward and forward through matter in the direction the wave is traveling.)

---

2. While this research focuses on science texts in particular, these challenges extend to other content areas as well.

Conditional phrases: Let's take a closer look at these three examples. In the most basic sense, conditional phrases are about facts and consequences. We tend to teach the conditional in very clear constructions using *if* and *then*. For example, "If blue and yellow pigment are mixed, then the result will be green." There is also the hypothetical situation in which *would* is used. For example, "If it were below 32 degrees outside, the rain *would* turn to snow." In academic texts, however, teachers may find the conditional in more complex structures, and it may be used in the negative or based on a false (counterfactual) condition. The following, more complex example may give even native speakers pause, "The children of the village would have been much worse off if not for the efforts of the educators."

In order to scaffold student comprehension of conditional phrases, teachers need to extend their repertoire beyond simplistic constructions so that ELs recognize complex conditionals. Teachers should certainly begin with the easy-to-understand examples, but then, they need to expose their ELs to the realities of the constructions found in academic texts. In order to do so effectively, teachers will need to break down this construction into "bite-sized" pieces of information. Looking at the previous example, we could support students in summarizing the information of each bite-sized piece of information, such as, "First the children in the village were suffering greatly. It could have been much worse. There were educators who made efforts. Those efforts helped the children's suffering. The youth continued to suffer, but the suffering was lessened due to the educators."

Comparisons are also used frequently in scientific and other academic texts. Similar to our approach to conditionals, we tend to teach comparisons in rather simplistic ways. In doing so, we don't meet the needs of our ELs, who must be able to navigate complex sentence structures that they encounter in academic texts. For example, "Julia has more pencils than Boubacar. Duong has fewer pencils than Boubacar. Julia has the most pencils." Students across the world are taught to add -er to the adjective to form the comparative for shorter-length adjectives (e.g., great and greater). In those cases, it is obvious what two items are being compared. In academic writing, however, the sentences containing comparisons are much more complex. For example, "People in many developing countries are becoming obese at a rapid pace, faster since 2010 than they did from 1980 to 2010." We need to break this down into manageable pieces of information and model for our students the strategies for recognizing comparisons and identifying what is being compared.

Relative clauses are a third common grammatical feature in academic texts. Relative clauses start with relative pronouns (who, whom, which, whose, that) and provide more information about nouns. Relative clauses enable writers to embed definitions and additional information in one sentence, often resulting in content-dense text. Relative clauses can be tricky because they frequently occur in academic writing, and one of their by-products is creating long *noun groups*, which increase the density of texts (Zhang, 2016). Relative clauses present a solid example of a feature of academic language at the sentence level that teachers across all content areas can address through their instruction. There are many ways teachers can point out relative clauses to ELs that do not take a lot of time yet increase ELs' awareness of what relative clauses are and how they can serve as a tool to help students unlock the meaning of challenging texts. In addition, taking a deeper look at relative clauses may also help students who are fluent in English comprehend complex texts on a deeper level.

The following science writing example demonstrates the density of information in one sentence: "Sound waves are compression waves that move backward and forward through matter in the direction the wave is traveling." This sentence provides information about sound waves and includes what they are (compression waves) and how they travel ("backward and forward through matter in the direction the wave is traveling"). Just as with the other two constructions, teachers need to instruct students in breaking down the sentence into understandable fragments and in identifying all of the rich information it contains. The big takeaway here is that teachers can start with explanations using less complex language, but we need to expose ELs to the realities of complex academic texts that contain these structures. Teachers need to teach ELs how to break down these complex structures into more manageable bite-sized pieces in order to access their content.

What Is the Discourse Level?

In our work with teachers, we have found that the concept of the discourse level can be the most abstract and, by default, the most challenging to grasp, as compared with the word and sentence levels. The discourse level means the organization, structure, and purpose of text or talk as a whole. In addition, discourse entails the amount of text, its density, and its coherence, as well as cohesion. Within an organized text, there will be different sentence types to form that text (WIDA, 2012). Zwiers (2008) describes the discourse level as the "message level" of communication, which takes a more comprehensive view of the message, as well as how that message is constructed, including the level of clarity for a particular audience. Some components of academic discourse include voice and register; clarity and coherence; and purpose, functions, and audience. These nuances at the discourse level, such as register (e.g., the level of formality used in language when speaking with an adult versus a peer), can make the discourse level especially challenging for ELs who may be acquiring a level of English needed to be aware of such components of discourse and use them consistently.

In terms of what ELs need to be able to do with language at the discourse level, they will need to navigate academic text to understand the gist, summarize or explain the meaning of a text, and also extract key information from text. They also need to be able to understand the distinct structures of a variety of texts used in different content areas, such as arguments, sequences in problem solving, research reports, persuasive letters, webpages, lab reports, and expository texts (Moughamian, Rivera, & Francis, 2009). In addition to understanding discourse-level features of texts, students will also need to be able to produce academic language at the discourse level. Two practices emphasized throughout the college- and career-readiness standards are that students need to be able to explain and argue based on evidence at the discourse level (CCSSO, 2012; Christie, 2012; Nippold & Scott, 2010). Other ways students will need to produce language (either orally or in writing) at the discourse level across content areas include ordering events into a chronological sequence and using connecting ideas to clarify the links between their ideas in speaking or in writing.

Figure 5.5 summarizes the levels of academic language, their features, and their meaning and provides some examples of their use.

> *Reflection: Draw a picture that includes the elements related to academic language presented so far in this chapter, and label what the parts of the picture relate to which elements of academic language. What are you still wondering about?*

FIGURE 5.5 Levels and Features of Academic Language, Meaning, and Examples

Level of Academic Language	Feature of Academic Language	Meaning	Examples
Word	Lexical	Precision of general, specific, and technical vocabulary; linguistic properties of words	• Tier 1 (e.g., book or run), Tier 2 (e.g., measure or entertainment), and Tier 3 (e.g., isotope or revolutionary) vocabulary • Syllables, prefixes, suffixes
Sentence	Grammatical	Types and variety of grammatical structures; grammatical devices used	• Conditional tense (e.g., If it rains, the grass gets wet.) • Embedded clauses (e.g., Two species of armadillo, *which are found in Central America*, are the northern naked-tailed armadillo and the nine-banded armadillo.) • Compound sentences (e.g., Manuel waited for the train, but the train was late.)
Discourse	Organization and functions	Organization and purpose of text or talk	• Structure and purpose of a debate, a persuasive essay, explanation of a mathematical equation, or a science lab report • Discourse connectors for sequencing text (e.g., first, next, etc.) and conveying relationships between ideas (e.g., however and moreover).

Source: Adapted from Bailey (2012); Beck, McKeown, and Kucan (2002); WIDA (2012).

Why Is Academic Language Important?

College- and career-readiness content standards (including the Common Core State Standards) call for all teachers to be teachers of academic language.[3] Moughamian and colleagues (2009) describe academic language as the vocabulary and semantics involved in particular content area literacy that is fundamental to students' academic success in all areas. They note that academic language is the primary source of ELs' challenges with academic content regardless of the grade. Even after ELs are considered English proficient, they may still face challenges with academic language. Academic language also influences how well ELs tend to perform on all content and English language proficiency assessments. In addition to the pure linguistic features of academic language, educators must also acknowledge that the acquisition of academic language takes place within a sociocultural context (WIDA, 2012). Such factors as ELs' background knowledge on a particular topic, the teacher's level of expectations for ELs, students' home language use in the classroom, and the impact of ELs' culture on their understanding of the content may influence their use of academic language.

It is critical for ELs to have a command of the forms and functions of academic language to gain access to challenging academic content and to express their knowledge of subject matter in the content areas. Further, native or proficient speakers of English may not have a command of this specialized language that is crucial for academic success (Bailey, 2012). Thus, even teachers who don't work directly with ELs can pass along the benefits of academic language to their students.

Why Don't ELs Just Need Assistance With Vocabulary?

In order for ELs to comprehend complex content instruction, especially in the era of the college and career readiness standards, teachers will need to expand their repertoire to move beyond teaching ELs isolated vocabulary words that the students will encounter in instruction. In some cases, teachers will need to move out of their comfort zones, possibly dust off a grammar book or take a grammar course, and reacquaint themselves with features of

---

3. See Chapter 1 for the shifts in the CCRS for English language arts and literacy and the new demands on all teachers of ELs.

English grammar that their ELs will need to acquire. However, you don't need to spend a long time on the grammatical rules and terms; it's more important to help students understand the function and meaning of the language they're encountering. Further, content teachers should not feel that they are alone in analyzing and teaching academic language to ELs.

As more schools, districts, and states move toward a collaborative teaching model, and also recognize that ELs do not tend to spend their entire day in the presence of an ESOL teacher, content teachers will need to take on more shared responsibility for teaching ELs features of academic language at the sentence as well as discourse level. In addition, non-ELs will most likely benefit from instruction in academic language as well. Content teachers can leverage their ESOL teachers' expertise to consult them on which features of academic language at the sentence and discourse levels they may wish to focus on during instruction. ESOL teachers could provide guidance around minilessons content teachers could teach to focus on developing ELs' academic language at the sentence and discourse levels.

What Does It Mean That Acquisition of Academic Language Takes Place Within a Sociocultural Context?

While the field of EL education operates from a framework of academic language at the word, sentence, and discourse levels, teachers must remember that ELs' development of academic language does not take place within a vacuum. As with the way ELs' culture must always be taken into account when teaching content, teachers must also consider the context in which ELs acquire academic language. Thus, ELs' sociocultural context plays a distinct role in the way in which ELs acquire academic language. The sociocultural context means that "interactions between different people for specific purposes and across different learning environments influence how language is used" (WIDA, 2012, p. v). The sociocultural context honors the participants who are acquiring language, as well as their experiences, in a holistic way. We also argue that the sociocultural aspect encompasses ELs' background knowledge that they can leverage when learning English academic language. These aspects of academic language encompass the situation in which language is acquired, as well as participants' identities, cultures, and social roles within the classroom, school, and community.

For example, consider Rima, a Syrian girl who is encouraged to draw from Arabic, her home language, as a support in partner and group work. She is sometimes placed with a more English proficient Arabic speaker who helps confirm her understanding of complex concepts in her home language. Rima attends a school that has an Arabic/English bilingual parent liaison and has signs in Arabic posted in the hallways, as well as books in Arabic in the school library. Rima feels that her home language and culture are honored at her school, and she may acquire English academic language more effectively than ELs who are only allowed to use English in the classroom and do not see their language and culture reflected within the classroom and school environment. Teachers must recognize the many complexities involved with ELs acquiring academic language and how culture, motivation, home language, and positive learning environments affect its acquisition.

How Do I Increase My Awareness of the Academic Language ELs Need to Access Challenging Content?

Teachers must be aware of the academic language that is essential for their students' access of content before they can teach it. However, it's not always obvious that certain elements of academic language may pose challenges to ELs. This is because without training, many teachers may simply not be attuned to vocabulary, sentence structures, and discourse that may inhibit ELs' access to academic content. One way to become more aware of the vast quantity of academic language ELs encounter in their content classes is to analyze the academic language found in a text that students use during instruction. However, we would like to note that the notion of what exactly a text is has expanded in recent years. A text does not necessarily mean something that is written. A text can also encompass oral language, such as a speech, or even a visual, such as a painting or an advertisement. According to James Gee (2007), the concept of text also extends to media and *multimodal texts*, which are texts that mix images and/or sounds with words. As educators of ELs, we need to be clear with each other regarding what we mean by the word *text* and think about possible implications for teaching.

We recommend that content teachers collaborate with ESOL teachers to analyze texts in order to discover which elements of academic language may present barriers to ELs comprehending and working with these texts. When direct collaboration with an ESOL teacher is not possible, we recommend content teachers collaborate with other content teachers, reading specialists, instructional coaches, and/or special education teachers to unlock the academic language necessary for instruction. Academic language is aligned and intertwined with the content, ELD standards, objectives, texts, and assessments.

How Can I Figure Out What Academic Language Might Be Challenging for My ELs?

One way you can develop a general sense of what aspects of language might make ELs' access to content challenging is by collaborating with a teacher to determine which aspects of smaller chunks of content and language might present the most barriers. Teachers can analyze any content to help tease apart the content from the academic language. Consider the following math problem:

Addison wants to ride her scooter more than 100 miles this month. She has already ridden her scooter 12 miles. Which inequality could be used to determine the mean number of miles, m, she would need to ride her scooter each day for 20 more days to achieve her goal?

$20m + 12 < 100$

$20m - 12 < 100$

$20m + 12 > 100$

$20m - 12 < 100$

Source: Adapted from New York State Testing Program. (2016). 2016 Common Core mathematics test. Retrieved from http://edinformatics.com/testing/2016-released-items-math-grade7.pdf

In collaboration, an ESOL teacher and a math teacher could discuss the following:

1. What might be difficult for your students in terms of the content?

2. What might be difficult for your students in terms of the language expectations?

3. Are there any assessment vocabulary words that should be taught explicitly before testing?

4. How can we make this problem more accessible for ELs?

5. How can we scaffold this problem so that ELs can access its meaning and answer it?

This series of questions can be used with any content area material.

Checklist for Increasing Academic-Language Awareness

Another way educators can increase their awareness of academic language is through completing Figure 5.6, the "Checklist for Increasing Academic-Language Awareness." We suggest educators collaborate with an ESOL teacher and/or content teacher to do a "deep dive" and analyze the many types of academic language found in a text together that they use in their instruction. By working through this checklist, educators can develop a deeper understanding of the levels of academic language in their authentic texts and prioritize which features of academic language are important for lessons based on a particular text and purpose for using the text. They can prioritize which features of academic language to teach in minilessons or point out to students during instruction. After taking this step to build awareness, we provide some suggestions for weaving the instruction of sentence- and discourse-level academic language seamlessly with content instruction.[4]

Let's look at the takeaways Juan and Amanda, an ESOL and third-grade teacher, had when using this checklist with the following text excerpt recommended for the second- to third-grade level.

Moonshot: The Flight of Apollo 11 by Brian Floca (2009)

High above there is the Moon, cold and quiet, no air, no life, but glowing in the sky.

Here below there are three men who close themselves in special clothes, who—click—lock hands in heavy gloves, who—click—lock heads in large round helmets.

It is summer here in Florida, hot, and near the sea. But now these men are dressed for colder, stranger places. They walk with stiff and awkward steps in suits not made for Earth.

They have studied and practiced and trained, and said good-bye to family and friends. If all goes well, they will be gone for one week, gone where no one has been.

Their two small spaceships are Columbia and Eagle. They sit atop the rocket that will raise them into space, a monster of a machine: It stands thirty stories, it weighs six million pounds, a tower full of fuel and fire and valves and pipes and engines, too big to believe, but built to fly—the mighty, massive Saturn V.

(Excerpt continues on page 130.)

---

4. Since Chapter 6 focuses solely on vocabulary, we do not provide suggestions for teaching vocabulary in this chapter.

FIGURE 5.6   Checklist for Increasing Academic-Language Awareness

1. Find a text you will be using with your students.

2. Note the purpose for teaching this text. You can cite content and/or language standards or provide a general purpose.

3. Analyze the various elements of the text's academic language, and complete the checklist.

Awareness-Building Questions	Text Info	Example(s) Found in Text	Teach This Feature?
Vocabulary (Word Level)			
Are there everyday Tier 1 words (e.g., cat) that may be unfamiliar to students?	Yes/No		Yes/No
Are there general academic Tier 2 words (e.g., analyze or describe) that may be unfamiliar?	Yes/No		Yes/No
Does the vocabulary in the text lend itself to any minilessons on word-learning strategies (e.g., words with multiple meanings, determining meaning of words in context, or affixes)?	Yes/No		Yes/No
Are there Tier 3 words specific to the content you're teaching that may be unfamiliar?	Yes/No		Yes/No
Grammar or Syntax (Sentence Level)			
Are there aspects of grammar (e.g., clauses, verb tense, or interrogatives) that may be challenging for ELs?	Yes/No		Yes/No
Is there any syntax (arrangement of words and phrases) that might be confusing?	Yes/No		Yes/No
Are there any conventions that may be new or confusing (e.g., punctuation, spelling, etc.)?	Yes/No		Yes/No
Organization (Discourse Level)			
What is the type of text (e.g., lab report or blog post)?			Yes/No
How is the text organized or structured (e.g., description or cause and effect)?			Yes/No
How do the ideas hang together cohesively?			Yes/No
Are there any markers of sequence or relationships between ideas (e.g., in addition or likewise)?	Yes/No		Yes/No
What is the purpose of text (e.g., to persuade or to inform)?			Yes/No
Sociocultural Level			
Does the text assume any experience, background knowledge, and/or awareness for students to understand it?	Yes/No		Yes/No
Could students' first language and/or home culture impact their understanding of the text?	Yes/No		Yes/No

(Continued from page 128.)

The astronauts squeeze in to Columbia's sideways seats, lying on their backs, facing toward the sky—Neil Armstrong on the left, Michael Collins in the right, Buzz Aldrin in the middle.

Click and they fasten straps.

Click and the hatch is sealed.

There they wait, while the Saturn hums beneath them.

Near the rocket, in Launch Control, and far away in Houston, in Mission Control, there are numbers, screens, and charts, ways of watching and checking every piece of the rocket and ships, the fuel, the valves, the pipes, the engines, the beats of the astronauts' hearts.

As the countdown closes, each man watching is asked the question: GO/NO GO? And each man answers back: "GO." "GO." "GO." Apollo 11 is GO for launch.

Teacher Takeaways

Background and Purpose for Using the Text: Juan and Amanda coteach a third-grade English language arts class that has a total of twenty-five students, ten of whom are ELs who speak Spanish, Vietnamese, and Hmong at the beginning and intermediate levels. The teacher team referred to their content and English language development standards and decided the purpose for which their students would read this text would be to demonstrate their understanding of it. They would also focus on having the students determine the meaning of some key words and phrases in the text that help unlock the meaning for students.

Vocabulary: Juan and Amanda decided to focus on Tier 2 vocabulary words and also make sure their students grasped key words that would help them unlock the meaning of the text. Based on that approach, they chose the Tier 2[5] words *practiced*, *trained*, *weighs*, *tower*, *launch*, and *mission*. In addition, they chose the word *click*, which is not a Tier 2 word but is key for understanding the text.

Sentence Level: At the sentence level, they noted the use of the present perfect verb tense (*have studied* and *has been*) and decided to highlight this structure for students, realizing that their ELs, as well as their fluent English speakers, would benefit from knowing more about this verb tense. They also noted some complex sentences ("If all goes well, they will be gone for one week, gone where no one has been"). They decided to have students break this complex sentence into more manageable pieces to dig deeper into its meaning.

---

5. One way to locate Tier 2 vocabulary by grade level is to use Achieve the Core's online Academic Word Finder.

Juan also pointed out that there were participle phrases ("lying on their backs," "facing toward the sky"), but the team decided not to focus on participle phrases at this point in time.

Discourse Level: At the discourse level, Amanda pointed out that the text is organized as a narrative, nonfiction text. Juan noticed its use of stanzas, similar to a poem. The team also recognized how the word *click* is used to signify the sequence of events, which underscores the importance of students knowing the meaning of the word *click* in this context. They decided to focus on eliciting students' observations on how the text uses language to form a cohesive message.

Sociocultural Context: The teacher team recognized that their ELs will need to bring some background knowledge to their approach to this text, including some knowledge of space exploration and who the astronauts are. In addition, they will need to be as familiar as non-ELs with NASA (e.g., Mission Control and Houston). The teachers recognized that Juan, the ESOL teacher, can concisely preteach some essential background the ELs will need to fully access the text. In addition, the teachers noted how their ELs are encouraged to use their home languages in summarizing and accessing complex texts, which they intend to intentionally build into their instruction using this text.

How Do I Teach Sentence-Level Academic Language to ELs?

Once you have completed the checklist and determined an area of priority in teaching sentence-level academic language, it's time to add some tools to your toolbox so your ELs can focus on unlocking academic language. There are many ways to teach sentence-level academic language to ELs, and we'll share two ways to do so in this chapter.[6] One way is to focus on sentences from grade-level texts that may be particularly challenging and have students unlock these sentences' meanings. Application Activity 5.2, "Unpacking Juicy Sentences," draws from Wong Fillmore and Fillmore's (2012) *juicy sentences* term and also from the California Department of Education's (2014) "Sentence Detectives" activity.[7] While it isn't possible to unpack every juicy sentence students come across in their encounters with texts, teachers can teach students how to do this on their own. Students' skills in deconstructing and unpacking dense sentences will serve them well across multiple content areas.

---

6. Chapter 6 focuses on selecting and teaching academic vocabulary to ELs. For that reason, we do not go in depth on vocabulary in this chapter.

7. See http://readingapprenticeship.org/publications/downloadable-resources.

APPLICATION ACTIVITY 5.2

Unpacking Juicy Sentences

We'll use the following scientific sentence to model the activity: "Since most owls feed upon a variety of animals, owl abundance is not limited by the rise and fall in numbers of any one prey species" (Government of Alberta, 2002).

Students complete the following four steps:

1. Have students select one particularly challenging sentence, or provide a sentence for them. Write the sentence on a poster paper, or display it on an interactive whiteboard.

2. Work with students to break the sentence into smaller chunks.

3. "Unpack" the meaning of each sentence chunk, summarizing each chunk in their own words (in either the home language, English, or a combination of the two). To do so, work with students to point out which elements of each chunk in the sentence are helpful in illuminating the meaning, such as punctuation and transition words.

4. Finally, have students summarize the entire sentence as a whole, discussing how they were able to unpack its meaning.

Figure 5.7 presents a sample of students' work on the sentence that was given.

FIGURE 5.7 Chunk of Text and Summary in My Own Words

Chunk of Text	Summary in My Own Words
Since most owls feed upon	Because the majority of owls eat
a variety of animals	lots of different kinds of animals,
owl abundance	how many owls there are
is not limited	is not made less
by the rise and fall in numbers	from more or fewer
of any one prey species.	kinds of animals that owls eat.

APPLICATION ACTIVITY 5.3

Finding and Teaching Relative Clauses

As we mentioned earlier, relative clauses can be challenging for ELs and a barrier to their accessing complex text. A clause is the smallest grammatical unit that can express a complete preposition; it contains a subject and a verb. Relative clauses begin with relative pronouns, such as who, whom, which, whose, or that, and provide more information about a noun. Relative clauses frequently occur in academic writing and create long *noun groups*, which increase the density of a text (Zhang, 2016). An example of a relative clause is the underlined portion of this sentence: *Roughly 20,000 years ago the great ice sheets <u>that buried much of Asia, Europe and North America</u> stopped their creeping advance.* The relative pronoun in the sentence is *that*. The relative clause "that buried much of Asia, Europe and North America" provides us more information about the great ice sheets. One way to help raise students' awareness as to what relative clauses are and how understanding how they're structured can provide a clue to unlocking the meaning of sentence-level academic language is through the following activity. The activity can be used with any type of text, but we model its use in one example of a scientific text. You can then continue working through the rest of the activity.

Use the steps below to practice analyzing relative clauses in the following text.

1. Highlight clauses beginning with *that*.
2. Identify the noun by circling it and relative clause using the graphic organizer.
3. Write the information in separate sentences.

Text: "What Thawed the Last Ice Age?"

Roughly 20,000 years ago the great ice sheets that buried much of Asia, Europe and North America stopped their creeping advance. Within a few hundred years, sea levels in some places had risen by as much as 10 meters—more than if the ice sheet that still covers Greenland were to melt today. This freshwater flood filled the North Atlantic and also shut down the ocean currents that conveyed warmer water from equatorial regions northward. The equatorial heat warmed the precincts of Antarctica in the Southern Hemisphere instead, shrinking the fringing sea ice and changing the circumpolar winds. As a result—and for reasons that remain unexplained—the waters of the Southern Ocean may have begun to release carbon dioxide, enough to raise concentrations in the atmosphere by more than 100 parts per million over millennia—roughly equivalent to the rise in the last 200 years. That CO_2 then warmed the globe, melting back the continental ice sheets and ushering in the current climate that enabled humanity to thrive.

Source: Biello, D. (2012, April 4). What thawed the last ice age? *Scientific American.* Retrieved from http://www .scientificamerican.com/article/what-thawed-the-last-ice-age

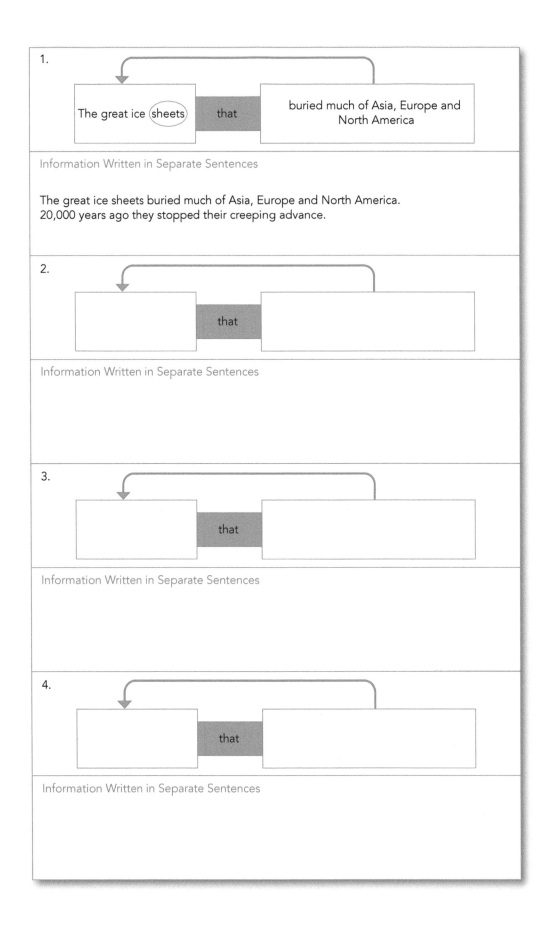

1.

| The great ice (sheets) | that | buried much of Asia, Europe and North America |

Information Written in Separate Sentences

The great ice sheets buried much of Asia, Europe and North America.
20,000 years ago they stopped their creeping advance.

2.

| | that | |

Information Written in Separate Sentences

3.

| | that | |

Information Written in Separate Sentences

4.

| | that | |

Information Written in Separate Sentences

How Do I Teach Discourse-Level Academic Language to ELs?

The first thing to keep in mind when teaching academic language to ELs is that language and content should be taught in tandem. Using a smaller portion of the same Ice Age text from before, we illustrate how teachers can explore different features of discourse-level academic language with their ELs through two different activities. The first application activity is called "I Speak Science" for short, but the structure of it can be used with other content areas as well.

APPLICATION ACTIVITY 5.4

Scaffolded Summary: I Speak Science

Purpose: This application is designed to guide ELs to understand the gist or main idea of a text and its details through summarizing academic text.

Instructions for Students

Your science reading homework begins with the following passage. What can you do to make sure you understand it? One strategy is to summarize or "translate" what you read into everyday English. Take the following steps to do so:

1. Locate information in the text using the graphic organizer.

2. Copy the text language exactly as it's written into the "Copied Text Information" column.

3. Rewrite the concepts into everyday English.

4. Use the everyday English to write the "Translated Summary."

What Thawed the Last Ice Age?

Roughly 20,000 years ago the great ice sheets that buried much of Asia, Europe and North America stopped their creeping advance. Within a few hundred years, sea levels in some places had risen by as much as 10 meters—more than if the ice sheet that still covers Greenland were to melt today.

Graphic Organizer

Questions	Copied Text Information	Everyday English
When did it happen?	Roughly 20,000 years ago	Around 20,000 years ago
What thing is the text about?	The great ice sheets that buried	The big sheets of ice that covered
Where did it happen?	Much of Asia, Europe and North America	
What happened?	Stopped their creeping advance	
When did it happen?	Within a few hundred years	
What was the result?		
What would that be like today?		

Translated Summary

Around 20,000 years ago, the big ice sheets that covered . . .

APPLICATION ACTIVITY 5.5

Sequencing in Paragraphs

As we noted earlier, one aspect of discourse is recognizing the sequence of events. ELs will need to build their awareness of how texts are sequenced, and they can apply this knowledge across content areas to help them unlock the meaning of challenging academic texts. One way teachers can help ELs learn about the order in which events take place in a text is by using sentence strips to determine the proper order of a text. Teachers can provide extra scaffolding by giving students the first and last sentences and by working with a shorter text. In this case, in working with the same Ice Age text, students could build their awareness of the sequence words in each sentence. To do so, the teacher would have to have worked with students on what sequence words are.

Instructions

It is important to understand the sequence (order) of events in what you read and to pay attention to clues in the text itself. This activity will help you develop the strategy of using sequence words in order to sequence events as you read.

1. Highlight the sequence words in each sentence. The first two are done for you ("Roughly 20,000 years ago")

2. Using the sequence words, map the events on a timeline.

3. Share how you can use this strategy when you read independently.

Sequence Words	What the Sequence Words Mean (in English or Home Language)	What Happened (in English or Home Language)
20,000 years ago	Hace 20.000 años	The ice sheets stopped moving forward
Within a few hundred years	Dentro de unos pocos cientos de años	Sea levels had risen by up to 10 meters
Over milennia		
In the last 200 years		
Then warmed the globe		
Ushering in the current climate		

Timeline:

20,000 years ago

What Steps Should I Follow When Planning Instruction That Integrates Instruction of Academic Language Simultaneously With Content?

Once students are aware of a feature of academic language in one content area, they can transfer this knowledge to other content areas. Thus, teachers across content areas should incorporate a discussion and plan of attack around teaching academic language into their planning to help ELs unlock the meaning of challenging texts and increase their academic language across the content areas. Figure 5.8 provides an example of how teachers planning at the second-grade level may wish to ensure they are incorporating the instruction of academic language throughout all content areas during their weekly planning meeting. In this way, all content teachers do not need to teach all features of academic language but can coordinate with each other to make sure they are exposing ELs to different aspects of academic language that are appropriate to their grade level and/or content area.

FIGURE 5.8   Sample Grade 2 Academic-Language Team-Planning Template

Feature of Academic Language	Mathematics	Science	Social Studies	English Language Arts	ESOL
Tier 2 Words (Word)	✓ Examples: estimate, interpret, and measure		✓ Example: describe		
Sentence		✓ Examples: Relative clauses		✓ Examples: Compare and contrast two versions of Cinderella	✓ Collaborating with science teacher on relative clauses and coteaching Cinderella stories that are culturally relevant
Organization of discourse . . . how ideas hang together . . . linear progression . . . (Discourse)	✓ Describe steps in a process to solve a word problem		✓ Discourse features of a text on George Washington Carver		

While Figure 5.8 lends itself to grade-level meetings at the elementary level, secondary teachers can also "divide and conquer" to ensure that different features of academic language are taught to ELs within content areas. An ESOL teacher can be instrumental in supporting content area teachers at the elementary as well as secondary levels to suggest minilessons around academic-language features that can be incorporated into the instruction of content.

Developing and implementing lessons that integrate academic-language instruction with content instruction is a multistep process that benefits from close collaboration between ESOL and content teachers. This collaboration, built upon a framework of distributed expertise (Edwards, 2005, 2011), recognizes both types of teachers' strengths, builds upon them, and is shown in Figure 5.9.

FIGURE 5.9 Steps to Collaboratively Plan and Teach Content That Integrates Instruction of Academic Language and Content

Step	Possible Lead Teacher
1. Identify content standards that guide the lesson, and create content objectives.	Content teacher
2. Identify ELD standards that support linguistic demands of the content standards and lesson, and create language objectives where appropriate.	ESOL teacher
3. Analyze the text(s)[8] you'll use during instruction, highlighting features of academic language ELs at different levels of ELP will need to access the text(s) to meet content and ELD standards.	Content and ESOL teacher
4. Design (a) minilesson(s) to teach challenging academic language from a text, focusing on a limited number of lessons.	ESOL and content teacher
5. Integrate scaffolds to support instruction for ELs at different levels of English proficiency.	ESOL teacher
6. Teach the lesson.	Content and ESOL teacher
7. Reflect on what was effective and what needs improvement in terms of ELs learning academic language and content simultaneously.	Content and ESOL teacher
8. Revise the lesson based on reflection. Repeat Steps 1–8 as needed.	Content and ESOL teacher

How Can I Coplan Instruction of Academic Language When My Time Is Limited?

While we like to present the optimal model for coplanning instruction between content and ESOL teachers, we also recognize that not all teachers are afforded the luxury of a block of time set aside for weekly or even

---

8. A text may be written (e.g., a blog post or a scientific journal article) or verbal (e.g., a speech or a video clip).

monthly planning. For example, itinerant ESOL teachers who have more than one school in their caseload may find it nearly impossible to plan together with the content teachers they support in multiple schools. In cases where a time and place has not been reserved for planning purposes, teachers will need to draw from their own creativity and flexibility to ensure that the importance of academic language is elevated through collaborative planning. When teachers do not have the time to meet in person, there are several ways we recommend that teachers can still accomplish planning to incorporate the instruction of academic language through content.

One way we recommend for teachers to plan together is online. They can use file sharing or e-mail to share their lessons with each other and solicit feedback and input. Many teachers we work with recommend Google Docs specifically for this purpose so that multiple teachers can work on lessons together in real time. In cases where it may be overwhelming to meet face to face on a weekly basis, teachers can plan to meet monthly and divide their workload in order to identify features of academic language they'd like to focus on in their instruction. Whatever meeting structure teachers choose (face to face or online), teachers will need to identify specific as well as shared tasks for the ESOL teacher and content teachers to support ELs' acquisition of academic language. In addition to coplanning, we encourage teachers to observe each other's instruction to see how colleagues are integrating the teaching of academic language with content teaching and debrief on what they saw. Finally, teachers can look for informal ways to check in and plan, such as after school.

In cases where administrators have not yet set aside time for content and ESOL teachers to plan together, an opportunity for teachers arises to advocate for the allowance of planning time in service of ELs. In order for teachers to advocate for this time, we suggest that more than one teacher approach an administrator or two who may be sympathetic to better supporting ELs during instruction. Then, we recommend that teachers create a short set of rehearsed talking points that underscore the need for time to meet so that all teachers develop instruction to support ELs' acquisition of academic language across content areas. We also recommend that teachers approach administrators with a proposal for a planning schedule that may work for the teachers involved, taking into account that school and district guidelines for scheduling are being met.

How Can I Infuse Equity, Advocacy, and Leadership to Promote Academic Language?

As many researchers point out (e.g., Bailey, 2012; Shanahan, 2013; Wong Fillmore & Fillmore, 2012), educators must expose ELs to the discourse and content of the content areas. Providing ELs limited access to the content that their grade-level peers receive puts them on a remedial track that may deny them access to the coursework they will need to graduate and experience success after Grade 12. Further, only providing ELs texts at their reading level also does them a disservice. While college and career readiness standards focus on grade-level reading, educators must strike a balance between providing ELs access only to grade-level texts, which may frustrate ELs if sufficient scaffolding is not provided, and giving them texts at their reading level, which may not provide enough challenge. On the other end of the continuum, educators must not give ELs texts only at their reading level, denying them access to the complex academic language and content that their grade-level English-fluent peers are exposed to.

For example, if ELs at a beginning or intermediate level are given a grade-level complex text without instructional support, they will not comprehend it. Many ELs will then "tune out" instruction and may even present classroom management issues for their teachers. Teachers must take extra steps, as necessary, to adapt instruction, such as providing additional resources and giving students adapted materials that complement the grade-level texts at a reduced linguistic load. In this way, teachers can construct a framework for ELs so they can eventually access the same texts as their grade-level non-EL peers without additional support. Teachers' ability to adapt instruction for ELs to incorporate the instruction of academic language hinges upon their knowledge of their students' background experiences, literacy level, culture, and level of English proficiency (among other factors).

We suggest that educators supplement grade-level texts with texts at ELs' reading levels to preview and reinforce content, academic language, and concepts they encounter in grade-appropriate content instruction. In this way, ELs gain confidence in content through working with texts at their reading level (and/or in their home language) and also benefit from exposure to challenging grade-level content and texts. We also caution educators to keep in mind that a focus on the academic language that ELs lack falls into the deficit perspective. It is always important to recognize the language ELs bring with them, whether in the home language or in English. Many times, ELs may not be literate in their home language, but they may bring with them rich oral traditions that can be leveraged in their acquisition of academic language.

> *Reflect on your approach to instructing academic language for your ELs. How have you identified their strengths?*

Next Steps

The following application activity will help you synthesize your learning on academic language for ELs through a collaborative framework.

Cooperative Lesson-Planning Tool

Directions: Find a text you use for instruction. Using the planning template in Figure 5.10, complete the following steps.

FIGURE 5.10   Academic-Language Planning Template

Steps:

1. Analyze the text to determine which aspects of the academic language and/or cultural references used in the text might be challenging for ELs.

    Text name and grade level:

    Word-level challenges for ELs:

    Sentence-level challenges for ELs:

    Discourse-level challenges for ELs:

    Challenging cultural references for ELs:

2. Decide which vocabulary you will focus on from the text and how you will teach and practice the new vocabulary.

Vocabulary Word	How to Teach and Practice It

Vocabulary Word	How to Teach and Practice It

3. Decide which academic-language linguistic features of the text you will teach at the sentence and discourse level.

Linguistic Feature of Text	How to Teach This Feature
Sentence level:	
Discourse level:	

4. Drawing from the potentially challenging aspects of the text, decide on appropriate scaffolds[9] that you will develop to support ELs at different levels of proficiency in understanding the text. Scaffolds might include the following:

   a. Embedded glossaries with easy-to-understand definitions of key academic vocabulary in English

   b. Translations in the home language, if available and appropriate

   c. Images

   d. Graphic organizers

   e. Sentence frames or sentence starters

Level of Proficiency	Scaffolds
Beginning	
Intermediate	
Advanced	

---

9. See Chapter 3 for more information on scaffolds.

(Continued)

FIGURE 5.10 (Continued)

5. Discuss the roles that you (content, ESOL teacher, specialist, etc.) will have in implementing the lesson. How will you complement each other's strengths by leveraging your expertise?

Type of Teacher	Role in Implementing Lesson	Strengths and Expertise to Leverage
ESOL		
Content		
Specialist		
Other		

6. How will you reflect on the efficacy of the lesson and collaborate to revise the lesson?

Conclusion

This chapter highlighted what the concept of academic language entails and the importance of teaching academic language in tandem with content to ELs. It explained the concept of academic language at the word, sentence, and discourse level while encouraging teachers to teach beyond the word level. The chapter provided example activities that underscore how teachers can integrate academic-language instruction at the sentence and discourse levels. Part of the framework for academic language was the sociocultural aspect, which included ELs' background knowledge. In the next chapter, we will explore the concept of selecting and teaching vocabulary to ELs in more depth and show how vocabulary fits into the instructional framework established in this book.

Reflection Questions

1. What types of academic language from your content area at the word, sentence, and discourse levels might be challenging for ELs?

2. How can you build your content instruction around your students' linguistic strengths?

3. What are three ways you can collaborate with ESOL or content teachers to strengthen your teaching of academic language?

References

Bailey, A. L. (Ed.). (2007). *The language demands of school: Putting academic English to the test.* New Haven, CT: Yale University Press.

Bailey, A. L. (2012). Academic English. In J. Banks (Ed.), *Encyclopedia of diversity in education.* Thousand Oaks, CA: Sage.

Bailey, A. L., & Heritage, M. (2008). *Formative assessment for literacy, grades K–6: Building reading and academic language skills across the curriculum.* Thousand Oaks, CA: Corwin.

Beck, I. L., McKeown, M. G., & Kucan, L. (2002). *Bringing words to life.* New York, NY: Guilford Press.

California Department of Education. (2014). Figure collection of the English language arts/English language development framework for California public schools kindergarten through grade twelve, Chapter 3–Chapter 7. Retrieved from http://www.cde.ca.gov/ci/rl/cf/documents/figurescollectch3-7.pdf

Christie, F. (2012). *Language learning through the school years: A functional perspective.* Malden, MA: Wiley & Sons.

Cook, H. G., & Zhao, Y. (2011, April). How English language proficiency assessments manifest growth: An examination of language proficiency growth in a WIDA state. Paper presented at the Annual Meeting of the American Educational Research Association, New Orleans, LA.

Council of Chief State School Officers. (2012). Framework for English Language Proficiency Development Standards corresponding to the Common Core State Standards and the Next Generation Science Standards. Washington, DC: CCSSO.

Edwards, A. (2010). *Being an expert professional practitioner: The relational turn in expertise.* Dordrecht, Netherlands: Springer.

Edwards, A. (2005). Relational agency: Learning to be a resourceful practitioner. *International Journal of Educational Research, 4*(3), 168–182.

Floca, B. (2009). *Moonshot: The Flight of Apollo 11.* New York, NY: Atheneum.

Gee, J. P. (2007). *Good video games and good learning: Collected essays on video games, learning, and literacy.* New York, NY: Peter Lang.

Government of Alberta. (2002). Alberta's wild species. Alberta, Canada: Author. Retrieved from http://aep.alberta.ca/fish-wildlife/wild-species/birds/owls/documents/Owls-FoodChain-Jul17-2009.pdf

Hakuta, K., Butler, Y. G., & Witt, D. (2000) How long does it take English learners to attain proficiency? (Policy Report 2000-1). Stanford: University of California Linguistic Minority Research Institute.

Moughamian, A. C., Rivera, M. O., & Francis, D. J. (2009). *Instructional models and strategies for teaching English language learners.* Portsmouth, NH: RMC Research Corporation, Center on Instruction.

Nippold, M. A., & Scott, C. M. (Eds.). (2010). *Expository discourse in children, adolescents, and adults: Development and disorders.* New York, NY: Psychology Press/Taylor & Francis.

Scarcella, R. (2008). Academic language: Clarifying terms. *AccELLerate!, (1)*1, 5–6.

Shanahan, T. (2013). Letting the text take center stage: How the Common Core will transform English language arts instruction. *American Educator.* Retrieved from http://www.aft.org//sites/default/files/periodicals/Shanahan.pdf

Staehr Fenner, D. (2014). *Advocating for English learners: A guide for educators.* Thousand Oaks, CA, Corwin Press.

WIDA. (2012). WIDA's 2012 amplification of the English language development standards, kindergarten–grade 12. Madison: Board of Regents of the University of Wisconsin System.

Wong Fillmore, L., & Fillmore, C. J. (2012). What does text complexity mean for English learners and language minority students? Stanford, CA: Stanford University, Understanding Language. Retrieved from http://ell.stanford .edu/sites/default/files/pdf/academic-papers/06-LWF%20CJF%20Text%20 Complexity%20FINAL_0.pdf

Zhang, W. (2016, April). *Science language in action: Instructional strategies to teach science language.* Session presented at TESOL International Convention, Baltimore, MD.

Zwiers, J. (2005). *Building reading comprehension habits in grades 6–12.* Newark, DE: International Reading Association.

Zwiers, J. (2008). *Building academic language: Essential practices for content classrooms.* San Francisco, CA: Jossey-Bass.

Vocabulary Instruction and ELs

Alejandro slumps down at his desk and looks at the clock. There are still thirty minutes before the end of his English class, and he has to finish writing the definitions and example sentences for twenty new vocabulary words. They are working on "m" vocabulary words, so the list includes such words as *meager* and *maelstrom*. He will have to try to memorize all of these new words for the test on Friday. He never does very well on the vocabulary tests.

Teaching vocabulary is not a new idea in the field of education. How many of us, at one point in our education, were given a task like the one that Alejandro has in this scenario, where we were asked to memorize a large list of vocabulary words that were not related or only tangentially related to the content we were studying? Assuming we all speak English fluently, how well did that approach work in teaching us new vocabulary? If we want ELs to acquire the academic vocabulary that they need to successfully engage with content-based material, we must be even more intentional about how we approach vocabulary instruction. This chapter will begin with a discussion of why focused teaching of academic vocabulary is critical to ELs' academic achievement. It will also include guidelines on selecting what vocabulary to teach, as well as strategies for teaching and reinforcing new words. You will have an opportunity to practice these strategies throughout the chapter.

> What are your beliefs about teaching academic vocabulary? What questions do you have about teaching vocabulary?

What Is Academic Vocabulary?

As you recall, in Chapter 5, we highlighted the differences between academic language and social language and explained that academic language is the language that is needed to participate in the school curriculum. Similarly, *academic vocabulary* is defined as words used in an academic context, such as in a text or academic discussion. These words, unlike words used informally in conversation, are specialized and are more likely to have multiple meanings across content areas (WIDA, 2012).

Why Teach Academic Vocabulary to ELs?

As described earlier, it can be challenging for ELs to have a solid understanding of and successfully acquire academic vocabulary, which is key to their academic success. Knowledge of academic vocabulary in English is linked to proficiency in reading and writing (August & Shanahan, 2006). If ELs are to be able to effectively engage with complex, grade-level texts and complete standards-based content tasks, they need to develop understanding of the academic—and frequently abstract—vocabulary necessary for these tasks. However, many ELs do not have the opportunities to learn and practice academic vocabulary (August & Shanahan, 2006). All students—but ELs, in particular—need many and varied opportunities to practice their skills with assistance from the teacher, as well as independently (Grabe, 1991; McLaughlin, 1987).

Based on their synthesis of research of effective instructional practices for teaching content and literacy to ELs, Baker et al. (2014) recommend teaching a set of academic vocabulary words intensively over the course of several days using a variety of instructional activities. The strategic teaching of academic vocabulary and the opportunities to use this new vocabulary in varied academic activities will provide ELs the support they need in order to fully understand the meaning of these words and use them in standards-based tasks.

How Should I Select Vocabulary for In-Depth Instruction?

When selecting vocabulary for in-depth focus, Baker et al. (2014) recommend using a brief, informational text that is connected to the content being addressed in class as a platform for vocabulary instruction. The use of these texts or text excerpts can serve as a basis for the acquisition of discipline-specific vocabulary and academic language. Baker et al. (2014) suggest texts such as a magazine or newspaper article, a letter to the editor, an informative piece from the Web, or an excerpt from an academic text or trade book. The texts should be engaging grade-level texts, contain a variety of target academic words, and include ideas that can be discussed from multiple viewpoints. Although all ELs may not be able to independently read grade-level texts, instruction should be scaffolded so as to support ELs of all levels of proficiency in understanding and discussing the text. Information on how to effectively scaffold instruction of a text is provided in Chapters 3 and 8.

Once you have chosen the text that you will use, select five to ten words that you will focus on over the course of several lessons (Baker et al., 2014). When too many new vocabulary words are taught to students, it can be challenging for them to gain a deeper understanding of these words and have sufficient practice with the new words. According to Stahl (2005), students most likely need to see a word more than once to place it firmly in their long-term memories. Additionally, they should not be exposed to the word through repetition or drill of the word only but should practice with the word in different and multiple contexts.

Other vocabulary from the text that may be challenging for ELs can be taught during the work with the text but should not be focused on in the same way as the selected set of words. For example, when reading a text aloud, a teacher might stop and provide a short definition of an unfamiliar word or show a visual to support understanding.

In selecting which words to focus on, Baker et al. (2014) recommend choosing words that meet the following criteria:

1. Are central to understanding the text

2. Appear frequently in the text

3. May appear in other content areas

4. Have multiple meanings

5. Have affixes (prefixes and suffixes)

In other words, it is important to select vocabulary that will both help ELs in accessing the content of a particular text and support them in their learning across disciplines. (We like to call this selecting words that help students get the most "bang for their buck.") For example, learning words with multiple meanings is an effective tool to help students recognize that the meaning of a word may vary depending on the content being studied. Similarly, the study of words with affixes (i.e., prefixes and suffixes) provides students with opportunities to understand the way in which affixes can change a word's meaning or grammatical form (e.g., adding *dis-* to *like; exhibit* and *exhibition*). Figure 6.1 is an example of a type of activity that you could use with students to help them build knowledge of how word parts change the grammatical function of a word.

FIGURE 6.1 Using Word Parts to Understand Word Meaning

Verbs (Action)	Nouns (Person, Place, Thing, or Idea)	Adjectives (Words to Describe Nouns)	Adverbs (Words to Describe Actions)
Investigate	Investigation Investigator	Investigative	
Exhibit	Exhibit Exhibition	Exhibitory	
Pursue	Pursuit	Pursuant	Pursuantly
Opt	Option	Optional	Optionally

Source: Adapted from Baker, S., Lesaux, N., Jayanthi, M., Dimino, J., Proctor, C. P., Morris, J., & Newman-Gonchar, R. (2014). *Teaching academic content and literacy to English learners in elementary and middle school* (NCEE 2014-4012) (p. 23). Washington, DC: U.S. Department of Education, Institute for Education Sciences, National Center for Education Evaluation and Regional Assistance. Retrieved from http://ies.ed.gov/ncee/wwc/pdf/practice_guides/english_learners_pg_040114.pdf

APPLICATION ACTIVITY 6.1

Selecting Words for In-Depth Focus

Read the following Grade 2–3 text excerpt from Sarah Thomson's (2010) *Where Do Polar Bears Live?* Then, decide which five to ten words you would choose for in-depth focus during a unit on animals of the Arctic. Include a short explanation of why you chose each word, citing Criteria 1–5 from Baker et al. (2014), listed previously. Complete Figure 6.2.

A mother polar bear heaves herself out of her den. A cub scrambles after her. When the cub was born four months ago, he was no bigger than a guinea pig. Blind and helpless, he snuggled in his mother's fur. He drank her milk and grew, safe from the long Arctic winter. Outside the den, on some days, it was fifty degrees below zero. From October to February, the sun never rose. Now it is spring—even though snow still covers the land. The cub is about the size of a cocker spaniel. He's ready to leave the den. For the first time, he sees bright sunlight and feels the wind ruffle his fur. The cub tumbles and slides down icy hills. His play makes him strong and teaches him to walk and run in snow.

Like his mother, the cub is built to survive in the Arctic. His white fur will grow to be six inches thick—longer than your hand. The skin beneath the cub's fur is black. It soaks up the heat of the sun. Under the skin is a layer of fat. Like a snug blanket, this blubber keeps in the heat of the bear's body.

FIGURE 6.2 Vocabulary Word, Why Chosen, and Recommendation Cited

Vocabulary Word	Why Chosen	Recommendation Cited
survive	may appear in other content areas	#3

What additional words might you teach in context as you and the students are working on the text? For example, a word such as *cocker spaniel* (from the *Where Do Polar Bears Live?* text) would be helpful for students to understand, but you would not need to spend a lot of time having students study the word. You could provide a simple definition such as, "A cocker spaniel is a type of dog," and show a picture. It is also important to consider what additional words you might teach in context as you and your students are working on a particular text.

APPLICATION ACTIVITY 6.2

Additional Words to Teach

Review the *Where Do Polar Bears Live?* text again, and decide on five additional words that you might teach to students directly as you are working together on the text. These are words that you may only spend one to two minutes teaching to the class and would most likely not include in further instruction.

1.

2.

3.

4.

5.

How Can I Assess Students' Initial Understanding of These New Words?

Before beginning focused instruction on new vocabulary, you should assess student familiarity and understanding of the new words. In performing this initial assessment, you don't want to set students up to fail or to feel that they should already know these words. Instead, you can work with students to help them self-assess their knowledge, explaining that the whole class is going to be learning the meaning of some new words, and you want to know which words they might already know.

For example, you might ask students to sort words into three categories: (1) words that they don't know or have never heard before, (2) words that they have heard of but can't define or use in a sentence, and (3) words that they can accurately use in writing and speaking. You could also have them do a similar activity as a checklist. See Figure 6.3 for an example. In both cases, you should model how to do the self-assessment and walk students through your thought process (e.g., *Hmm, this is a word that I have heard before, but I can't really define it or use it in a sentence. I am going to check the middle column.*)

Another self-assessment option would be to have students do a thumbs up (I know the word or term and can use it), thumbs to the side (I've heard of the word or term, but I don't feel comfortable using it), or thumbs down (I don't know the word or term). You have to be careful that some students might not be entirely truthful in front of other students due to possible stigma associated with not knowing the word.

After you have taught and practiced the new vocabulary, you may wish to have students complete

> What strategies do you use to assess your students' familiarity with content vocabulary?

FIGURE 6.3 Student Vocabulary Self-Assessment Example

Vocabulary Self-Assessment

Directions:

1. Read each word.

2. Decide if . . .

   - You don't know the word

   - You have heard of the word but can't use it

   - You know and feel comfortable using the new word

3. Check the appropriate column.

Vocabulary word or term	I don't know this word or term.	I have heard this word or term, but I can't use it in a sentence.	I know this word or term and feel comfortable using it.
1. adaptation			
2. carnivore			
3. food web			
4. herbivore			

another self-assessment, so they can identify the progress they have made and also identify any words that they still need more practice with. You can also use other formative strategies (e.g., having students match pictures with words) to assess student learning as you are teaching and practicing the new words. For recommendations on more formative-assessment strategies, see Chapter 9.

What Strategies Should I Use for Teaching Academic Vocabulary?

When teaching academic vocabulary, Baker et al. (2014) recommend the use of student-friendly definitions, examples and nonexamples, and concrete representations to support students in gaining an in-depth understanding of the new words.

1. Provide student-friendly definitions.

It is important when learning new vocabulary that ELs have a clear and concrete definition of each new vocabulary word that aligns with the meaning of the word as it is used in the text. Student-friendly definitions will most likely need to be adapted from traditional dictionary definitions. For example, *Merriam-Webster* online provides the following definitions for the word *survive:* "(1) to remain alive: to continue to live; (2) to continue to exist; (3) to remain alive after the death of (someone)." If you were teaching the meaning of the word *survive* using the earlier text, you would want to focus on definitions one and two. However, words such as *remain*, *alive*, and *exist* may present obstacles to ELs being able to understand the meaning. So the most student-friendly definition for the word *survive* would be "to continue to live." Student-friendly definitions should be accompanied by visuals, examples, and translations of the word in students' home languages (as appropriate). The "Tools and Resources" section of this chapter on page 171 provides an online tool that can be helpful in developing student-friendly definitions.

Figure 6.4 provides an example of how a teacher might introduce a new vocabulary word. In this example, taken from a curricular unit focused on the book *Dreaming in Cuban* (García, 1992), the teacher can present a new vocabulary word by showing two pictures, providing the Spanish translation and an explanation of the word, and making a connection to the story. Notice that the teacher provides a student-friendly definition of

FIGURE 6.4   Introducing a New Vocabulary Word

Profits	ganancias
The customers pay money	The store owners make profits

Picture : Look at the picture. The customers pay money to buy something at the store. The person who owns the store collects the money. Some of this money is profits.

Explanation : Let's talk about the word profits. Profits are money that a business earns. After the business pays the workers and pays all the bills, the money left over is called profits. All types of business can make profits—a big company, supermarket, and even a lemonade stand.

Partner talk : If you had a store and earned profits what would you do with your profits? Use this sentence frame: If my business earned profits I would_____. *(Call on one or two students to share their responses.)*

Story connection : In the text, Abuela tells Pilar about life in Cuba before the revolution. Abuela says, "There was one product, sugar, and all the profits went to a few Cubans, and, of course, to the Americans."

Source: August, D., Golden, L., & Pook, D. (2015). *Secondary curricular units for New York City Department of Education* (p. 18). Reprinted with permission of American Institutes for Research. Retrieved from http://schools.nyc.gov/NR/rdonlyres/0A89D8C6-8B99-426A-B2CF-D7426ABF75C4/0/DreaminginCubanHSUnit.pdf

the word in her explanation: "Profits are the money that a business earns." In addition, students have an opportunity to practice the word through the "Partner Talk" activity.

APPLICATION ACTIVITY 6.3

Writing Student-Friendly Definitions

Return to the work that you did in Application Activity 6.1. Write student-friendly definitions for five of the words that you selected.

1.

2.

3.

4.

5.

2. Use examples, nonexamples, and concrete representations

In addition to student-friendly definitions, during explicit instruction of vocabulary it is also important to provide students with examples, nonexamples, and concrete representations of the word. For example, in the Frayer Model in Figure 6.5, you can see both examples and nonexamples of an *equation*. Similarly, in the word map in Figure 6.6, students have provided examples, nonexamples, synonyms, and antonyms of the word *enormous*. Concrete representations, such as pictures, gestures, and actions, can also help reinforce the meaning of a word.

As explained in the introduction to this chapter, abstract words are frequently more challenging to explain and teach than objects that can be easily exemplified by pictures. Let's take another example from the *Where Do Polar Bears Live?* reading used earlier in the chapter to complete Application Activity 6.4.

FIGURE 6.5 Example of Frayer Model

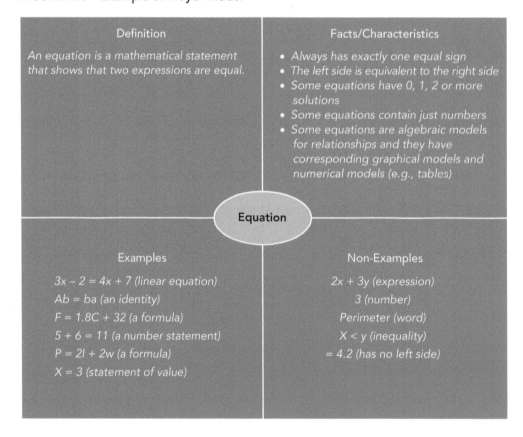

Definition	Facts/Characteristics
An equation is a mathematical statement that shows that two expressions are equal.	• Always has exactly one equal sign • The left side is equivalent to the right side • Some equations have 0, 1, 2 or more solutions • Some equations contain just numbers • Some equations are algebraic models for relationships and they have corresponding graphical models and numerical models (e.g., tables)

Equation

Examples	Non-Examples
$3x - 2 = 4x + 7$ (linear equation) $Ab = ba$ (an identity) $F = 1.8C + 32$ (a formula) $5 + 6 = 11$ (a number statement) $P = 2l + 2w$ (a formula) $X = 3$ (statement of value)	$2x + 3y$ (expression) 3 (number) Perimeter (word) $X < y$ (inequality) $= 4.2$ (has no left side)

FIGURE 6.6 Example of Word Map

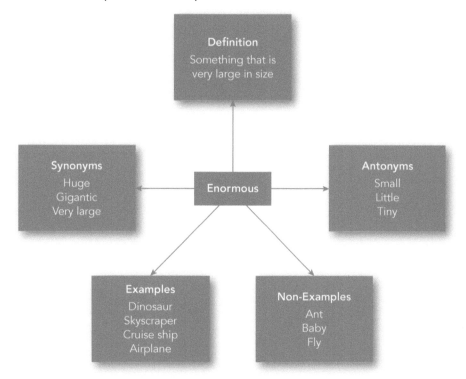

Source: Baker, S., Lesaux, N., Jayanthi, M., Dimino, J., Proctor, C. P., Morris, J., & Newman-Gonchar, R. (2014). *Teaching academic content and literacy to English learners in elementary and middle school* (NCEE 2014-4012). Washington, DC: U.S. Department of Education, Institute for Education Sciences, National Center for Education Evaluation and Regional Assistance. Retrieved from http://ies.ed.gov/ncee/wwc/pdf/practice_guides/english_learners_pg_040114.pdf

APPLICATION ACTIVITY 6.4

Vocabulary Practice. Reread this excerpt from the text: *A mother polar bear heaves herself out of her den. A cub scrambles after her.* What does *heaves* mean in this sentence? Using context clues, a dictionary, and a bilingual dictionary, complete the following:

- Student-friendly definition:

- Synonym:

- Antonym:

- An example:

- A nonexample:

- Concrete images you could provide students:

- Other meanings:

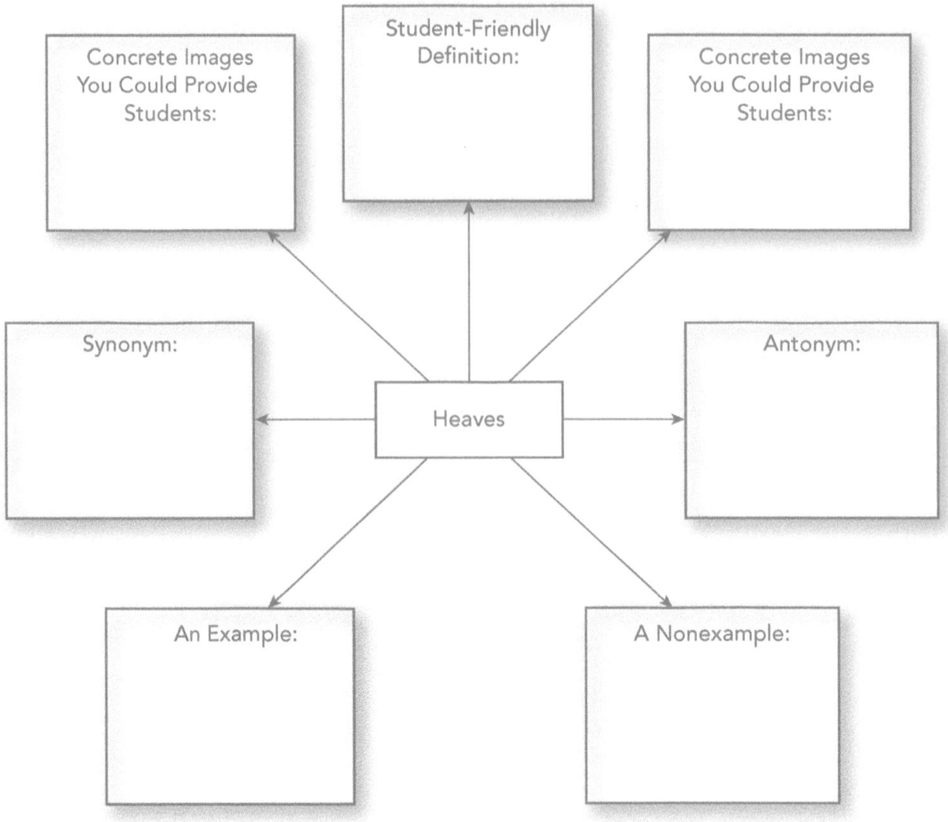
Concrete Images You Could Provide Students:
Student-Friendly Definition:
Concrete Images You Could Provide Students:
Synonym:
Heaves
Antonym:
An Example:
A Nonexample:

What Activities Can I Use to Help My ELs Practice New Vocabulary?

It is important that ELs have focused opportunities to practice the new vocabulary that they have been taught through a variety of listening, speaking, reading, and writing activities (Baker et al., 2014). In other words, once new vocabulary has been introduced through an engaging, content-specific text, students will need to test their understanding of the words over the course of several days in order to really cement their knowledge of the word. It is important to create a classroom culture in which trying out new academic words in speech and writing is encouraged and students are not expected to use words correctly the first time. There are many different activities that teachers can use to practice new vocabulary, but we have included descriptions of a few of our favorites. Some of these activities may be more appropriate for students in certain grade levels than others. The vignette on page 161, "Mr. Bellow's Classroom," provides an example of what vocabulary instruction might look like in a kindergarten classroom. The list of "Additional Tools and Resources" at the end of the chapter offers some tools for developing these activities.

Listening and Speaking Activities to Develop ELs' Vocabulary

- **Interactive word wall:** For this activity, students are placed in groups of three or four. Each group is given a piece of poster paper, some tape, markers, and vocabulary words on index cards. Students take turns choosing a vocabulary word and making a connection to another word (e.g., A *predator* hunts for its *prey*). As they make the connection, they tape both words to the poster paper and draw an arrow between them. The next student then must make a connection between one of those words and a new word (e.g., A *predator* is *carnivore*). Connections can be made to more than one word.

- **Pair discussion questions:** The teacher develops discussion questions that include the new vocabulary. Students work in pairs to discuss the questions and write an answer.

- **Video clips:** Students watch short video clips that include the new vocabulary and discuss what they saw. Teachers should preview the video discussion questions with their ELs prior to watching the video. ELs may also benefit from sentence stems, sentence frames, and a word bank to support their discussion.

- **Word experts:** Students (or pairs of students) are assigned to present on a new vocabulary word that the teacher assigns them. Students should provide a student-friendly definition, the part of speech, an image to help remember the word, any suffixes or prefixes that can help in understanding the word, and the use of new word. If you only have a small number of words, you could have students present in small groups. You could also incorporate technology into this activity by having students make a short PowerPoint presentation about their word. ELs will need to have this activity modeled for them and could also benefit from the use of bilingual dictionaries, if appropriate.

- **Information gap:** Students are paired and given information involving new vocabulary words, but within the pair, Student A has information that Student B doesn't have and vice versa. They need to use new vocabulary words and exchange information in order to complete the information gap activity. ELs could benefit from the use of sentence stems or sentence frames during this activity.

- **Dramatic representations:** Students work individually, in pairs, or in groups to act out new words. For example, if the new word is *revolve*, the person acting as the Earth would revolve around the person acting as the Sun. ELs would benefit from having this activity modeled and may also benefit from working with a partner that speaks their same home language.

Reading and Writing Activities to Develop ELs' Vocabulary

- **Responding to a content-related prompt using a word bank:** Students can be given a prompt connected to the content they are studying and be asked to write a response using the vocabulary words in the word bank. ELs may need sentence frames or paragraph frames as additional support.

- **Glossary:** Students can be asked to create a glossary to support their understanding of new content. The glossary can include a student-friendly definition, the use of the word in the text, an image to represent the word, whether or not the word is a cognate in their home language, and another example of how the word could be used in a sentence. For an example of a glossary, see page 63.

- **Text-dependent questions:** Text-dependent questions are an excellent way for ELs to practice their understanding of new words using a text. A teacher might develop a question such as the following: Sentence 2 says, "Like a snug blanket, this blubber keeps in the heat of the bear's body." What do you think *blubber* means in this sentence? Students can be given sentence frames, sentence stems, and word banks to support their work. For more on creating text-dependent questions for ELs, see Chapter 8.

- **Gallery walk:** Students or pairs of students can be assigned one aspect of the content that they are studying. They should create a poster that explains their topic. Students can also be asked to use a certain number of vocabulary words from a word bank on their poster as well as images that help explain both the topic and the vocabulary. When students are finished, they can move around the room, looking at others' posters. They can write comments or questions on sticky notes, and these can be discussed with the large group. ELs may benefit from such scaffolds as a word bank, sentence stems, and working with students that speak their home language.

Games and Activities to Develop ELs' Vocabulary

- **Memory:** For this game, vocabulary words can be written on one card, and a definition, picture, or example can be written on another. Students play memory to match the vocabulary word with its pair. As students play the game, they should say the vocabulary word aloud for the pictures and definitions to reinforce their understanding and practice with the words.

- **Vocab Jeopardy!:** In a modified version of the game show *Jeopardy!*, students are given a clue and need to determine the correct vocabulary word based on the clue given. Clues can be placed in a grid of different categories (e.g., definitions, examples, and antonyms). Students can be grouped in teams. When it is their turn, each team can select which category they want and for how many points (e.g., "Definitions" for 300). The team is given the clue and tries to figure out the answer. ELs may benefit from having a word bank or bilingual glossary to refer to during the game.

- **Vocab jigsaw:** For this activity, students are placed in groups of four. Each person on the team gets one clue about the word (e.g., what letter the word starts with, the number of syllables in the word, an antonym, or definition). Students take turns reading their clues, and as a group, they try to figure out the mystery vocabulary word.

- **Vocabulary bingo:** Students write or glue their vocabulary words on bingo cards. The teacher or a student reads a definition or provides an example of the word, and students put a marker on their bingo card if they have that word. A student wins when he or she has marked five vocabulary words in a row.

- **What's my word?:** Students have a vocabulary word on their back, and they have to figure out what their word is by asking yes/no questions (e.g., *Is my word a noun? Does my word mean "to live"?*). ELs may benefit from having sentence stems or sentence frames to refer to.

> *What other strategies do you use to practice key vocabulary? Does your practice include opportunities for students to use the new vocabulary when speaking, reading, writing, and listening?*

Mr. Bellow's Class: Teaching Vocabulary in a Kindergarten Classroom

Mr. Bellow teaches kindergarten in a suburban elementary school. He has many Spanish-speaking students who are considered *dual language learners* because of their young age and the fact that they are learning their home language and English simultaneously. Mr. Bellow, who teaches primarily in English, knows that academic vocabulary instruction is critical for students of this age. During a unit on emotions, Mr. Bellow selects a story to use for a read-aloud that contains several adjectives describing emotions (e.g., *excited*, *unhappy*, or *frustrated*). He identifies six words to preteach. He introduces each word by showing a picture and providing examples of when someone might feel that emotion. He also has the students act out the emotions and share situations in which they felt that particular emotion. Mr. Bellow has also created a word wall with the new vocabulary word in both English and Spanish, as well as a picture of a person or situation that represents that emotion. As Mr. Bellow reads the story, he highlights the new vocabulary as it comes up in the story.

The following day, Mr. Bellow reads the story again in Spanish. In order to provide students opportunities to practice the new vocabulary throughout the day, Mr. Bellow includes varied vocabulary activities in his centers. For example, at one center students work in pairs to cut out pictures of people and animals feeling different emotions. They then sort these pictures into the different emotions and paste them into a table. Finally, they tally the number of how many of each emotion they found (e.g., two people and three animals feel afraid). Mr. Bellow, with the assistance of the school's ESOL teacher, also researches online apps for young learners that reinforce the vocabulary of emotions. Students can also listen to the story again (either in Spanish or English) as part of a listening center. When transitioning between centers or other activities, Mr. Bellow also asks students to move in ways that represent the new vocabulary (e.g., *Walk like you are unhappy*). By the end of the week, Mr. Bellow's students are able to complete a vocabulary sort in which they match the written word with a picture that represents the word, and they are able to describe how they or other students may feel in particular situations using the new vocabulary.

How Can I Help My ELs Become Independent Learners of New Vocabulary?

In addition to intensively teaching new academic vocabulary, it is also important to give students opportunities to practice skills that will help them figure out the meaning of unfamiliar words and acquire new vocabulary independently (Baker et al., 2014). Such skills include the following:

- Using context clues
- Understanding word parts and compound words
- Understanding cognates and false cognates
- Recognizing proper nouns

We describe each skill in more depth in the following sections.

Using Context Clues

One strategy to support ELs' independent learning of new words is to provide them with opportunities to practice determining the meaning of unfamiliar words using clues from the sentence that include the unfamiliar word or using clues from surrounding sentences. The teacher can provide a think-aloud to model how he or she uses context clues to determine the

FIGURE 6.7 Minilesson on Using Context Clues

Context Clues

Mystery Word	Location	Clues
1. jerrybuilt affairs	Line 5	Lines 5–6
Clues: *looked solid, but stone or brick exteriors hid wooden frames and floors*		
Definition: structures built in a cheap way		
2. stately	Line 19	Lines 19–20
Clues:		
Definition:		
3. lined	Line 21	Lines 21–22
Clues:		
Definition:		
4. soggy	Line 25	Lines 24–25
Clues:		
Definition:		
5. showers	Line 35	Lines 35–36
Clues:		
Definition:		
6. drooped	Line 36	Lines 36–37
Clues:		
Definition:		

Source: August, D., Golden, L., Staehr Fenner, D., & Snyder, S. (2015). *Secondary curricular units for New York City Department of Education* (p. 128). Reprinted with permission of American Institutes for Research. Washington, DC: American Institutes of Research. Retrieved from http://schools.nyc.gov/NR/rdonlyres/5A960901-7DC4-42AF-8D82-7CE911CFD328/0/GreatFireMSUnit.pdf

meaning of an unfamiliar word and develop minilessons, such as the one in Figure 6.7, to give students opportunities to practice this skill. As you can see in Figure 6.7, the students are provided with a short list of words that may be unfamiliar, the location of the word, and the location of the clues. Working in pairs, the students read the sentences that contain the word and the clues, select clues that help them determine the meaning, and write a definition for the word. This activity is designed to support secondary students' work with excerpts from a text called *The Great Fire* (Murphy, 1995).

Understanding Word Parts and Compound Words

In addition to practice discerning the meaning of new words using context, ELs (as well as non-ELs) will also benefit from explicit instruction of word parts including prefixes, suffixes, and root words[1] as a tool to make predictions about the meaning of unknown words. Again, the teacher should model his or her thought process aloud to students in order to demonstrate how to make such predictions. Students can also practice using different forms of words that they are learning. In the following vignette from Mr. Clark's class, the teacher incorporates understanding of word parts into his teaching on a regular basis. Students add to a list of the meaning of word parts throughout the year, and the teacher gives them opportunities to practice their understanding through short in-class exercises.

Mr. Clark's Class: Understanding Word Parts

Mr. Clark's ninth-grade history class is studying different forms of government. Seven out of twenty-three students in the class are ELs. They are all at an intermediate or advanced level of language proficiency. The students have learned the definition for the term *democracy*. Mr. Clark writes the following terms on the board: *democratic*, *democratically*, and *undemocratic*. He asks his students to work in pairs and use their knowledge of word parts that he has already taught to determine a meaning for each of the words. They should write an example of how the word might be used based on the content that they are studying. Students have practiced using word parts previously and have a list in their notebooks of the meanings of different affixes that they have studied. The students know that the suffixes *-ic* and *-ly* indicate the part of speech. They also know that the prefix *un-* is used to indicate what something is not. They discuss the words in pairs. While they are working, Mr. Clark checks in with groups that are struggling.

The strategy used in this vignette will support ELs in recognizing and understanding the meaning of words that come from the same word families (e.g., *patience*, *patiently*, and *impatient*). Teachers who speak ELs' home languages can also point out similar types of affixes if they occur in the home language. For example, the prefix *ante-* means *before* in Spanish. In addition, ELs can also benefit from explicit instruction in determining the meaning of compound words, two words joined together to make a new word (e.g., *firefly* and *softball*). According to Hiebert (2013), the addition of compound words is one of the central ways that new words are added to the English language. Consider such words as *software*, *playlist*, and *upgrade*. Compound words such as these have connections to their root words, but they also may have idiomatic meanings. Accordingly, compound words need to be taught differently than words coming from the same word family. Teachers should work with students in determining the meaning of words

---

1. A root word is the base word to which prefixes and suffixes can be added. It can also stand on its own. For example, in the word *lovely*, *love* is the root word and *-ly* is the suffix.

that share the same headwords, the first word in the compound word (e.g., *uproar*, *upset*, and *uptight*) (Hiebert, 2013).

Understanding Cognates and False Cognates

Cognates are words in different languages that are derived from the same original word or root. In addition to having the same meaning, the words look and sound similar. For example, *conclusion* in English is *conclusión* in Spanish. While it might seem like the use of cognates is a tool that ELs will use naturally and without prompting, it is beneficial for them to be given explicit instruction in recognizing and using cognates in their work. Students also need to be aware of false cognates, or "false friends" as they are sometimes called. These are words that look and sound similar in two languages but actually have very different meanings. For example, the word *assist* in English means to help, but the phrase *assister à* in French means to attend an event. Additionally, students who have had interrupted schooling or who have not had the benefit of extensive formal education in their home language may be familiar with an academic word that is a cognate but may not understand the meaning of the word (e.g., *electrode* in English and *electrodo* in Spanish). Teachers can't assume this knowledge, which underscores the importance of all teachers of ELs knowing their students' background experiences.

Recognizing Proper Nouns

Similar to the instruction of cognates, ELs also benefit from explicit instruction in the recognition of proper nouns (Hiebert, 2013). Unfamiliar proper nouns can be a stumbling block in students' comprehension of texts. ELs need to be taught that capitalized words in the middle of sentences are most likely proper nouns and may or may not be critical to understanding the meaning of the text. ELs can be taught to recognize proper nouns and determine based on the context whether the word is the name of a person, place, or something else. Let's look at a sample text.

Glacier Peak, also known as Takobia to the Sauk Native American tribe, is the fourth-largest but most active volcano in the state of Washington. Located in Glacier Peak Wilderness, it can be seen from Seattle and suburbs of Vancouver, such as Coquitlam. This little-known volcano was formed during the Pleistocene epoch and during the most recent ice age. When the ice retreated, Glacier Peak began to erupt regularly, including five explosive eruptions and two of the state's largest.

Students can be taught strategies to help them understand the function of unfamiliar proper nouns in the sentence so that they can understand the gist and not get tripped up over decoding often large, unfamiliar words. In this example, there are context clues that indicate that the word Takobia is from the Sauk language and is a synonym for Glacier Peak. Other linguistic clues tell the reader that other proper nouns in the text are names of locations and time periods.

How Do I Put All of the EL Vocabulary Strategies Together?

In this chapter, we have provided several recommendations for teaching and practicing academic vocabulary. It may be helpful to begin by using one or two strategies in order to not get overwhelmed by all of the possible strategies that you might use. In order to help you remember and use the strategies, we have developed a "Vocabulary Instruction Checklist" (Figure 6.8) that you may find helpful when teaching vocabulary. You could use a checklist such as this to keep track of vocabulary that you have taught, as well as to take notes on specific activities that worked well or did not work well in order to refine your instruction. You could also use the checklist to keep track of word-learning strategies that you have practiced with students and any challenges that they had. Using the "Vocabulary Instruction Checklist" will support you as you continue to bolster students' understanding and use of academic vocabulary.

FIGURE 6.8 Vocabulary Instruction Checklist

Unit Vocabulary:		
Steps	Completed	Notes
1. I have selected a short, engaging, content-related text to use for vocabulary selection.		
2. I have selected five to ten words that are central to understanding the text, appear frequently in the text, may appear in other content areas, have multiple meanings, and/or have affixes.		
3. I have assessed students' initial understanding of these words.		
4. I have taught the words using student-friendly definitions, visuals or actions, synonyms, antonyms, examples, and nonexamples.		
5. I have given student opportunities to practice the words in varied ways using varied modalities (i.e., speaking, reading, writing, and listening).		
6. I have given students opportunities to practice word-learning strategies (e.g., use of context clues, morphology, and cognates).		
7. I have reassessed student understanding of the new words.		

What Is the Role of Collaboration in Teaching Academic Vocabulary to ELs?

As we described in Chapter 1, when ESOL teachers and content teachers collaborate, it can be highly beneficial to both ELs and the teachers of ELs (Honigsfeld & Dove, 2010). Sharing responsibility for planning for and teaching vocabulary is an excellent opportunity to build such collaboration. Content teachers and ESOL teachers can share their expertise as they work together to select a set of vocabulary that is both essential to the content being covered and that may present challenges to ELs. Content teachers can provide their expertise in determining content-specific texts that will allow students to see the new vocabulary embedded in rich content material. They can also provide information to the ESOL teacher on the key vocab that students need to know in the unit. ESOL teachers can suggest concrete ways of teaching and practicing the new vocabulary. ESOL teachers can also provide explicit instruction on the pronunciation, morphology, syntax, and function of the new word, as well as address its word family members or root of the word. Both teachers can work together to develop activities and materials that will support ELs of varying proficiency levels in gaining deeper understanding of the new vocabulary and practicing using the new words in multiple modalities. School librarians can also be an excellent resource.

What Is the Role of Equity, Advocacy, and Leadership in Teaching Academic Vocabulary to ELs?

In order to comprehend instruction and access challenging grade-level texts, ELs need a solid grasp of the academic vocabulary connected to the content and the texts. Non-ELs may already have a working knowledge of this vocabulary, so it's each teacher's responsibility to teach ELs the vocabulary they need to fully engage in instruction. Teaching ELs vocabulary the same ways you teach non-ELs vocabulary may not be effective, so you will need to try out and adopt new strategies that are effective with the ELs in your classroom. It is also essential that you give ELs multiple opportunities to practice this new vocabulary in the four domains (i.e., reading, writing, listening, and speaking). Furthermore, you can leverage your leadership skills to ensure that all teachers are aware of ELs' strengths and needs in terms of academic vocabulary and collaborate with other teachers in your grade level or content area. You can also make sure administrators are on board to provide the support in academic vocabulary that ELs need.

Next Steps

In order to practice and adopt the strategies outlined in this chapter, complete the following application activity. We recommend working with another teacher when possible to discuss and answer the questions in the activity. Another possibility would be to have a small group of teachers complete the activity individually and then share responses with each other, making revisions as appropriate.

APPLICATION ACTIVITY 6.5

Planning to Teach Academic Vocabulary

Select a short, engaging text that you could use to accompany one of your lessons. Then, complete the template (Figure 6.9).

FIGURE 6.9 Academic Vocabulary Template

Text:	
Content topic:	
A. Select five to ten words that you will teach. For each word, write a student-friendly definition.	
Word	**Student-Friendly Definition**
1.	
2.	
3.	
4.	
5.	
6.	
7.	
8.	
9.	
10.	

Text:
Content topic:
B. Explain how you will assess the students' understanding and use of the vocabulary (prior to instruction).
C. Explain how you will introduce or teach this set of vocabulary words.
D. Explain what activities you will use help students learn and practice these new words (e.g., word map, use of visuals, vocabulary bingo, or information gap).
E. Determine what, if any, word-learning skills (e.g., understanding cognates, determining meaning from context, or understanding word parts) you will have students practice. What will the activity include?

Conclusion

In this chapter, we have explained why the explicit and strategic instruction of academic vocabulary is so important to ELs' acquisition of language and learning of content. We have also provided some recommendations for how to select the vocabulary you will teach, as well as given you some strategies for teaching and practicing new vocabulary. In the next chapter, we will be providing information on how to select what background knowledge to teach. As you explore that chapter, keep in mind that background knowledge instruction and vocabulary instruction work hand in hand to help prepare ELs for learning new content.

Reflection Questions

1. How do you plan to adapt your current strategies for teaching new vocabulary to ELs based on the material in this chapter?

2. What is one new activity for practicing vocabulary that you would like to use? How will you adapt it for your context?

References

August, D., & Shanahan, T. (Eds.). (2006). *Developing literacy in second-language learners: Report of the national literacy panel on language-minority children and youth*. Mahwah, NJ: Lawrence Erlbaum.

Baker, S., Lesaux, N., Jayanthi, M., Dimino, J., Proctor, C. P., Morris, J., & Newman-Gonchar, R. (2014). *Teaching academic content and literacy to English learners in elementary and middle school* (NCEE 2014-4012). Washington, DC: U.S. Department of Education, Institute for Education Sciences, National Center for Education Evaluation and Regional Assistance. Retrieved from http://ies.ed.gov/ncee/wwc/pdf/practice_guides/english_learners_pg_040114.pdf

García, C. (1992). *Dreaming in Cuban*. New York, NY: Knopf.

Grabe, W. (1991). Current developments in second language reading research. *TESOL Quarterly, 25*(3), 375–406.

Hiebert, E. (2013). Text matters: Text complexity and English learners—Building vocabulary. Retrieved from http://textproject.org/professional-development/text-matters/text-complexity-and-english-learners-building-vocabulary

Honigsfeld, A., & Dove, M. G. (2010). *Collaboration and co-teaching: Strategies for English learners*. Thousand Oaks, CA: Corwin.

McLaughlin, B. (1987). *Theories of second language learning*. London, UK: Edward Arnold.

Murphy, J. (1995). *The great fire*. New York, NY: Scholastic.

Stahl, S. A. (2005). Four problems with teaching word meanings (and what to do to make vocabulary an integral part of instruction). In E. H. Hiebert & M. L. Kamil (Eds.), *Teaching and learning vocabulary: Bringing research to practice* (pp. 95–115). Mahwah, NJ: Lawrence Erlbaum.

survive. (2016). Retrieved from http://www.merriam-webster.com/dictionary/survive

Thomson, S. L. (2010). *Where do polar bears live?* New York, NY: HarperCollins.

WIDA. (2012). *WIDA's 2012 amplification of the English language development standards, kindergarten–grade 12*. Madison: Board of Regents of the University of Wisconsin System.

Additional Tools and Resources

Tools

Achieve the Core's Academic Word Finder: This tool supports teachers in determining which Tier 2 academic words they may want to focus on in relation to a particular text. You can insert a text and select a grade level, and the tool analyzes the text and identifies academic words for you to consider at and above grade level (http://achievethecore.org/academic-word-finder).

flashcardstash.com: This site provides a quick way to create flashcards.

Lingro.com: An online dictionary that remembers words you have already looked up in order to allow you to easily review them. It also provides translations of words in eleven different languages.

The Visual Thesaurus is an interactive dictionary and thesaurus. It creates word maps that help you explore the meanings of words, and it provides links to related words (https://www.visualthesaurus.com/vocabgrabber).

Wordsmyth.net is an online dictionary that provides three levels of definitions (beginner, intermediate, and advanced) for every word. This website can be a helpful starting point for creating student-friendly definitions.

Resources

Colorín Colorado. (n.d.). Selecting vocabulary words to teach English language learners. Retrieved from http://www.colorincolorado.org/article/selecting-vocabulary-words- teach-english-language-learners

Colorín Colorado. (n.d.). Tips for educators of ELLs: Teaching vocabulary in grades 4–12. Retrieved from http://www.colorincolorado.org/article/tips-educators-ells-teaching- vocabulary-grades-4-12

Colorín Colorado. (n.d.). Vocabulary development. Retrieved from http://www.colorincolorado.org/article/vocabulary-development

Teaching Channel. (n.d.). Frontloading for English language learners [video]. Retrieved from https://www.teachingchannel.org/videos/vocabulary-english-language-learners

Teaching ELs Background Knowledge

Viktor, a Ukrainian middle school student at a high beginning level of proficiency who has been in the United States for six months, is beginning a unit on the Great Depression in the United States in his social studies class. To prepare him for the unit, Ms. Moussa and Mr. Lopez, his social studies and ESOL teachers, devote several class periods building his and his EL classmates' background knowledge on the consumer economy of the 1920s, what the stock market is, "Black Tuesday," and President Hoover. However, Ms. Moussa is beginning to grow frustrated with building background knowledge since she has a district social studies pacing guide she needs to follow and is falling behind. She is also concerned that her native English speakers are getting bored with all the background knowledge instruction since they already know much of this material. Both teachers wonder if there is a better way to help Viktor gain enough background knowledge so he can be an active participant in the content unit while developing his academic-language skills in English.

Ms. Moussa and Mr. Lopez are not alone in wondering how to choose and teach background knowledge to ELs when more is asked of all students, including ELs, yet teachers' time constraints are so pressing. This chapter will help you take a deeper look at how you select and teach background knowledge to ELs. It explores the time investment and potential benefit to ELs when background knowledge is chosen carefully and taught succinctly. The chapter will address the need to develop a new approach to or reconceptualize the teaching of background knowledge to ELs within a focus of close reading or challenging topics. The chapter will first briefly define close reading and will share considerations in close reading for ELs. It will

Think of one lesson in which you teach some background knowledge to ELs. What background do you see as essential? Why do you choose to teach it? How do you teach it, and how long do you spend on instruction of background knowledge as part of this lesson?

then highlight a four-step framework for deciding which types of background knowledge to teach ELs and ways to activate and teach background knowledge concisely. The chapter includes a flowchart, tables, and models for educators to use in deciding which background knowledge to teach and how to teach it. It also includes and models several activities that you can use in your own planning and instruction to help you put the framework into practice. Since background knowledge is also crucial for ELs to access mathematics instruction, we also include a special section on the unique areas of background knowledge and mathematics for ELs.

Reflection: How Do I Feel About Teaching Background Knowledge to ELs?

Part of effectively choosing and teaching background knowledge to ELs involves first getting a sense of where you fall along the continuum of beliefs about teaching background knowledge. Here we provide two avenues for you to do so: a continuum and an activity. First, consider the points on this continuum, and mark where you think you fall:

| 1. I believe ELs should not be taught background knowledge. They will gain that knowledge through reading the text. | 2. I believe ELs should be taught some background knowledge prior to reading texts on topics unfamiliar to them. | 3. I believe ELs should be taught ample background knowledge so that they are completely familiar with the nuances and topics of a text before working with it. |

Now, think about a rationale for your answer. Why did you choose your answer? Has this approach worked for you and your ELs? Why, or why not?

Another way to raise awareness about the impact of background knowledge on learning is to take part in an activity called "Describe the Apple." You can engage in this three-step activity either with teachers or your own students.

Step 1. The class should split up into five groups, and each group will receive one "support item" related to the topic of apples. Once each group receives their support item, they must write down as much as they can based on what they can gather from their support item to describe the apple.

Group 1: The word apple printed on an index card

Group 2: A black-and-white printed picture of an apple

Group 3: A color printed picture of an apple

Group 4: A short video clip of an apple being cut into slices

Group 5: A real apple with a label that says "apple" taped on to it, a paper plate, and apple slices

Step 2. Ask the groups to count their words that they have used to describe the apple.

Step 3. Ask each group to share their words, beginning with Group 1 and ending with Group 5. Group 5 gets to eat the apple, as well as smell and taste it, which are all very real experiences. It is likely that this group, who has been given the most real and applicable experience to activate and/or build their background knowledge, will produce the most words.

We've heard opinions that span both ends of the continuum when it comes to deciding how much background knowledge is appropriate for ELs—from no background knowledge whatsoever (and exclusive attention on the text) all the way to extensive preparation about the subject of the text, the author, or other topics that might or might not directly relate to the text. In our experience, ESOL teachers' responses typically tend to gravitate more toward Point 3 on the continuum, whereas content teachers' responses usually tend to align somewhere between Point 1 and Point 2. Naturally, there are outliers in both groups of teachers. While we know through the apple activity that providing more experiential-type background knowledge usually results in students' production of more language, it may take more class time to provide such experiences in depth. With more challenging standards in place and texts being used by teachers of ELs, we need to find a happy medium. Background knowledge is an issue that teachers, district leaders, policy makers, and curriculum writers seem to continue to struggle with when considering how to equitably teach ELs within a standards-based framework.

How Can I Raise My Awareness About the Importance of ELs' Background Knowledge?

Now that you have considered your own stance on teaching background knowledge to ELs, you can continue raising awareness about the importance of background knowledge for ELs by putting yourself in the shoes of a student who has not yet developed background knowledge on a topic. One way to do this is to first take a look at how background knowledge influences your own understanding of a text by reading a math word problem that's written in English. Unlike most ELs' experiences learning language and content simultaneously, your knowledge of language should not affect your comprehension of the following short text in Application Activity 7.1.

APPLICATION ACTIVITY 7.1

Math Word Problem

First, read this word problem, and then, discuss or think about your responses to the three reflection questions that follow.

Word Problem: *A cricketer whose bowling average is 12.4 runs per wicket takes 5 wickets for 26 runs and thereby decreases his average by 0.4. How many wickets were taken by him until the last match?*[1]

Reflection Questions

1. What would you need to know in order to answer this problem?

2. How does background knowledge play a part in your understanding of this problem?

3. How would you approach trying to solve this problem? What resources would you use?[2]

Maybe you were able to solve the problem without linguistic or mathematical supports, but consider how much "85 wickets taken before final match" actually means to you and the amount of information it provides. Now, suppose you're in a mathematics class in England where wickets and cricket vocabulary might be part of regular conversation. Would you ask the teacher what cricket is and what the rules are in front of the class? Would you interrupt instruction and also immediately expose yourself as a speaker of American English? What if you also did not have the math skills to solve this problem, let alone the understanding of the terms? This experience also underscores that you should not rely on ELs' responses to teachers' questions about contexts such as, "You know what a baseball field is, right?" or, "Have you ever heard of NASA?" Students may be self-conscious about sharing the range and depth of information that

---

1. See https://www.quora.com/A-cricketer-whose-bowling-average-is-12-4-runs-per-wicket-takes-5-wickets-for-26-runs-thereby-decreases-his-average-by-0-4.

2. Please see the end of the chapter for the solution.

is unfamiliar, and they may not be entirely candid in publicly identifying cultural or linguistic information they do not yet know (August, Staehr Fenner, & Bright, 2014).

What Does the Research Say About Background Knowledge?

Now that you've had the opportunity to see how your own background knowledge plays out in solving an algebra problem, let's take a look at some of the relevant research on the concept of background knowledge. According to Marzano (2004), "What students *already know* about the content is one of the strongest indicators of how well they will learn new information relative to the content" (p. 1). In addition, Guthrie (2008) states that reading comprehension is impossible without prior knowledge. Further, the National Academy of Sciences (2000) shares, "All learning involves transfer from previous experiences. Even initial learning involves transfer that is based on previous experiences and prior knowledge. . . . Effective teachers attempt to support positive transfer by actively identifying the strengths that students bring to a learning situation and building on them" (p. 236).[3]

It is generally true that what we know and are already familiar with can influence new learning and the comprehension of what we read (McNamara & Kintsch, 1996; Tobias, 1994). Background knowledge does not have to be knowledge gained from a text. It can also be built through a piece of art, a diagram, a cartoon, a picture, or a video. Further, peer discussion and interaction that foster intellectual engagement with a topic also support building the wide array of background knowledge that students need for success from one content class and text to the next (Fisher, Frey, & Lapp, 2012).

Students, in general, bring great diversity in terms of their background knowledge and experiences (Fisher et al., 2012). Specifically, for ELs who come from such diverse backgrounds, it is critical to provide targeted support in linking background knowledge that they have and addressing gaps in their background knowledge that may exist for them to acquire new content. Taking a few minutes to "jump-start" students' schema, finding out what they know or have experienced about a topic, and linking their knowledge directly to a lesson's objective will result in greater understanding for ELs (Echevarria, Vogt, & Short, 2004). Research supports that the relationship between students' background knowledge and comprehension increases

---

3. See http://www.ascd.org/publications/books/113005/chapters/Background-Knowledge@-The-Glue-That-Makes-Learning-Stick.aspx.

with age (Evans, Floyd, McGrew, & Leforgee, 2002). Also vocabulary and background knowledge have the potential to be two of the more powerful means of improving learning and comprehension, particularly for adolescent readers (Cromley & Azevedo, 2007). For these reasons, it is critical to learn what background knowledge ELs already have and also to find the gaps in ELs' background knowledge to provide explicit instruction or explanation in order to facilitate learning new content.

What Is the Close Reading of Texts?

To understand our new framework for selecting and teaching background knowledge to ELs, we must first take a quick look at the concept of close reading.[4] While the framework can be applied to any type of topic or content instruction, it is particularly applicable within a close-reading approach. Shanahan (2013) explains that *close reading* is a concept that indicates where meaning resides (in the text) and what readers must do to gain access to this meaning (read the text closely, weighing the author's words and ideas and relying heavily on the evidence in the text). He sees close reading as a way to place emphasis on readers figuring out a high-quality text and grappling with it. Fisher and Frey (2015) note that many interrelated practices combine to create a close-reading experience for students.

Close reading plays out in the classroom by shifting instruction off of strategies and skills and onto the texts themselves and ideas presented in texts. Instead of having students focus on their own personal connection to a text (e.g., How did the story remind you of a similar time from your childhood?), instruction focuses students' attention on reading, interpreting, and evaluating text. So close reading becomes an intensive analysis of a text in order to comprehend what it says, how it says it, and what it means. By engaging in close reading throughout their education, Shanahan says students are poised to develop a rich body of knowledge about the world, and their reading practices will become ingrained *habits of mind*.

What Is the Role of Background Knowledge in ELs' Close Reading of Texts?

Although there are multiple challenges for ELs at all levels of English proficiency in effectively partaking in the close reading of complex texts (e.g., academic language needed and unlocking the meaning of complex

---

4. We will examine close reading more fully in the next chapter.

texts), we focus, in this chapter, on the role of background knowledge. There has been some debate about whether to preteach elements of a text at all before students read it using a close-reading framework, with some saying students should not be given any background knowledge at all (Staehr Fenner, 2013a). For ELs, however, there are many more considerations to take into account than with native English speakers. The role of background knowledge cannot be ignored, and we truly believe it's an issue of equity for ELs. As a component of ELs taking part in a close reading of text, all teachers of ELs across content areas need to find out how much background their students have about a text's given topic and activate and/or build background where necessary. In a way, it's about finding out what the "sweet spot" is in terms of background knowledge, and we will provide you some guidance so you can determine what that practice may look like for your unique group of ELs.

Shanahan (2013) contends that readers use what they know to interpret text, which supports teaching background knowledge where necessary.[5] However, even though students use what they know when they read, he tempers his position on background knowledge by stating that any prereading activities should "give students as little preparation as required to engage with the text." In other words, providing students with background knowledge can't take the place of them making meaning from the text itself. This is especially true if the teacher is going to work with a text over time to help students understand it deeply. This area has gotten more "buzz" in the context of close reading, as some educators have incorrectly interpreted this to mean that teachers may not provide any background knowledge at all.

One of the many hats we wear as educators of ELs is to position our students so they can achieve academic success. While more attention is now being paid to the question of EL rigor and finding the right balance between scaffolding and independent learning, state content standards now call for teachers to be more cognizant of how we approach building background knowledge as part of close reading. So while building ELs' background knowledge definitely has its place in content standards, it is just one piece of the close-reading puzzle. After we build ELs' background knowledge, as necessary, we must then focus the majority of our instruction on having students working with the text itself so that they can unlock its meaning.[6]

> *How has your understanding of the teaching of background knowledge changed from the beginning of the chapter?*

---

5. See https://edexcellence.net/commentary/education-gadfly-daily/common-core-watch/how-bad-are-the-common-core-lessons-on-the.

6. Please see Chapter 8 for a more in-depth emphasis on helping ELs comprehend complex text.

How Do I Match ELs to Texts?

This focus on background knowledge is situated within a larger discussion about text complexity and challenge for ELs. Until recently, English language arts content standards usually ignored the fact that some texts are harder to read than others (Shanahan, 2013). Teachers, for the most part, had been taught to give students books at their instructional level, or a word accuracy rate of between 90 and 94 percent. However, Shanahan (2016)[7] says there is, in actuality, not a firm base of research to support matching students to texts at their instructional level (e.g., Jorgenson, Klein, & Kumar, 1977; Kuhn et al., 2006; Morgan, Wilcox, & Eldredge, 2000; O'Connor, Swanson, & Geraghty, 2010; Powell & Dunkeld, 1971; Stahl & Heubach, 2005; Stanley, 1986).

In addition, new, more challenging content standards constitute a reversal of the practice of giving students books at their instructional level, since content standards call for all students to read texts at their grade level. As teachers of ELs, we know this practice of having ELs read grade-level texts is challenging for ELs in general and very questionable specifically for ELs with lower levels of proficiency. By their nature of being classified as ELs, these students will not be reading on grade level. While the student and text level *do* matter, the amount a teacher can support or scaffold a text is also key, which should come as no surprise for many teachers. Depending on the context and purpose for learning, teachers can choose a variety of text levels, from frustration (less than 90 percent accuracy) to independent (95 percent word accuracy and above), for their students to use. The important point is that ELs should have access to grade-level text, which they will most likely not read at an independent level, but grade-level texts should not be the sole focus of the texts they engage with. They should also work with texts that build their ELs' confidence as readers in English, including text in their home language if they can read their home language, and that support their access to grade-level texts.

Since all students are now expected to read more challenging texts, this means other instructional supports will be needed to help and encourage ELs along this path—but without actually doing the work for them. This kind of expertise is exactly the kind of skill set many ESOL teachers bring to the classroom. However, ESOL teachers may still need support in not doing all the work for their students via providing too much background knowledge so ELs can gain more responsibility in negotiating the meaning of complex, challenging texts. The next section details a framework which will help you make this transition.

---

7. See http://www.shanahanonliteracy.com/2016/06/further-explanation-of-teaching_16.html.

What Is a Framework I Can Use for Building ELs' Background Knowledge?

Through our review of the research, as well as work with ELs and their teachers, we have developed a framework for building ELs' background knowledge when working with complex texts or topics. The framework consists of four sequential steps, each of which we outline in more detail in this chapter. The framework takes place within a context of collaboration among teachers. It is important to remember that not all background knowledge is created equal in terms of relevance when it comes to lesson planning and instruction, and this framework will provide a tool to you to determine what is most relevant for ELs and worth your precious time. Figure 7.1 provides a visual representation of the framework.

Step 1: How Do I Find out My ELs' Prior Knowledge on a Particular Topic or Text?

In order to maximize your instructional time on new content, assessing your ELs' background knowledge to gauge your students' level of familiarity on a certain topic can provide valuable insight for lesson planning. You will need to figure out how much ELs already know about a topic or text prior to your teaching it so you can determine whether to activate prior knowledge, build new background, or do a combination of both. This kind of informal

FIGURE 7.1 Framework for Building ELs' Background Knowledge

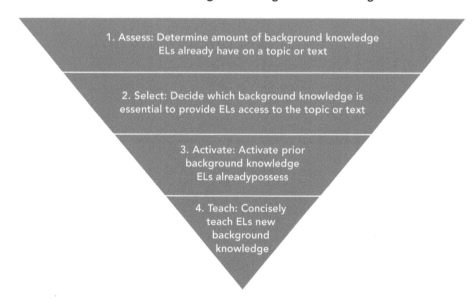

1. Assess: Determine amount of background knowledge ELs already have on a topic or text

2. Select: Decide which background knowledge is essential to provide ELs access to the topic or text

3. Activate: Activate prior background knowledge ELs alreadypossess

4. Teach: Concisely teach ELs new background knowledge

assessment can be done through many means that do not require much time and can be seamlessly woven into instruction. In addition, you should concentrate this informal assessment on background you already feel may be essential for ELs to fully engage with the topic and/or comprehend the text you're planning on basing your instruction on. For example, teachers can engage ELs in oral discussions, anticipation guides, checklists, and self-ratings to inform them of ELs' background knowledge and adjust instruction accordingly. In addition, Fisher et al. (2012) suggest cloze assessments, word sorts, opinionnaires, and caption writing to find out what students already know on a given topic. Let's look at one type of informal assessment in a little more depth.

Opinionnaires are a series of statements students can complete that demonstrate students' background knowledge on a particular topic. Teachers can use them before instruction on a topic and then again after instruction to see what students knew prior to instruction and what they learned. Figure 7.2 provides a sample opinionnaire that teachers could use to determine the level of students' background knowledge on a health lesson on nutrition before reading a text on health or discussing the topic. Students would answer the opinionnaire individually, then discuss their answers in pairs, and finally discuss with the entire class. This exercise, which can be used with all students, would allow teachers to see how much background individual ELs have on the topic without singling them out. To ensure ELs of varying proficiency levels can respond to the opinionnaire, you will need to write statements in a way so that they will be linguistically accessible to ELs. In addition, you may need to add scaffolds, such as glossaries in English or the home language, so that ELs can fully engage with opinionnaires.

FIGURE 7.2 Health Lesson Opinionnaire Example

Before Reading	Statement	After Reading
Yes No	1. I am active, so the kinds of food I eat do not matter.	Yes No
Yes No	2. Taste is more important than nutrition.	Yes No
Yes No	3. The government should limit the size of junk food and soda containers.	Yes No
Yes No	4. It's reasonable to exercise for thirty minutes a day.	Yes No

Step 2: How Do I Decide How Much Background Knowledge to Provide to ELs?

When trying to decide how much background knowledge to teach ELs, it's important to first figure out how critical the background knowledge is to ELs' understanding of the topic or text. This is the area that is the biggest departure from traditional thinking on ELs' background knowledge and can be the most challenging for teachers to change their practice. Fisher et al. (2012) note that *core background knowledge* is what students need to understand the new information to be learned. They contrast core knowledge with *incidental knowledge*, which is knowledge that is merely interesting and not likely to be used or recalled in the future. We refer to the background knowledge that is needed as *essential*. When you're considering preteaching some background about a text your ELs will be working with or a topic they will be discussing, use the following table and flowchart to help you decide whether knowledge fits into the essential category. Figure 7.3 provides considerations for determining which background knowledge to teach. Some of the considerations are applicable to ELs as well as non-ELs, and we point this information out in the final column of the table.

Since it's often helpful for us to see concepts presented visually, we have developed a flowchart to help you determine which background knowledge to teach ELs. While Figure 7.4 presents the four considerations from Figure 7.3 in a flowchart, you can adapt the flowchart to meet your needs.

These tools build upon Diane August's Common Core work in New York State.

FIGURE 7.3 Determining Which Background Knowledge to Teach ELs

Background Consideration	Comments	Applicable to ELs or ELs and non-ELs
1. Do non-ELs have background knowledge on the topic?	Teachers must ensure that ELs approach the text with comparable levels of background knowledge that non-ELs already have. If non-ELs already approach the text with certain background knowledge, teachers should make sure ELs have the same information as a matter of equity.	ELs
2. Does the background provide information in place of what the author is going to provide in the text?	The background information provided can't give away the text. (No spoilers!) Students must gather information from the text itself instead of learning it from background knowledge the teacher provides. ELs will still need support and scaffolding to gather information from the text itself.	ELs and non-ELs
3. Is the background knowledge about big issues that will help ELs make sense of the text?	Teachers must focus instruction only on the background knowledge that is critical to ELs comprehending the text. ELs don't need to know everything possible related to the topic. For example, when studying the Gettysburg Address, ELs don't need to be pretaught a full biography of Abraham Lincoln's life but will need to know enough about the big issue of the Civil War that will help them unlock the meaning of the text.	ELs and non-ELs
4. Is the background knowledge you'd like to provide to ELs concise?	The more concise the background information is, the better (e.g., you may wish to reconsider taking an entire class period to build ELs' background knowledge). For example, you could provide some background knowledge via homework that students complete prior to class time and briefly discuss the background the next day of class.	ELs

Source: Adapted from Staehr Fenner (2013b) (Colorincolorado.org/blog).

FIGURE 7.4 Flowchart for Determining Which Background Knowledge to Teach ELs

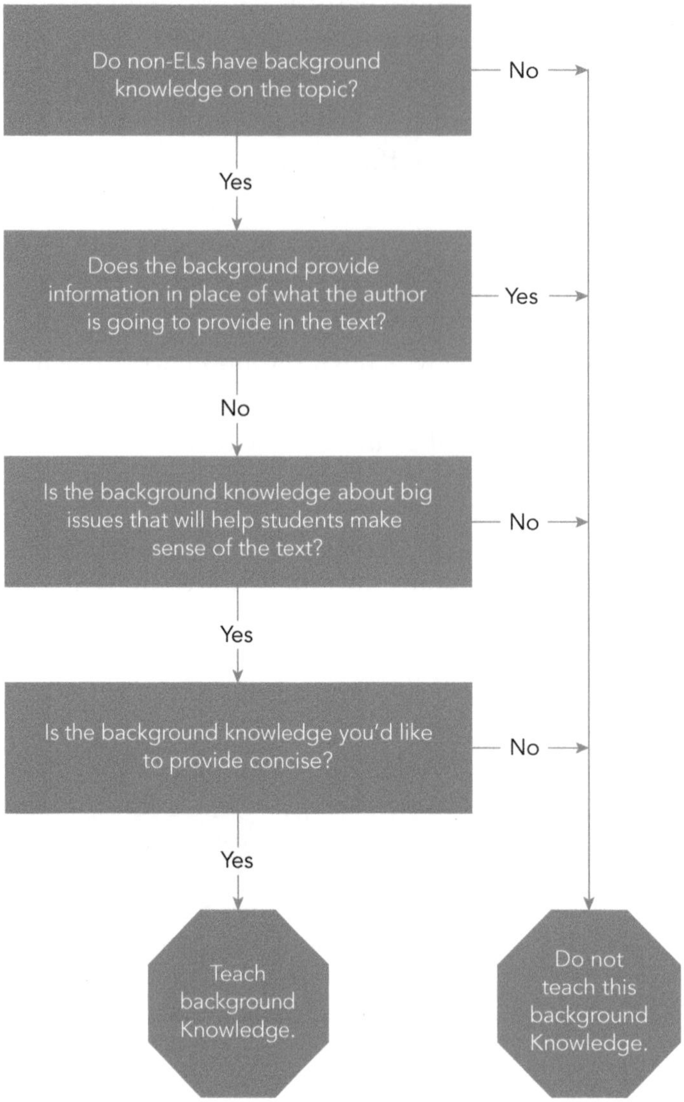

Source: *Adapted from Staehr Fenner (2013b) (Colorincolorado.org/blog).*

Step 3: How Do I Activate ELs' Background Knowledge That They Already Possess?

After taking part in Step 2, you may have a few areas of background knowledge you'd like to teach. However, some ELs may actually already have some related background knowledge you can tap into instead of teach outright. Shanahan (2013) outlines two essential areas of background knowledge that teachers can effectively utilize with students. One area is providing background knowledge where none previously exists. Readers need to integrate prior knowledge—when it exists—with text information

FIGURE 7.5 Differences Between Providing Background Knowledge and Activating Existing Prior Knowledge

Type of Background Knowledge	Definition	Examples
Providing background knowledge	Giving students background knowledge that they do not already have on a particular topic or text	• Showing students a visual of Inuit art prior to them engaging in a lesson on the topic • Showing students a video clip on Betsy Ross
Activating background knowledge	Finding out and leveraging pre-existing knowledge on a topic or text	• Having students discuss what they think the title of a text titled "Hurricane Katrina" means in pairs • Having students write a paragraph in their journals about what they previously learned about the Revolutionary War

in order to form a mental representation or memory. A second area is activating existing prior knowledge. Existing prior knowledge is also a form of background knowledge, and teachers can efficiently draw upon what students already know. For example, teachers can use the title of a text as a springboard to help the students make a connection between the title and their existing knowledge of a topic without giving away the text. Figure 7.5 provides further explanation and examples of the differences between providing background knowledge and activating existing prior knowledge.

Three ways to activate ELs', as well as non-ELs', prior knowledge are through carousel brainstorming, sentence starters, and categorized sticky notes.[8] There are many other ways as well.

> *What ways do you activate your ELs' background knowledge?*

- **Carousel brainstorming:** On chart paper around the room, have small groups of students respond to a question or statement posed at the top of the paper. These questions or statements should be written at a linguistic level that ELs can use to access their meaning and should represent components of students' upcoming texts. After a short period of time, student groups move on to another piece of chart paper, read what has been written about that topic, and add to or respond to it. You can use these charts and responses as lesson activators because they represent the prior knowledge and current understandings of the group.

- **Sentence starters:** Provide for students a sentence starter or prompt that requires them to complete a sentence or phrase on the topic or text you will be working on. Take this for example: One thing I already

---

8. Strategies selected and adapted from http://www.gcasd.org/Downloads/Activating_Strategies.pdf.

know about _____ is _____. You could post these starters around the room and have students view and discuss each other's sentence starters.

- **Categorized sticky notes:** Give students sticky notes and a question or topic related to the upcoming lesson. For example, when beginning a unit on bees, you can ask students, "What is one thing bees do?" Students respond to the question or topic on their sticky notes and then post their notes on the board, door, wall, or a chart. The space they post their notes to can be divided into positives and negatives, for example, so students will have to categorize their responses. (For example, the sticky note with "Bees give us honey" written on it would go in the "positive" section while the sticky note with "Bees sting" would go in the "negative" section). Students will return to those responses at the end of the lesson to confirm, revise, or add to their thinking and may need to move their sticky notes.

Step 4: What Are Some Strategies for Concisely Teaching ELs Background Knowledge?

After you have determined which background knowledge ELs already have on a topic or text (Step 1), decided which background knowledge is essential (Step 2), and activated ELs' prior background knowledge (Step 3), it is now time to focus on concisely teaching any new background knowledge that is necessary for ELs (Step 4). There are several strategies for teaching background knowledge (August, Staehr Fenner, & Snyder, 2014), which include the following:

1. Short, teacher-developed text, with guiding and supplementary questions
2. Web link (in English or home language)
3. Brief video clips or visuals
4. Text-based instruction
5. Home language support (e.g., text, Web link, or video)

Background knowledge instruction can be pretaught, or it can be embedded into instruction. How much background knowledge you teach depends on the amount of instruction that is needed, students' English language proficiency levels, and your lesson objectives. It's important to consider how to make the most out of limited instructional time and how to teach background knowledge concisely. Some ways to teach background knowledge to ELs that do not interrupt class time are for ESOL teachers to teach it during a stand-alone ESOL class or to assign it for homework prior to all students working with the content in the content teacher's classroom. This approach will require collaboration between content and ESOL teachers. Another option that we've seen work well with ELs is to hold a "lunch bunch" meeting for ELs in which they bring their lunches to the ESOL and/or content teacher, socialize a bit, and also work on a background knowledge lesson. This provides a setting in which ELs can feel safe to ask questions about the background, as well as take risks with the language.

What Are Some Examples of Teaching Background Knowledge?

In what follows, we present two different examples of how teachers of ELs can concisely teach background knowledge that will help ELs access the content of challenging, grade-level texts and topics. The first example is at the first-grade text level, and the second example is at the ninth-grade text level.

Grade 1 Text Example

The background knowledge we teach is related to the subsequent sample text that is meant to be read aloud to students.

A Father and His Son in Mesopotamia

Almost four thousand years ago, a father and a son were walking together on the banks of a great river, close to what was then possibly the biggest city in the world: Babylon. The father, whose name was Warad, said to his son Iddin, "See, my son, the great Euphrates River. If this river did not flow, there would be no wonderful city of Babylon, no palaces, no gardens, not even any houses . . . They dug ditches cut into the earth, which we call canals. The water flowed out of the river and through the canals to the areas of the city farther from the river. Then farmers could grow crops even where the rivers didn't flow." "Our great king, Hammurabi, did the same thing. He had canals dug to move water all over our country from the two great rivers, the Tigris and the Euphrates. And King Hammurabi and his helpers used an ancient way to collect rainwater. When the winter rains come, the water doesn't just wash away downstream. They made the waters run into a reservoir so that after the rains stopped, there would be water for drinking or for watering crops."

Source: Core Knowledge Foundation. (2013). Early World Civilizations: Tell It Again!™ Read-Aloud Anthology: Listening & Learning™ Strand: Grade 1: Core Knowledge Language Arts® New York Edition (p. 16). Charlottesville, VA: Author.

FIGURE 7.6 Background Knowledge Considerations and Comments on the Word *Ancient*

Background Knowledge Considerations	Comments
1. Do non-ELs have background knowledge on the topic?	Yes, non-ELs know what the word *ancient* means.
2. Does the background provide information in place of what the author is going to provide in the text?	No, it does not.
3. Is the background knowledge about big issues that will help students make sense of the text?	Yes, knowing what *ancient* means will help students make sense of the text.
4. Is the background knowledge you'd like to provide concise?	Yes, we will provide this background knowledge concisely by showing two visuals and having ELs discuss them.

Figure 7.6 shows how, in deciding which background knowledge to teach to ELs, we considered teaching the meaning of the word *ancient*. All students would be explained the similarities and differences between people today and people in ancient Mesopotamia.

Figure 7.7 shows how we concisely taught two meanings of the word ancient to ELs in an engaging way. We use two images, partner talk, and questions that are accessible to ELs as scaffolds for this activity.

FIGURE 7.7 Teaching Background Knowledge of the Word *Ancient*

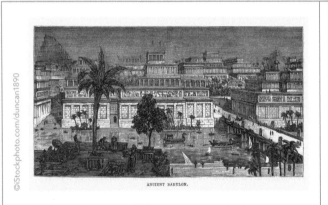 

Instructions for Teachers

- Show students the first picture.
- The picture shows a village, or town, in Mesopotamia from a long time ago.
- Partner Talk: How can you tell this village is from a very long time ago?
- Show students the second picture.
- Tell students that the word *ancient* can also mean very, very old. This picture shows a very old tree.

Partner Talk: How can you tell this tree is very old?

Source: Adapted from August, D., Staehr Fenner, D., & Snyder, S. (2014). Scaffolding instruction for English language learners: A resource guide for ELA (p. 25). Reprinted with permission of American Institutes for Research. Retrieved from https://www.engageny.org/resource/scaffolding-instruction-english-language-learners-resource-guides-english-language-arts-and

Grade 9 Text Example

The first lesson in this unit is centered on an excerpt of the first chapter of the book *Animals in Translation* (Grandin, 2005). Here is the text excerpt:

> *People who aren't autistic always ask me about the moment I realized I could understand the way animals think. They think I must have had an epiphany. But it wasn't like that. It took me a long time to figure out that I see things about animals other people don't. And it wasn't until I was in my forties that I finally realized I had one big advantage over the feedlot owners who were hiring me to manage their animals: being autistic. Autism made school and life hard, but it made animals easy. (Grandin, 2005, p. 1)*

The book draws from the author's own experiences with autism, which provides her insight into how animals think, act, and feel. However, the concept of autism will be unknown to some ELs. Some might not know the meaning of the word *autism* in English but may know it in their home language. Also, in some cultures, disabilities may not be acknowledged due to possible stigma, and the concept of autism will not exist in the home language. Thus, we worked through these considerations when deciding whether to teach background knowledge on autism. Figure 7.8 outlines our thinking using Step 2 of the framework.

FIGURE 7.8 Background Knowledge Considerations and Comments on Teaching Autism as Background to *Animals in Translation*

Background Knowledge Considerations	Comments
1. Do non-ELs have background knowledge on the topic?	Yes, we believe most non-ELs would know what autism is.
2. Does the background provide information in place of what the author is going to provide in the text?	No, knowing what autism is will not provide information in place of what the author will provide in the text.
3. Is the background knowledge about big issues that will help students make sense of the text?	Yes, knowing what autism is in general will be critical to ELs comprehending the text.
4. Is the background knowledge you'd like to provide concise?	Yes, we will present this information concisely in one paragraph with some guiding questions.

Based on our responses to these four questions, we recognize that ELs are more likely to be able to successfully engage with the first chapter of *Animals in Translation* if they are provided background knowledge about the concept of autism in a concise manner. Accordingly, we would develop a short text (seven or eight sentences) on autism that provides basic information about the disorder and the challenges, strengths, and behaviors of individuals with autism. We would also develop a glossary to support ELs in understanding key words of the autism text we would develop that may be unfamiliar to them. We would also create a few supporting questions to check for students' understanding. Depending on the levels of the ELs, we would use sentence stems and/or sentence frames and a work bank to scaffold the questions.

How Can I Apply the Four-Step Framework When Teaching Background Knowledge to ELs?

To better illustrate how to apply the four-step framework from start to finish, let's take a look at a sample social studies text. Erinn Banting's (2004) *England: The Land* is suggested to be at a Grade 4–5 reading level. Take a look at an excerpt from this informational text, and think about what kinds of background knowledge your ELs would need to fully access the meaning:

England: The Land Text Excerpt

Low fences, some of which are thousands of years old, divide much of England's countryside. These fences, called hedgerows, were fist built by the Anglo-Saxons, a group of warriors from Germany and Scandinavia who arrived in England around 410 A.D.

As they gained control of sections of land, they protected their property with walls made from wooden stakes and spiny plants. Dead hedgerows, as these fences were called, were eventually replaced by fences made from live bushes and trees.

Recently, people building large farms and homes in the countryside have destroyed many live hedgerows. Other people are working to save the hedgerows, which are home to a variety of wildlife, including birds, butterflies, hedgehogs, and hares.

Step 1: Determine the amount of background knowledge ELs already have.

If we were using Banting's text to teach fourth-grade ELs at varying levels of English proficiency, we might want to first find out their knowledge of the following:

- The history of the Anglo-Saxons
- What was happening during the time period described in the text (410 A.D.)
- Their knowledge of low fences or hedgerows
- The importance of protecting one's property in the time period described and today

- How large farms and homes in the English countryside look today
- The wildlife mentioned in the text

Previously, teachers might have developed lessons on all of the aforementioned topics in order to fully prepare ELs to read this text. However, as teachers preparing ELs to read this text, we would not spend the majority of our instruction on building our ELs' background knowledge, like we might have done before the adoption of challenging content standards. However, we would recognize that our ELs would likely have very little background knowledge on the many topics contained in this text, let alone be familiar with all of the terms and academic-language structures used in the text. But we would need to whittle down the topics somewhat and determine how much background knowledge they have on the topic of low fences.

One way we could determine ELs' existing knowledge on the topic would be to have all students do some caption writing individually and then assess how much background knowledge ELs have on three topics pertaining to low fences. We would determine these three topics in collaboration with the content and ESOL teacher. We could give students a visual of the English countryside from Anglo-Saxon times, a visual of English countryside today, and a visual of low fences and have them write a caption for each visual, first modeling our expectations for what a caption should look like. We would collaborate with content teachers on supporting ELs to engage with this task and could provide ELs scaffolds, such as sentence starters and word walls, to complete the captions. The image of a low fence visual is below:

Low Fence Visual

After determining what ELs already know about the topic through caption writing, we learned that they could all describe an image of the English countryside of today. They could not describe a visual of the English countryside during Anglo-Saxon times well and could only provide basic information on the low fence visual. Caption writing allowed us to note how their background knowledge might differ from a personal connection to a text. For example, one student had some knowledge about what the English countryside looks like today from a documentary she had seen about England. On the other hand, another student's personal connection to this image might be in the form of an event in the student's life that took place in the countryside. Where background knowledge will most likely support the student's understanding of the text, the student's personal connection might not accomplish the same goal (Staehr Fenner, 2013a).

Step 2: Decide what background knowledge is needed.

We met with the content teacher and determined that ELs might need more instruction on what low fences are. We then walked through the considerations that follow to determine whether we should teach background knowledge on low fences or not. Figure 7.9 outlines our decision-making process.

FIGURE 7.9   Background Considerations for Low Fences

Background Consideration	Comments
1. Do non-ELs have background knowledge on the topic?	Through Step 1, we determined that ELs do not have background knowledge on what low fences or hedgerows are.
2. Does the background provide information in place of what the author is going to provide in the text?	No, knowing what low fences or hedgerows are will not provide information in place of what students will read in the text.
3. Is the background knowledge about big issues that will help ELs make sense of the text?	Yes, knowing what low fences or hedgerows are will help students make sense of the text.
4. Is the background knowledge you'd like to provide ELs concise?	Yes, we can provide this background precisely through a guided group work discussion about the same visual we used in Step 1, caption writing.

Step 3: Activate the prior background knowledge ELs already possess.

Through taking part in the caption-writing process in Step 1, we learned that most ELs could write some key words about the English countryside. Some ELs wrote the word *fence* under the image of the low fence or hedgerow, and some wrote fence in their home language. That information told us that many

ELs knew what a fence was at a surface level of knowledge, and we decided to activate that specific prior knowledge about fences. We then decided to activate ELs' knowledge about fences by doing a carousel brainstorm. To do so, we created three poster papers with the following statements for our ELs to respond to, answering true, false, and then stating why.

- Fences are used to join two pieces of land together.
  - True or False
  - I think this statement is _____ because
  _____.

- Fences can be made of wood.
  - True or False
  - I think this statement is _____ because
  _____.

- Fences can be made of plants.
  - True or False
  - I think this statement is _____ because
  _____.

Students worked in pairs to provide answers to each poster paper, rotating through the papers. Then, we had students come together as a large group to their answers. This gave us the opportunity to listen to students as they discussed their previous knowledge on fences and also to introduce some new vocabulary to them to discuss fences (e.g., fence, join, and land). Bringing them together in the large group also provided an opportunity to respond to any misconceptions they might have about fences—for example, that they cannot be made of wood or plants.

Step 4: Concisely teach new background knowledge.

Next, after completing Steps 1 through 3, it was time to concisely teach some new background knowledge to prepare students to read an excerpt from *England: The Land*. We looked back at what we decided to do as a team in Step 2 and referred to the same visual we used for Step 1, caption writing. This time, we used the visual as a basis for a guided discussion around what low fences or hedgerows are. The entire discussion took fifteen minutes of time and was centered on the following questions, which students discussed in small groups while viewing the image:

1. What is the purpose of the *low fence* (or *hedgerow*) in the photo?

   The low fence or hedgerow in the photo is used to

   _____.

2. What is the low fence or hedgerow in the photo made of?

The low fence or hedgerow in the photo is made of

_____.

After the students discussed the answers to the questions, we brought them together as a large group to talk about what low fences or hedgerows are and what they are used for. We also elicited their responses to what low fences are made of. This conversation "primed the pump" for them to read and comprehend an excerpt from the text *England: The Land* without spoiling the meaning of the text.

Figure 7.10 captures how we used the four-step process to plan our instruction of background knowledge for ELs with this lesson.

FIGURE 7.10   Background-Planning Framework for Low-Fences Lesson

Step	Outcome	Next Step
1. Determine the amount of background knowledge ELs already have on a topic or text.	Through caption writing, we determined that ELs were already familiar with what fences are.	We wanted to determine what essential background knowledge we needed to provide to them.
2. Decide which essential background knowledge is needed to provide ELs access to the topic or text.	We decided that ELs needed to know about low fences or hedgerows in order to take part in this lesson.	We needed a quick way to teach this to them, so we decided we would use a visual and guided discussion.
3. Activate the prior background knowledge that ELs already possess.	Through the caption writing, we learned that our ELs already knew a little about fences, but we wanted to dig deeper and activate more detailed prior knowledge.	We activated that prior knowledge through carousel brainstorming about fences.
4. Teach the new background knowledge.	Our ELs needed new background knowledge on low fences or hedgerows.	We decided to show them a picture of a low fence and have a discussion about it using guiding questions.

How Do I Build or Activate ELs' Background Knowledge in Mathematics?

Now that we have focused on teaching ELs background knowledge in general, we'd like to narrow our focus for special considerations of ELs' background knowledge in mathematics. Many ELs will have developed mathematical concepts in their home language and/or in prior schooling. However, because ELs are unlikely to possess a level of background knowledge on par with fluent English speakers, they will need additional support to comprehend the stimulus or prompt texts used in many mathematics lessons (August, Staehr Fenner, & Bright, 2014). Not only might ELs be unfamiliar with vocabulary words but also they may be unfamiliar with linguistic constructs and the so-called "real-life" contexts used in mathematics problems, which may very well not relate to the ELs' lived experiences. As with our previous examples in English language arts and social studies, there may be times when ELs will need a succinct and purposeful explanation of a scenario, illustration, or other information that is not part of the mathematical content related to the lesson.

To support ELs in accessing the concise background information necessary to understand mathematical contexts, it can be useful to show them images and short video clips. Also, keep in mind that students may think they recognize a context but may not fully understand it. For example, when working with a problem about a state fair, students may say they know what it means, "Like when things are equal, they are fair, so it's one of the United States where things are fair" (August, Staehr Fenner, & Bright, 2014). It's important to clear up these misconceptions ELs may have while not singling them out or embarrassing them in front of their peers. Since most teachers of ELs have been educated in the United States, they may have limited familiarity with educational systems or how different mathematics content is taught in systems outside the United States. For example, although mathematics education has many similar characteristics around the world, there are, at times, significant differences in the ways and order in which mathematics content is presented (August, Staehr Fenner, & Bright, 2014).

How Do I Construct Less Biased Mathematics Problems for ELs?

The first step in providing background knowledge to ELs in mathematics is constructing or adapting problems so that they are less linguistically or contextually biased for ELs but maintain the same level of mathematical rigor. Less biased problems mean less of a need to spend time providing background knowledge. To help you get a sense of what less biased problems look like, take a look at Application Activity 7.2. For the answers, turn to page 200.

Analyzing Test Questions

Determine which three of the following six questions are less linguistically and/or culturally complex for ELs:

1a. How many minutes are equivalent to 5 hours?

OR

1b. Alex worked for 5 hours raking leaves in the fall. How many minutes are equivalent to 5 hours?

2a. A parking garage has 3 levels. Each level has 40 parking spaces for compact cars. What is the total number of parking spaces in the garage for compact cars?

OR

2b. A school has 3 floors. Each floor has 40 rooms. What is the total number of rooms in the school?

3a. A set of football jerseys contains only odd-numbered jerseys. Which could be 3 of the jersey numbers from this set of uniforms?

OR

3b. A set contains only odd numbers. What are 3 numbers that can be in this set?

> What did you notice about the ways the problems were more or less linguistically or contextually biased?

Figure 7.11 details tips, explanations, and examples to build ELs' mathematics background knowledge.

FIGURE 7.11 Mathematics EL Background Knowledge Tips and Explanations

Mathematics EL Background Knowledge Tip	Explanation	Examples
Build knowledge from real-world examples.	Revise unfamiliar situations in word problem scenarios to make them more familiar. Try to reinforce concepts with examples that students can picture, and talk students through the situation.	Look for familiar ideas or props that can be used to engage students, such as recipes of familiar foods or school current events.

Mathematics EL Background Knowledge Tip	Explanation	Examples
Modify the linguistic complexity of language, and rephrase math problems.	Students will understand the problem better if it is stated in shorter sentences and in language they understand.	See examples in Application Activity 7.2.
Guide students to cross out the unnecessary vocabulary in word problems and circle the necessary vocabulary.	Crossing out unnecessary words and circling necessary vocabulary allow students to focus on the math function required instead of getting bogged down with unnecessary language.	One problem refers to a *school assembly*. Even though the meaning of that term isn't important in solving the math problem, students don't know that term isn't important, and the lack of understanding may contribute to their confusion.
Use manipulatives purposefully.	Manipulatives can be very useful in having students represent the numbers in the problems and manipulating them to get the answer.	A teacher uses cubes and the terms *hot numbers* and *cold numbers* when teaching with the concept of negative numbers. Students use the red cubes as hot, or positive, numbers and the blue cubes as cold, or negative, numbers. As students lay out the number of hot cubes and cold cubes represented, they can easily see if the answer would be a positive or negative number by which color had the most cubes.

Source: *Adapted from Robertson (http://www.colorincolorado.org/article/math-instruction-english-language-learners) and the Virginia Department of Education (http://www.doe.virginia.gov/testing/sol/standards_docs/mathematics/plain_english_information.pdf).*

What Is the Role of Collaboration in Teaching Background Knowledge?

Our teachers Ms. Moussa and Mr. Lopez, whom we introduced at the beginning of this chapter, had already decided they would coteach background knowledge to Viktor and his other EL classmates. However, there are different options that you might wish to explore to utilize your precious instructional and planning time, as well as your colleagues' time, when selecting and teaching background knowledge to ELs. Which option you use depends on the type of ESOL program that is in place at your school, the grade level(s) you teach, your students' level of proficiency, and the content you're working on. Figure 7.12 describes different background teaching options for program models and suggests roles the content teacher and ESOL teacher can take in selecting and teaching background knowledge to ELs.

FIGURE 7.12 Program Models and Teachers' Possible Roles in Teaching Background Knowledge

Program Model	Content Teacher's Role	ESOL Teacher's Role
Cotaught (inclusive) elementary or secondary class	Determine which background knowledge non-ELs already have, share essential learning from the text, lesson, or unit; coteach background knowledge	Determine which background knowledge ELs need and at what point in instruction; develop activities to assess it, activate it, and teach it; coteach background knowledge
Sheltered instruction or small-group elementary-level ESOL	Share relevant, grade-level content standards and classroom materials with ESOL teachers who teach ELs at that grade level; reinforce background knowledge throughout content instruction	Determine which background knowledge ELs already have and need; develop activities to activate it and teach it as part of ESOL instruction
Sheltered instruction or small-group secondary-level ESOL	Share relevant content standards and classroom materials with ESOL teachers who teach ELs enrolled in those content classes (e.g., algebra or world history); reinforce background knowledge throughout content instruction	Determine which background knowledge ELs already have and need in key content classes; develop activities to activate it and teach it as part of ESOL instruction

What Is the Role of Equity, Advocacy, and Leadership in Teaching Background Knowledge?

Activating and concisely teaching background knowledge to ELs requires a more defined skill set and targeted training for all educators who work with ELs. Engaging ELs in the close reading of texts and challenging topics often presents challenges that go beyond balancing the building of background knowledge with working with the actual text. Such challenges for educators of ELs include choosing appropriate grade-level texts, supplying ELs with supplementary texts at different reading levels and/or texts in the home language, scaffolding instruction, and creating text-dependent questions that ELs can access to help them unlock the meaning of texts. We recognize that background knowledge is just one piece of the puzzle that gives ELs a greater chance at accessing equitable instruction.

In addition to learning about ELs' level of background knowledge, teachers themselves will benefit from building their own background knowledge of their students. In particular, teachers will need to learn about their students' and students' families' cultures to have a sense of what valuable background knowledge ELs bring. In addition, teachers of ELs should learn about the ways in which mathematics, social studies, science, and language concepts are approached in students' or their families' home countries or communities to the degree possible. When teachers of ELs employ an assets-based approach that highlights what students already know and can do, teachers may shift instruction appropriately to be more inclusive of ELs. Many opportunities exist for you to leverage your leadership skills when sharing this framework with colleagues and also if conflicts arise in terms of your colleagues' approach to assessing, selecting, activating, and teaching background knowledge. Your focus on the students and support of colleagues as they reflect on their practice will be key in treating background knowledge in a different way.

Conclusion

This chapter focused on the need to rethink the way we frame the selection and instruction of background knowledge for ELs within the context of time constraints and challenging texts and topics. The chapter recognizes the shift in the emphasis and role of background knowledge in teaching ELs, especially within a close-reading context. We provide a four-step framework to assess background knowledge, select essential background knowledge, activate ELs' existing background knowledge, and teach background knowledge concisely through modeling and examples. We also highlight the specific issues of teaching background knowledge in mathematics and considerations for advocacy, equity, and collaboration when teaching background knowledge to ELs. The next chapter builds on this learning around background knowledge as a vehicle to support ELs' access and understanding of lessons and texts. Chapter 8 deepens our conversation, focusing on developing scaffolded text-dependent questions to help ELs unlock the meaning of complex texts.

Reflection Questions

1. How will you change how you approach the teaching of background knowledge to ELs?

2. Who will you collaborate with in teaching background knowledge, and how will you collaborate?

Application Activity Responses

Solution to Mathematics Problem in Application Activity 7.1

Here's one way to solve the problem:

x = number of wickets before final match

(x wickets)(12.4 runs/wicket) = 12.4x runs

After taking another 5 wickets for 26 runs, his average is $12.4 - 0.4 = 12$ runs/wicket

Total runs = 12.4x + 26

Total wickets = x + 5

$(12.4x + 26)/(x + 5) = 12$

$x = 85$

85 wickets taken before final match

Application Activity 7.2

Answers: 1a, 2b, and 3b are less linguistically complex for ELs.

References

August, D., Staehr Fenner, D., & Bright, A. (2014). *Scaffolding instruction for English language learners: A resource guide for mathematics*. Washington, DC: American Institutes for Research. Retrieved from https://www.engageny.org/resource/ scaffolding-instruction-english-language-learners-resource-guides-english-language-arts-and

August, D., Staehr Fenner, D., & Snyder, S. (2014). *Scaffolding instruction for English language learners: A resource guide for English language arts*. Washington, DC: American Institutes for Research. Retrieved from https://www.engageny .org/resource/scaffolding-instruction-english-language-learners-resource-guides-english-language-arts-and

Banting, E. (2004). *England: The land*. New York, NY: Crabtree Publishing.

Cromley, J. G., & Azevedo, R. (2007). Testing and refining the direct and inferential mediation model of reading comprehension. *Journal of Educational Psychology*, *99*, 311–325.

Echevarria, J., Vogt. M., & Short. D. (2004). Making content comprehensible for English language learners: The SIOP model. Boston, MA: Pearson.

Evans, J. J., Floyd, R. G., McGrew, K. S., & Leforgee, M. H. (2002). The relations between measures of Cattell-Horn-Carroll (CHC) cognitive abilities and reading achievement during childhood and adolescence. *School Psychology Review, 31*, 246–262.

Fisher, D., & Frey, N. (2015). *Text-dependent questions: Pathways to close and critical reading.* Thousand Oaks, CA: Corwin.

Fisher, D., Frey, N., & Lapp, D. (2012, January). Building and activating students' background knowledge: It's what they already know that counts. *Middle School Journal*, 22–31.

Grandin, T. (2005). *Animals in translation: Using the mysteries of autism to decode animal behavior.* New York, NY: Scribner.

Guthrie, J. R. (2008). *Engaging adolescents in reading.* Thousand Oaks, CA: Corwin.

Jorgenson, G. W., Klein, N., & Kumar, V. K. (1977). Achievement and behavioral correlates of matched levels of student ability and materials difficulty. *Journal of Educational Research, 71*, 100–103.

Kuhn, M. R., Schwanenflugel, P. J., Morris, R. D., Morrow, L. M., Woo, D. G., Meisinger, E. B., . . . Stahl, S. A. (2006). Teaching children to become fluent and automatic readers. *Journal of Literacy Research, 38*, 357–387.

Marzano, R. J. (2004). *Building background knowledge for academic achievement: Research on what works in schools.* Alexandria, VA: ASCD.

McNamara, D., & Kintsch, W. (1996). Learning from texts: Effects of prior knowledge and text coherence. *Discourse Processes, 22*(3), 247–288.

Morgan, A., Wilcox, B. R., & Eldredge, J. L. (2000). Effect of difficulty levels on second-grade delayed readers using dyad reading. *Journal of Educational Research, 94*(2), 113–119.

National Academy of Sciences. (2000). *How people learn: Brain, mind, experience, and school* (Exp. ed.). Washington, DC: National Academy Press.

O'Connor, R. E., Swanson, L. H., & Geraghty, C. (2010). Improvement in reading rate under independent and difficult text levels: Influences on word and comprehension skills. *Journal of Educational Psychology, 102*, 1–19.

Powell, W. R., & Dunkeld, C. G. (1971). Validity of the IRI reading levels. *Elementary English, 48*, 637–642.

Shanahan, T. (2013). Letting the text take center stage: How the Common Core State Standards will transform English language arts instruction. *American Educator, 37*(3), 4–11.

Staehr Fenner, D. (2013a). Background knowledge: A key to close reading for ELLs [Web log post]. Retrieved from http://www.colorincolorado.org/blog/background-knowledge-key-close-reading-ells

Staehr Fenner, D. (2013b). Determining how much background knowledge to provide for ELLs [Web log post]. Retrieved from http://www.colorincolorado.org/blog/determining-how-much-background-knowledge-provide-ells

Stahl, S. A., & Heubach, K. M. (2005). Fluency-oriented reading instruction. *Journal of Literacy Research, 37*, 25–60.

Stanley, N. V. (1986). *A concurrent validity study of the emergent reading level* (Unpublished doctoral dissertation). University of Florida, Gainesville.

Tobias, S. (1994). Interest, prior knowledge, and learning. *Review of Educational Research, 64*, 37–54.

Supporting ELs' Reading for Multiple Purposes Through Use of Scaffolded Text-Dependent Questions

Ms. Baxter's eleventh-grade English class is beginning a unit that will include close reading of excerpts from Malcolm Gladwell's book *The Tipping Point.* To prepare for her first lesson in the unit, Ms. Baxter rereads the introduction of the book to herself for a second time. She notes parts of the text that she finds important, interesting, or confusing. She also highlights academic words that may be unfamiliar to some students in her class but could be understood using context clues from the text. She considers which pieces of the text will help students identify the themes of the book and also which ideas connect to past class discussions. Based on her notes, Ms. Baxter develops a set of text-dependent questions (TDQs) that students will use during the close reading of the introduction. Thinking about her ELs in particular, she also develops sentence frames and word banks that students can use to support their work.

Ms. Baxter recognizes that standards-based instruction requires students to read for multiple purposes (i.e., understanding key ideas and details, analyzing craft and structure, and integrating knowledge and ideas).[1] In order to be able to do this, ELs need explicit instruction on what it means to read for different purposes. They also need opportunities to engage in close reading of a text and guidance to support them while doing so (August & Shanahan, 2008). One way to provide them with this level of access to unlock multiple meanings of texts and successfully read for different purposes is to provide them with TDQs. However, teachers of ELs will need to provide another layer of support beyond the "usual" TDQs so that ELs can have the same level of access to complex text and its meanings. They will need to scaffold TDQs for ELs at different levels of proficiency. Scaffolded TDQs are one very important tool that teachers can use to support ELs as they engage with and make sense of complex texts.

In this chapter, we will highlight what it means for all students to read for multiple purposes, and we will also provide a unique look into what it means for ELs to read for multiple purposes, in particular. We provide an overlay framework of the approach to teaching ELs to read for multiple purposes that allows ELs access to unlocking the meaning of complex text. In order to do so, we also explain what text-dependent questions are in depth and how they are a tool to support reading for multiple purposes.

> *How do you support your ELs in understanding grade-level text? What is going well? What would you like to improve?*

Then, we describe how to develop and scaffold TDQs to support ELs of varying proficiency levels. In doing so, we provide examples of TDQs at different grade levels and offer opportunities for you to practice writing your own TDQs, ideally in collaboration with other teachers of ELs. We would like to note that the content of this chapter draws from the content and tools we have shared in several chapters that precede it. Teachers will note how this chapter synthesizes learning in areas such as scaffolding,

---

1. See Chapter 7 (background knowledge) for a more in-depth explanation of reading for multiple purposes within the context of close reading.

academic language, vocabulary, and background knowledge. Teachers will need to draw from all of these areas to design effective TDQs for ELs.

What Does It Mean to Read for Multiple Purposes?

Reading for multiple purposes can happen through students going through several "close reads" of a complex text. Although we have introduced the concept of close reading in the previous chapter, we would like to explore the concept a bit further and also provide an EL teaching perspective on the concept. As described by Shanahan (2012), close reading focuses on readers "figuring out high quality text" (para. 2), which requires students to carefully read and discuss a text from different perspectives. It is concept that indicates where meaning resides (in the text) and what readers must to do gain access to this meaning (read the text closely, weighing the author's words and ideas and relying heavily on the evidence in the text). Fisher and Frey (2015) note that there are several features necessary for all students to be successful in reading closely, which include reading short, complex passages; repeated reading; student annotation; having collaborative conversations about the text; and using text-dependent questions. The authors also remind us that not all texts are deserving of a close read. For example, texts read for pleasure or to find specific pieces of information or those that are accessible most likely don't warrant close reading. On the other hand, complex texts that do not "give up their meaning easily or quickly" (p. 2) tend to be deserving of a close read.

As students engage in several close reads of a text, Shanahan (2012) suggests what they should be focusing on during each close read. Similarly, Fisher and Frey (2015) frame the focused discussion of a text with each close read using a succinct question. We'd like to note that this framework is for all students, which includes ELs. While this framework may be familiar to many, we will later provide an EL "twist" on it so that teachers can support ELs during the close reading of texts across content areas by scaffolding TDQs to support their ELs' learning. Shanahan suggests that the following take place during a particular close-reading sequence of three steps:

1. **The first reading** allows the reader to determine what a text says. During this read, the focus is on understanding key ideas and details. If students are reading fiction, for example, they should be able to explain the plot. If it is a nonfiction text, students should be able to recount the main ideas and details of the text. (Fisher and Frey ask, "What does the text say?")

2. **The second reading** allows the reader to determine how a text works. During this read, the focus is on analyzing craft and structure. Students can be asked to analyze such aspects as how a text is organized, what literary devices are used, the author's word choice and the effect of those choices, and the type and quality of the evidence provided. (Fisher and Frey ask, "How does the text work?")

3. **The third reading** allows the reader to evaluate the quality and value of the text and to connect the text to other texts. The focus of this read is on integrating knowledge and ideas. During the third close read, students should determine what the text means on a deeper level. Students can focus on the author's purpose in writing the text, how the text relates to the student's life, and other things that he or she has studied. Students should also use this close read to evaluate the writing. (Fisher and Frey ask, "What does the text mean?"[2])

How Can I Specifically Scaffold My Instruction of ELs to Support Their Reading for Multiple Purposes?

Now that teachers are aware of a suggested sequence for all students' reading for multiple purposes, we offer some scaffolds to help provide ELs access to this framework (or the "EL twist" we referred to earlier in the chapter). These scaffolds recognize teachers' and students' limited time and the need to maximize that time during instruction so that ELs can acquire academic language and content simultaneously.

---

2. Fisher and Frey (2015) include a fourth question, "What does the text inspire you to do?" to extend students' learning and take action.

The scaffolds are applicable to all content areas and types of teachers. We also recommend using smaller chunks of text that are more manageable for students and that allow students to gain the full meaning of a text. In terms of how often to develop scaffolded TDQs, we recommend that teachers who tend to work with shorter texts try to incorporate them regularly into instruction. When using longer texts, we recommend using scaffolded TDQs to help ELs unlock the meaning of those texts you feel to be essential and then supplement other texts with TDQs on an as-needed basis. In order to support ELs in reading for multiple purposes, August, Staehr Fenner, and Snyder (2014) make the following recommendations:

1. Before ELs begin reading, support them in acquiring the background knowledge necessary to successfully engage with the text.[3]

2. Teachers should read the text aloud once (or as needed) in order to model fluent reading. As a teacher reads aloud, students should follow along in the text. While reading, teachers can also take an opportunity to define certain key vocabulary words and phrases in context.[4]

3. ELs read the text independently or in pairs to answer scaffolded questions about key ideas and details in the text.

4. ELs reread the text independently or in pairs to identify vocabulary and sections they did not understand. There are a variety of ways a teacher could structure this activity. For example, teachers might ask the class to work in pairs to complete bilingual glossaries of challenging vocabulary, have the class vote on and define the three to five most challenging words, or ask students to pull out one or two challenging passages and deconstruct these as a class.[5]

5. ELs read the text two or more times to answer questions that require them to analyze the craft and structure of the text and then integrate knowledge and ideas about the text as a whole.

For ease of reference, Figure 8.1 presents an overlay of a close-reading sequence with a suggested approach and supports that teachers can provide ELs so that they can access challenging texts.

---

3. For more information on how to select and concisely teach background knowledge, see Chapter 7.

4. See Chapter 6 for a focus on teaching ELs academic vocabulary.

5. See Chapter 5 for more support on "unpacking juicy sentences."

FIGURE 8.1 Close-Read Steps, Purposes, and Supports for ELs

Close-Read Step and Purpose	To Explore	Supports for ELs
1. To determine what a text says	Key ideas and details	• Support them in acquiring the background knowledge necessary to successfully engage with the text.[6] • Teachers read the text aloud once (or as needed). While reading, they define certain key vocabulary words and phrases. • ELs read the text independently or in pairs to answer scaffolded TDQs about key ideas and details in the text.
2. To determine how a text works	Craft and structure	• ELs read the text two or more times. • ELs reread the text independently or in pairs to identify vocabulary and sections they did not understand. • ELs complete glossaries (bilingual or English) of challenging vocabulary. • ELs pull out one or two challenging passages and "unpack" these as a class. • ELs answer scaffolded TDQs in pairs or groups that require them to analyze the craft and structure of the text.
3. To evaluate the quality and value of the text	Integrate knowledge and ideas	• ELs read the text two or more times. • ELs answer scaffolded questions in pairs or groups to integrate knowledge and ideas about the text.

What Are TDQs?

To accomplish a close read of complex text for ELs, as framed in Figure 8.1, teachers will need to develop TDQs and supporting scaffolds. TDQs are questions that cannot be answered without having read the text on which the questions are based (Shanahan, 2013). This idea of the crucial connection between questions and text actually comes from the field of assessment. One way to evaluate whether a TDQ is a true TDQ is by giving students test questions without the accompanying text in order to see if they can correctly answer the questions (Tuinman, 1973). If they can answer the question without needing to refer to the text, then it is not a true TDQ. However, in order to most effectively support students' understanding of a text, the TDQs also need to be purposeful and not random, trivia-type questions based on the text. Although teachers may be familiar with how to develop questions based on a specific text, they may not necessarily understand how to develop scaffolded TDQs that will specifically support their ELs in being able to better understand the many layers of challenging texts that are on grade level.[7]

---

6. For more information on how to select and concisely teach background knowledge, see Chapter 7.

7. See Chapter 7 for suggestions on providing ELs access to grade-level text and also providing supplementary texts in English and/or their home language.

What Type of Questions Should I Ask to Create TDQs for ELs?

Creating TDQs for any student is complex and requires a great deal of thought and ideally collaboration among different types of teachers. In creating TDQs, there are two overarching criteria that you should use when developing them (Shanahan, 2013):

1. **Students need to use the text to answer the question.** In order to answer the TDQ, students must refer to the text, not their own background knowledge.

2. **The question is worth asking.** Not all questions that depend on the text for their answer are important within each text. TDQs should support students in figuring out a text, not help them win a game of trivia. In addition, TDQs scaffolded for ELs should also help ELs learn academic language in support of the lesson objectives or standards.

As explained previously, well-developed TDQs require students not only to demonstrate their understanding of key ideas and details but also to speak to the craft and structure of the text and demonstrate their ability to integrate knowledge and ideas (Shanahan, 2013). Accordingly, when developing TDQs, teachers can develop three sets of questions that correspond to each of the three recommended close reads. To help determine which TDQs are trivia based and which are not, Application Activity 8.1 can give you a sense of how to begin.

APPLICATION ACTIVITY 8.1

Choosing the "Real" TDQ

Think about the story of *Rumpelstiltskin*, and decide which one of these three questions best fits the two TDQ criteria outlined beforehand.

1. What did the miller's daughter give Rumpelstiltskin the first time he turned straw into gold?

2. Why did the miller tell the king his daughter could spin (or turn) straw into gold?

3. If you were Rumpelstiltskin, what would you have asked the miller's daughter to give you in order to turn straw into gold?

The question that best meets both the TDQ criteria is Question 2, "Why did the miller tell the king his daughter could spin straw into gold?" The response to this question can be found in the text, and answering this question can also lead the reader to think more deeply about the story. In reviewing what TDQs are, it is also helpful to get a sense of what they are not. The response to Question 1, "What did the miller's daughter give Rumpelstilskin the first time he turned straw into gold?" can be found in the text, but it is not an important detail of the story. Thus, this question does not meet both TDQ criteria. Question 3, "If you were Rumpelstiltskin, what would you have asked the miller's daughter to give you in order to turn straw into gold?" does not require the reader to have read the text in order to be able to answer it, so it does not meet the first criterion for being a true TDQ.

> Think of another fairy tale, and write three questions, one of which is a TDQ. Ask a partner to select the true TDQ. Or design a Frayer model of a true TDQ, with an example and a nonexample from a fairy tale of your choice.

How Do I Scaffold My ELs' Responses to TDQs?

As teachers who work with ELs, you will need to consider what aspects of using the TDQ technique are different for ELs. Another way to distinguish scaffolded TDQs for ELs from TDQs for non-ELs is to consider not only how TDQs are constructed so that ELs can read for multiple purposes but also the way in which ELs respond to TDQs. In addition to crafting TDQs carefully so that they serve as a tool for ELs to unlock complex text, teachers also need to think about how they support ELs to respond to TDQs. Teachers need to provide ELs with supports so that ELs are poised to respond to TDQs, either orally, in writing, or both. These supports can encompass all three types of scaffolds presented in Chapter 3 (materials and resources, instruction, and student groupings).

In terms of materials and resources, ELs can be given such scaffolds as English or bilingual glossaries, as well as home language materials and sentence frames, to assist them with answering TDQs designed for different close reads of a text. In the instruction category of scaffolds, teachers can provide concise background knowledge to ELs to support their answering of TDQs, as well as paraphrasing TDQs or modeling responses to TDQs. We also recommend teachers using a think-aloud model to help ELs become more comfortable with answering TDQs. As far as student groupings go, teachers can incorporate structures and supports so that ELs have the opportunity to practice working on and answering TDQs in a way in which they are encouraged to take risks while developing their English

> Which scaffolds are you already using with TDQs? Which two to three would you like to add to your instruction?

language skills. For example, students who share the same home language but differ in English proficiency levels could work in pairs so that they can draw from their home language skills to support their work. Alternatively, students from different home language backgrounds could be purposefully grouped in small groups so that they have to use their English skills. As with all scaffolds, teachers will need to consider the backgrounds and English proficiency levels of their students when offering them scaffolds to support their use of TDQs.

APPLICATION ACTIVITY 8.2

Assigning TDQs to Close-Reading Categories

For this activity, we have selected a text at the sixth- to eighth-grade level in the category of "Informational Texts: Science, Mathematics and Technology" titled "The Evolution of the Grocery Bag" by Henry Petroski (2003).

Step 1: Read the text and the TDQs that follow it.

"The Evolution of the Grocery Bag" by H. Petroski (2003)

That much-reviled bottleneck known as the American supermarket checkout lane would be an even greater exercise in frustration were it not for several technological advances. The Universal Product Code and the decoding laser scanner, introduced in 1974, tally a shopper's groceries far more quickly and accurately than the old method of inputting each purchase manually into a cash register. But beeping a large order past the scanner would have led only to a faster pileup of cans and boxes down the line, where the bagger works, had it not been for the introduction, more than a century earlier, of an even greater technological masterpiece: the square-bottomed paper bag.

The geometry of paper bags continues to hold a magical appeal for those of us who are fascinated by how ordinary things are designed and made. Originally, grocery bags were created on demand by storekeepers, who cut, folded, and pasted sheets of paper, making versatile containers into which purchases could be loaded for carrying home. The first paper bags manufactured commercially are said to have been made in Bristol, England, in the 1840s. In 1852, a "Machine for Making Bags of Paper" was patented in America by Francis Wolle, of Bethlehem, Pennsylvania. According to Wolle's own description of the machine's operation, "pieces of paper of suitable length are given out from a roll of the required width, cut off from the roll and otherwise suitably cut to the required shape, folded, their edges pasted and lapped, and formed into complete and perfect bags."

The "perfect bags" produced at the rate of eighteen hundred per hour by Wolle's machine were, of course, not perfect, nor was his machine. The history of design has yet to see the development of a perfect object, though it has seen many satisfactory ones and many substantially improved ones. The concept of comparative improvement is embedded in the paradigm for invention, the better mousetrap. No one is ever likely to lay claim to a "best" mousetrap, for that would preclude the inventor himself from coming up with a still better mousetrap without suffering the embarrassment of having previously declared the search complete. As with the mousetrap, so with the bag.

Source: Petroski, H. (2003). The evolution of the grocery bag. American Scholar 72, 4. http://www.jstor.org/stable/41221195?seq=1#page_scan_tab_contents The article is from pp. 99–111.

Step 2: For each question, determine whether the question corresponds to one of three close-reading categories: (1) key ideas and details, (2) craft and structure, or (3) integration of knowledge and ideas. Usually, we would group the type of TDQs together, but for this purpose, the questions are not in a particular order.

Text-Dependent Questions

A. What two inventions made it faster to add up the cost of groceries?

Two inventions that made it faster to add up the cost of groceries were _____ and _____.

B. Why does the author say there is no perfect object?

He says there is no perfect object because _____.

C. What image or comparison does the author use to describe the grocery store checkout lanes?

He uses the word _____ to describe the checkout lane.

D. What emotion or feeling do you associate with his description of the grocery store checkout lane? Why?

Based on the author's description, I think of the word _____ when I read his description of the grocery store checkout lane because _____.

E. What is the concept of *comparative improvement*?

The concept of comparative improvement is the idea that _____.

F. How were bags made originally?

They were made _____ _____ by_____.

G. Why did the system of making paper bags by hand change?

It changed because _____ invented _____.

H. Based on the reading, what do you think the word *tally* means in this phrase: "The Universal Product Code and the decoding laser scanner, introduced in 1974, tally a shopper's groceries far more quickly and accurately."?

The word *tally* means _____. I think this

because _____.

I. Who described the bags from Wolfe's machine as "perfect"?

_____ described the bags as perfect.

J. What is the comparison the author makes between the mousetrap and the paper bag?

The author says the paper bag is like the mousetrap because _____

_____.

K. In this phrase—"*It* has seen many satisfactory ones and many substantially improved ones"—what does *it* refer to? What does *ones* refer to?

It refers to _____.

Ones refers to _____.

Step 3: Place the letter of each question under the correct close-reading heading that indicates what type of TDQ it is. The first question has been modeled for you. We have also provided examples of sentence frames that could be used to scaffold this activity for ELs that need additional support in responding to TDQs. You'll find the answers at the end of the chapter.

First Read (Key Ideas and Details)

Letters that correspond to the four TDQs that elicit key ideas and details:

____A____ _____ _____ _____

Second Read (Craft and Structure)

Letters that correspond to the four TDQs that elicit craft and structure:

_____ _____ _____ _____

Third Read (Integration of Knowledge and Ideas)

Letters that correspond to the three TDQs that elicit the integration of knowledge and ideas: _____ _____ _____

What Steps Should I Take to Create TDQs for ELs?

Now that we have considered close reading, what constitutes a genuine TDQ, and scaffolding ELs' responses to TDQs, it's time to create TDQs for ELs. In order to develop TDQs and the necessary scaffolds for ELs, we recommend following the five steps, which are further detailed in subsequent paragraphs. The steps are as follows:

1. Consider TDQ guidelines, and thoroughly analyze the text for ELs.

2. Decide on additional supports for ELs to accompany the TDQs.

3. Develop a guiding question or two to frame instruction for ELs.

4. Map the TDQs to close reads, and provide sentence starters for ELs.

5. Develop a culminating activity scaffolded for ELs.

We provide examples to model how we use these steps when working with the same text, "The Evolution of the Grocery Bag," that we used in Application Activity 8.2.[8]

Step 1: Consider TDQ guidelines and thoroughly analyze the text for ELs.

There are many resources available to support teachers in creating TDQs. However, most resources have not been developed with ELs in mind. For example, the Achieve the Core (n.d.b) group's resources related to TDQs are intended for work with non-ELs. Staehr Fenner (2014) adapted the Achieve the Core guidelines to add some considerations for using these guidelines with ELs. Teachers of ELs can use these guidelines when preparing to write TDQs and considering the additional support ELs may need to successfully work with TDQs and close reading in general. While it may be time consuming at first to consider the guidelines, as you become more familiar with them, they will help you conceptualize the complex process of creating effective, scaffolded TDQs to support ELs' close reading of texts.

Teachers should use the guidelines and the text that they are going to be teaching in tandem. Just as teachers have to ask their students to go back to the text to find the answers to the questions they develop, teachers must also closely analyze the text they are going to use, reading it multiple times for different purposes. It may be helpful to write directly on a copy of the text, noting key ideas of the text, challenging vocabulary, sentences that students may struggle with, idiomatic expressions, and literary devices used. Teachers can also jot down connections that students might make to other texts that they have read or other content that they have studied in class. The notes that teachers take during this step of the preparation will be essential as they begin to write the TDQs to accompany the text. Figure 8.2, "Guidelines for Creating TDQs," presents general considerations to follow when creating TDQs and specific suggestions targeted at ELs.

---

8. The examples we provide to support the steps were adapted from our blog post on TDQs, included in the references (Staehr Fenner & Snyder, 2014).

FIGURE 8.2 Guidelines for Creating TDQs and EL Suggestions

Achieve the Core TDQ Guideline	EL Suggestion
1. Think about what you think is the most important learning to be drawn from the text. Note this as raw material for the culminating assignment and the focal point for other activities to build toward.	1. Depending on their level of English language proficiency, ELs will need different amounts of scaffolding to access the most important learning. They may also require some additional steps to get to this level of learning.
2. Determine the key ideas of the text. Create a series of questions structured to bring the reader to an understanding of these.	2. ELs might need to be provided with some concise background knowledge to access the key ideas of the text. See Chapter 7 for more information on providing background knowledge. TDQs will also need to be scaffolded so that ELs at different levels of English language proficiency can understand them. ELs might need sentence frames and a word bank or sentence starters to support their answers to the questions.
3. Locate the most powerful academic words in the text and integrate questions and discussions that explore their role into the set of questions above.	3. Teachers of ELs will need to decide which academic words to teach ELs. See Chapters 5 and 6 for more information on vocabulary. Some additional resources include Colorín Colorado's (n.d.) "Selecting Vocabulary Words to Teach English Language Learners," the University of Nottingham's (n.d.), Academic Word List Highlighter, and Achieve the Core's (n.d.a) Academic Word Finder. See the "References" section at the end of this chapter for links to these resources.
4. Take stock of what standards are being addressed in the series of questions above. Then, decide if any other standards are suited to be a focus for this text. If so, form questions that exercise those standards.	4. In addition to content standards, English language proficiency and development standards will also need to guide the creation of TDQs. ESOL teachers should collaborate with content teachers to help them integrate English language proficiency and development standards into their TDQs.
5. Consider if there are any other academic words that students would profit from focusing on. Build discussion planning or additional questions to focus attention on them.	5. Teachers of ELs will need to decide which other academic words to teach ELs. They must be careful not to teach too many words in the text, or ELs could become overwhelmed. See Chapters 5 and 6 for more ideas on this topic.
6. Find the sections of the text that will present the greatest difficulty, and craft questions that support students in mastering these sections. These could be sections with difficult syntax, particularly dense information, and tricky transitions or places that offer a variety of possible inferences.	6. The sections of text that will present the greatest difficulty to ELs may differ from those that will present the greatest difficulty for non-ELs. Teachers should analyze the academic language found in each text and teach the academic language to the ELs, as well as the non-ELs. See Chapter 5 for more information on this topic.
7. Develop a culminating activity around the idea or learning identified in Guideline 1. A good task should reflect mastery of one or more of the standards, involve writing, and be structured to be done by students independently.	7. The culminating activity should incorporate content, as well as English language proficiency and development standards for ELs. Classroom-based assessments should be scaffolded so that ELs can demonstrate what they know and can do. In order for ELs to take part in the task, they will need scaffolding. The amount and type of scaffolding needed will depend on their level of English proficiency.

Source: Adapted from Achieve the Core. (n.d.). Short guide to creating questions for close analytical reading. Retrieved from http://achievethecore.org/category/1158/ela-literacy-text-dependent-questions; Staehr Fenner, D. (2014). Text-dependent questions for ELLs (Part 1) [Web log post]. Retrieved from http://www.colorincolorado.org/blog/text-dependent-questions-ells-part-1

Figure 8.3, "Example of TDQ Guidelines and EL Suggestions and Examples From 'The Evolution of the Grocery Bag,'" provides an example of how we applied these guidelines to a complex text aimed at Grades 6–8 as a model of our rationale.

FIGURE 8.3 Example of TDQ Guidelines and EL Suggestions and Examples From "The Evolution of the Grocery Bag"

Achieve the Core TDQ Guideline	EL Suggestions and Examples from "The Evolution of the Grocery Bag"
1. Think about what you believe to be the most important learning to be drawn from the text. Note this as raw material for the culminating assignment and the focal point for other activities to build toward.	1. Students should be able to explain the evolution of the paper bag and why the version of the paper bag that we know now cannot be called "perfect." They should also consider how this same concept applies to other technological advances. In order to meet these objectives, ELs will need scaffolding to understand the vocabulary and syntax used in this text, as well as the analogy that the author draws between the paper bag and the mousetrap.
2. Determine the key ideas of the text. Create a series of questions structured to bring the reader to an understanding of these.	2. The key ideas of the text include the following: • The Universal Product Code and the decoding laser scanner improved the grocery checkout system. • Grocery bags were originally made by hand by storekeepers. • In the 1800s, machines were invented for making the paper bag. • There is no perfect invention. Background knowledge could focus on how customers pay for groceries and carry them home.
3. Locate the most powerful academic words in the text, and integrate questions and discussions that explore their role into the set of questions above.	3. Achieve the Core's (n.d.a) Academic Word Finder identified seventeen Tier 2 words below the seventh-grade level and twenty Tier 2 words on grade level. Using our criteria from Chapter 6, we chose the words *product*, *code*, *manual*, *origin*, *demand*, and *manufacture* to focus on during instruction.
4. Take stock of what standards are being addressed in the series of questions above. Then, decide if any other standards are suited to be a focus for this text. If so, form questions that exercise those standards.	4. Several content standards are addressed: • Determine the central ideas or conclusions of a text; provide an accurate summary of the text distinct from prior knowledge or opinions. • Determine the meaning of symbols, key terms, and other domain-specific words and phrases as they are used in a specific scientific or technical context relevant to *Grades 6–8 texts and topics*. • Distinguish among facts, reasoned judgment based on research findings, and speculation in a text. • WIDA ELD Standard 5: ELLs communicate information, ideas, and concepts necessary for academic success in the content area of Social Studies.[9]

9. This is a sample ELD standard from WIDA. Other ELD standards include ELPA21 ELP Standards, as well as independently developed state-specific standards (e.g., Arizona, California, New York, and Texas).

Achieve the Core TDQ Guideline	EL Suggestions and Examples from "The Evolution of the Grocery Bag"
5. Consider if there are any other academic words that students would profit from focusing on. Build discussion planning or additional questions to focus attention on them.	5. Other important vocabulary from the text includes *severe*, *universal*, *introduce*, *input*, *purchase*, and *register*. However, teachers of ELs will need to be mindful not to overwhelm students with too many words and choose their words to teach carefully.
6. Find the sections of the text that will present the greatest difficulty, and craft questions that support students in mastering these sections. These could be sections with difficult syntax, particularly dense information, and tricky transitions or places that offer a variety of possible inferences.	6. The length and syntax of some sentences may be challenging to students, as in the example of this passage: "The concept of comparative improvement is embedded in the paradigm for invention, the better mousetrap. No one is ever likely to lay claim to a 'best' mousetrap, for that would preclude the inventor himself from coming up with a still better mousetrap without suffering the embarrassment of having previously declared the search complete. As with the mousetrap, so with the bag."
7. Develop a culminating activity around the idea or learning identified in Guideline 1. A good task should reflect mastery of one or more of the standards, involve writing, and be structured to be done by students independently.	7. In the culminating activity, students answer the guiding questions. • How has the design of the paper bag evolved? • Why is the design of today's paper bag not considered perfect?

Source: Adapted from Staehr Fenner, D., & Snyder, S. (2015). Creating text-dependent questions for ELLs: Examples for 6th–8th grade (Part 3) [Web log post]. Retrieved from http://www.colorincolorado.org/blog/creating-text-dependent-questions-ells-examples-6th-8th-grade-part-3

Step 2: Decide on additional supports for ELs to accompany the TDQs.

In this step, it is important to decide on the supports (in addition to the TDQs) that you will provide to ELs in order help them better engage with the text. Examples of these types of supports include the concise teaching of background knowledge and explicit vocabulary instruction. During Step 1, you will have identified background knowledge that may be necessary for preteaching, as well vocabulary that you want to focus on. In our example of "The Evolution of the Paper Bag" text, we want to build or activate students' prior knowledge about the topic, but we do not want to give away meaning of the text. So we recommend beginning the lesson with a brief discussion on how customers pay for groceries and carry them home to offer some context for the topic. We would also show them a paper bag from the grocery store so as to either build or activate their prior knowledge but not spoil the meaning of the text.

For introducing new vocabulary, we recommend using *realia* (real objects) or pictures to teach vocabulary that is central to understanding the text, such as a Universal Product Code, a cash register, a laser scanner, and a mousetrap. We also recommend providing and encouraging the use of a glossary (either bilingual or English) for other difficult vocabulary. If we wanted to do an intense focus on a small set of new vocabulary (as we described in Chapter 6),

Universal Product Code

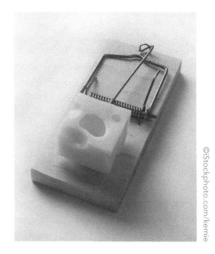
Mousetrap

we would select Tier 2 words that students could use across content areas. For example, we might select words such as *product, code, manual, origin, demand,* and *manufacture*.

Step 3: Develop a guiding question or two to frame instruction for ELs.

Guiding questions are an important step to help frame the lesson and give students a sense of purpose for the reading. These questions can often be developed by looking at what you wrote down for the most important learning that students will take from the text as part of Step 1. Guiding questions should also be returned to during the culminating activity. Returning to our example of "The Evolution of the Paper Bag," we recommend two possible guiding questions to frame the discussion. We ensure that the language of the guiding question lends itself to ELs being able to answer it. Teachers can further embed the use of scaffolds, such as glossaries, visuals, or students' home language, to provide more support to ELs in understanding the guiding question(s). These questions are based on our response to Guideline 1 in Step 1.

- How has the design of the paper bag evolved?

- Why is the design of today's paper bag not considered perfect?

Step 4: Map the TDQs to close reads, and provide sentence starters for ELs.

The fourth step is to develop the TDQs that map to each of the three close reads of the text. The TDQs should address the content and English language proficiency or development standards students will be working toward. As you are writing your questions, go back to the notes that you took during

Step 1 of the process and the guidelines for creating TDQs with suggestions for ELs. Remember that while some TDQs will have one correct answer, many will not. There should be space for students to respond to TDQs based on their individual analysis of a text. It can definitely be challenging to write TDQs that will help students effectively deconstruct and analyze a text. If you find you are struggling with your TDQ design, reach out to other teachers familiar with the context, and ask for their feedback. It is also important to note that all students, including ELs, most likely will not answer all of these TDQs in one lesson, depending on how much time you have allotted for instruction of different content areas. It might take a couple of lessons for students to gain a deeper understanding of the text's meaning. It is always a good idea to consider what the students who complete the TDQs earlier than others should do while other students continue to work on them.

Once you have developed your questions, write sentence stems for ELs at an intermediate level. The idea is for students to spend their time focusing on the text and not on producing language for a complete response. ELs at a beginning or low intermediate level may need sentence frames and word banks, instead of sentence stems. The challenge with including sentence frames and word banks is that you should not restrict all questions to right or wrong answers. However, you may need to provide these scaffolds to some students until they develop a higher level of language proficiency and the scaffolds can be removed.

Our example of TDQs is provided in Application Activity 8.2 on pages 211–213. We scaffolded these TDQs for ELs at the intermediate level of English language proficiency by embedding some vocabulary definitions into the TDQ itself and by providing sentence stems. For example, we embedded the definition of *emotion* into question D. TDQ. (What emotion or feeling do you associate with his description of the grocery store checkout lane?) In addition to providing sentence stems, if the ELs were at a lower level of proficiency, we would give a sentence frame and provide a word bank.

Step 5: Develop a culminating activity.

The final step in preparing to use TDQs with a class is to decide on a culminating activity. This activity could be as simple as asking students to discuss and answer the guiding questions. However, you could also take this opportunity to have students engage in a more in-depth writing task. For example, you might ask students to respond, in writing, to the guiding question and provide evidence from the text to support their responses. ELs will need specific language-based supports to complete the writing tasks (e.g., graphic organizers, paragraph frames, and word banks) (Baker et al., 2014). They will also need explicit instruction on how to go from ideas on a graphic organizer to the production of clear and coherent sentences (Baker et al., 2014).

McCarty (2014) also makes the following recommendations for following up with students on their answers to TDQs:

- Ask about specific words or phrases that students give in their responses.

- Have students indicate in the text where they found the evidence to support their opinion.

- Ask students to remark or elaborate on the ideas of another student.

- Ask students to find another piece of evidence in the text that supports their opinion.

- Ask students to consider what someone with an alternative position or viewpoint might say to their argument.

These recommendations can provide opportunities for students to delve deeper into the text. They can also support ELs in hearing the content and academic language repeated, which will help both their understanding of the material and their language development. However, teachers will need to ensure that they provide sufficient scaffolding and support in this follow-up phase.

How Do I Apply What I Have Learned About Creating TDQs for ELs?

Once you have completed these five steps and prepared the corresponding materials, you should be ready to teach your lesson(s). Application Activity 8.3 is an opportunity for you to gain some practice working through these five steps and actually writing TDQs. To complete the activity, you can use the text provided, or you can also use your own text. This activity would be an excellent opportunity for content and ESOL teachers to work together and discuss in pairs or small groups. It would also be a good fit for a school's professional learning community (PLC).

APPLICATION ACTIVITY 8.3

Creating TDQs Using a Template

Using an excerpt from Judith St. George's (2000) text *So You Want to Be President?* or your own text excerpt, complete the following template in order to develop three sets of TDQs for the text provided. These three sets of scaffolded TDQs should align to the three close reads students will undergo (i.e., [1] *key ideas and details*, [2] *craft and structure*, and [3] *integration of knowledge and ideas*). We provide you the structure to carefully analyze the text and the context in which ELs are reading to create the scaffolded TDQs. We also help you connect your analysis to ideas for instruction. We suggest creating three questions for each close read for a total of nine questions. This is a suggestion for getting started that you can later adapt depending on the text and your students to the number of TDQs that you feel are necessary for ELs to use.

Featured Text Excerpt: *So You Want to Be President?*

Every single President has taken this oath: "I do solemnly swear (or affirm) that I will faithfully execute the office of President of the United States, and will to the best of my ability, preserve, protect, and defend the Constitution of the United States."

Only thirty-five words! But it's a big order if you're President of this country. Abraham Lincoln was tops at filling that order. "I know very well that many others might in this matter or as in others, do better than I can," he said. "But . . . I am here. I must do the best I can, and bear the responsibility of taking the course which I feel I ought to take."

That's the bottom line. Tall, short, fat, thin, talkative, quiet, vain, humble, lawyer, teacher, or soldier—this is what most of our Presidents have tried to do, each in his own way. Some succeeded. Some failed. If you want to be President—a good President—pattern yourself after the best. Our best have asked more of themselves than they thought they could give. They have had the courage, spirit, and will to do what they knew was right. Most of all, their first priority has always been the people and the country they served.

Text: _____

Step 1: Consider these TDQ guidelines for ELs.

Achieve the Core Guideline	EL Suggestion	Example(s) from Text and Ideas for Instruction
1. Think about what you believe to be the most important learning to be drawn from the text. Note this as raw material for the culminating assignment and the focal point for other activities to build toward.	Depending on their level of English language proficiency, ELs will need different amounts of scaffolding to comprehend the text on a deep level. ELs may require some additional steps to get to this level of learning.	Most important learning: Scaffolding for ELs:

(Continued)

Achieve the Core Guideline	EL Suggestion	Example(s) from Text and Ideas for Instruction
2. Determine the key ideas of the text. Create a series of questions structured to bring the reader to an understanding of these.	ELs might need to be provided with some concise background knowledge to access the key ideas of the text. TDQs will need to be scaffolded so that ELs at different levels of English language proficiency can understand them. ELs might need sentence frames or sentence starters to support their answers to the questions.	Key ideas: Background knowledge:
3. Locate the most powerful academic words in the text, and integrate questions and discussions that explore their role into the set of questions above.	Teachers of ELs will need to decide which academic words to teach ELs. Some resources include Colorín Colorado's (n.d.) "Selecting Vocabulary Words to Teach English Language Learners," the University of Nottingham's (n.d.) Academic Word List Highlighter, and Achieve the Core's (n.d.a) Academic Word Finder.	Most powerful academic words for ELs:
4. Take stock of what standards are being addressed in the series of questions above. Then, decide if any other standards are suited to be a focus for this text. If so, form questions that exercise those standards.	In addition to content standards, English language proficiency and development standards will also need to guide the creation of TDQs. ESOL teachers will need to collaborate with content teachers to help them integrate English language proficiency and development standards into their TDQs.	Content standard(s): ELD standard(s):
5. Consider if there are any other academic words that students would profit from focusing on. Build discussion planning or additional questions to focus attention on them.	Teachers of ELs will need to decide which other academic words to teach ELs. They must be careful not to teach too many words in the text, or ELs could become overwhelmed.	Other academic words to teach ELs:
6. Find the sections of the text that will present the greatest difficulty, and craft questions that support students in mastering these sections. These could be sections with difficult syntax, particularly dense information, and tricky transitions or places that offer a variety of possible inferences.	The sections of text that will present the greatest difficulty to ELs may differ from those that will present the greatest difficulty for non-ELs. Teachers should analyze the academic language found in each text and teach the academic language to the ELs, as well as the non-ELs.	Academic language to teach:
7. Develop a culminating activity around the idea or learning identified in Guideline 1. A good task should reflect mastery of one or more of the standards, involve writing, and be structured to be done by students independently.	The culminating activity should incorporate content standards, as well as English language proficiency and development standards for ELs. Classroom-based assessments should be scaffolded so that ELs can demonstrate what they know and can do. In order for ELs to take part in the task, they will need scaffolding in order to do sos The amount and type of scaffolding needed will depend on their level of English proficiency.	Culminating activity that incorporates content and ELD standards: Scaffolding for task:

Step 2: Provide additional support for ELs.

Background knowledge instruction (What background knowledge, if any, will you teach? How will you teach it?)

[ ]

Academic vocabulary instruction (What vocabulary will you focus on, and how will you teach it? Will you provide a glossary? If so, what words will you include?)

[ ]

Step 3: Provide a guiding question or questions to frame instruction.

Guiding question or questions:

[ ]

Step 4: Outline the TDQs, and provide sentence frames or starters for ELs. (Write three questions for each step.)

First Read (Key Ideas and Details)

TDQ 1:

Sentence frame or starter:

TDQ 2:

Sentence frame or starter:

TDQ 3:

Sentence frame or starter:

Second Read (Craft and Structure)

TDQ 4:

Sentence frame or starter:

TDQ 5:

Sentence frame or starter:

TDQ 6:

Sentence frame or starter:

Third Read (Integration of Knowledge and Ideas)

TDQ 7:

Sentence frame or starter:

TDQ 8:

Sentence frame or starter:

TDQ 9:

Sentence frame or starter:

How Do I Collaborate to Create Effective Scaffolded TDQs for ELs?

Based on our own experience, we know that developing important and effective text-dependent questions can be very challenging work for teachers, just as answering them can be challenging for students. We found it very helpful to work together to create them. We suggest that ESOL and content teachers use the development of TDQs as a way to collaborate, with each bringing their respective expertise to the table. For example, content teachers might feel more comfortable determining the most important learning or key ideas from a particular text they have used previously in instruction. ESOL teachers may bring expertise in reviewing the language of the TDQs to make sure it will allow ELs to understand it and answer the questions. ESOL teachers may also wish to create sentence stems or frames to provide ELs support in answering the TDQs. Through taking part in such a collaborative process, teachers can develop TDQs that both address the key learning that students should take from a text and the specific linguistic challenges that might prevent ELs from understanding the text. This type of collaboration and discussion during the collaboration process allows ample opportunity for teachers to learn through "unofficial," or grassroots, professional development. By doing so, content teachers become more familiar with the strategies that should be used to support English learners, and ESOL teachers become familiar with key content and vocabulary to provide additional support for ELs—a win-win for both types of teachers. In addition to providing deeper learning for teachers, creating effective TDQs will allow ELs to gain a deeper understanding of texts they read.

What Is the Role of Equity, Advocacy, and Leadership in Creating TDQs?

There are several ways that scaffolded TDQs can lead to equity for ELs, advocacy for their appropriate instruction, and opportunities for teachers to develop their leadership skills. Appropriately scaffolded TDQs will provide ELs one more avenue to access grade-level complex text and engage more meaningfully with content instruction. Using carefully constructed TDQs that are scaffolded for ELs will enable ELs at different levels of proficiency to become more involved in classroom instruction, and many non-ELs may also benefit from the scaffolds designed with ELs in mind. The opportunity to collaborate around the creation and implementation of TDQs allows ESOL and content teachers to leverage their unique expertise and hone their leadership skills both inside and outside the classroom. Teachers we have supported in developing TDQs have consistently mentioned how beneficial it has been to collaborate across ESOL and content areas and how this collaboration has strengthened their professional relationships with each other. Ultimately, their students have seen the benefits of their collaborative efforts.

Conclusion

In this chapter, we outlined how teachers can create TDQs to help ELs unlock the meaning of complex text through multiple close reads. We outline a process by which teachers can consider supports and scaffolds for ELs and ultimately design TDQs that will assist ELs in developing a deeper understanding of the multiple layers of complex texts at grade level. Although we will readily admit that it can be somewhat time consuming and labor intensive to develop scaffolded TDQs, your ELs will benefit from their use, and you will benefit through collaborating with other teachers and sharing your expertise. Our next chapter, "Formative Assessment for ELs," will allow you to explore ways to gauge how well ELs are learning and use that information to adjust your instruction.

Reflection Questions

1. In preparing to write and use scaffolded TDQs with your ELs, what is the biggest challenge that you face? What support could you get to mitigate that challenge?

2. How do you think the use of scaffolded TDQs will benefit the ELs and non-ELs you work with?

Application Activity Responses

Application Activity 8.2 Answers

First Read (Key Ideas and Details)

____A____ ____F____ ____G____ ____I____

Second Read (Craft and Structure)

____C____ ____D____ ____H____ ____K____

Third Read (Integration of Knowledge and Ideas)

____B____ ____E____ ____J____

References

Achieve the Core. (n.d.a). Academic word finder. Retrieved from http://achievethecore.org/page/1027/academic-word-finder

Achieve the Core. (n.d.b). Text-dependent question resources. Retrieved from http://achievethecore.org/category/1158/ela-literacy-text-dependent-questions

August, D., & Shanahan, T. (Eds.). (2008). *Developing reading and writing in second-language learners*. New York: Routledge.

August, D., Staehr Fenner, D., & Snyder, S. (2014). *Scaffolding instruction for English language learners: A resource guide for ELA*. Retrieved from https://www.engageny.org/resource/scaffolding-instruction-english-language-learners-resource-guides-english-language-arts-and

Baker, S., Lesaux, N., Jayanthi, M., Dimino, J., Proctor, C. P., Morris, J., & Newman-Gonchar, R. (2014). *Teaching academic content and literacy to English learners in elementary and middle school* (NCEE 2014-4012). Washington, DC: National Center for Education Evaluation and Regional Assistance (NCEE), Institute of Education Sciences, U.S. Department of Education. Retrieved from http://ies.ed.gov/ncee/wwc/publications_reviews.aspx

Colorín Colorado. (n.d.). Selecting vocabulary words to teach English language learners. Retrieved from http://www.colorincolorado.org/article/selecting-vocabulary-words-teach-english-language-learners

Fisher, D., & Frey, N. (2015). *Text-dependent questions: Pathways to close and critical reading*. Thousand Oaks, CA: Corwin.

McCarty, R. (2014). Tackling the misconceptions of text-dependent questions [Blog post]. Retrieved from https://www.teachingchannel.org/blog/2014/11/13/tackling-misconceptions-of-text-dependent-question

Petroski, H. (2003). The evolution of the grocery bag. *American Scholar, 72*, 4.

Shanahan, T. (2012). What is close reading? [Blog post]. Shanahan on Literacy. Retrieved from http://www.shanahanonliteracy.com/2012/06/what-is-close-reading.html

Shanahan, T. (2013). Letting the text take center stage: How the Common Core State Standards will transform English language arts instruction. *American Educator, 37*.

St. George, J. (2000). *So you want to be president?* New York, NY: Philomel Books.

Staehr Fenner, D. (2014). Text-dependent questions for ELLs (Part 1) [Web log post]. Retrieved from http://www.colorincolorado.org/blog/text-dependent-questions-ells-part-1

Staehr Fenner, D., & Snyder, S. (2015). Creating text-dependent questions for ELLs: Examples for 6th–8th grade (Part 3) [Web log post]. Retrieved from http://www.colorincolorado.org/blog/creating-text-dependent-questions-ells-examples-6th-8th-grade-part-3

Tuinman, J. (1973). Determining the passage dependency of comprehension questions in 5 major tests. *Reading Research Quarterly, 9*(2), 206–223.

University of Nottingham. (n.d.). Academic word list highlighter. Retrieved from https://www.nottingham.ac.uk/alzsh3/acvocab/awlhighlighter.htm

Formative Assessment for ELs

Ms. Weber teaches biology in a suburban high school in Washington State, and this is her third year in the classroom. Her class contains a large number of ELs at all levels of proficiency who bring varying amounts of knowledge in biology from their previous education. While she is working with her school's ESOL teacher to scaffold her lessons so that her ELs can access the biology content and develop academic language, she is at a loss as to what she should do on her classroom assessments. Her students have to take an end-of-year biology multiple-choice content test in English, and she wants to prepare her students for that assessment measure. However, she recognizes that her students' developing proficiency in English does not always allow them to accurately show what they know and can do in biology. Ms. Weber wants to find a way to create classroom assessments that provide her ELs with a means to demonstrate what they have learned in biology and also give her some insights into where she might need to adapt her instruction.

> *What are some challenges you face assessing your ELs' acquisition of language and/or content? What do you do to address these challenges?*

This chapter will highlight the necessity of creating classroom-based or formative assessments that assess ELs' acquisition of academic language, as well as content to support all teachers sharing the responsibility and joy of teaching ELs. We will first define formative assessment and provide a summary of relevant research on the practice of formative assessment for ELs. We will provide opportunities for you to apply the topic, including guidance on creating appropriate classroom assessments for ELs based on ELs' proficiency levels. We will give you examples and practical guidance on ensuring ELs are prepared for computer-based content assessments and how you can use formative-assessment results to inform instructional planning for ELs. While there are many purposes that assessment can serve ELs, this chapter will focus on formative assessment.[1] You already may be scaffolding assessments, as well as instruction of ELs, embedding assessments in instruction to tailor and guide your instruction and thinking of instructional activities as formative assessments to monitor and measure ELs' progress in language and content. No matter where you are in terms of your expertise on developing and using formative assessment for ELs, this chapter aims to scaffold you to the next level.

What Is Assessment as, of, and for Learning?

To begin our exploration of formative assessment for ELs, let's first situate formative assessment within the larger context. In her framework of assessment, Margo Gottlieb (2016) conceptualizes assessment in three main types: assessment *as* learning, assessment *for* learning, and assessment *of* learning. Assessment *as* learning generates data to increase the students' metacognitive and metalinguistic awareness. Assessment *as* learning is more personalized, as it recognizes students as an important data source. Assessment *for* learning generates data on an ongoing basis to inform instruction. Assessment *for* learning embraces the role of teachers in making everyday decisions from instructionally embedded data. Assessment *of* learning generates data for summative purposes. Assessment *of* learning affords administrators a sense of their school or district's position in relation to standards-referenced data.

> For what purposes do you use assessment for ELs in your classroom? In your school? In your district?

Assessment *for* learning honors teachers as decision makers and leverages their expertise. Embedded in teaching routines, it is a direct expression of instruction, inviting student voice and revolving around providing descriptive, helpful feedback to teachers (Gottlieb, 2016; Stiggins, 2005). In this chapter, we examine formative assessment for teachers of ELs as an example of assessment *for* learning, in that it holds the promise of empowering teachers to design, implement, and integrate assessments that are valid and reliable and, most importantly, provide valuable information to inform their instruction of ELs. Figure 9.1 displays the features of Gottlieb's framework of assessment in more detail.

---

1. For broader information on assessment for ELs, see Gottlieb (2016) or Valdez Pierce (2003).

FIGURE 9.1 Assessment *as*, *for*, and *of* Learning

Assessment *as* Learning	Assessment *for* Learning	Assessment *of* Learning
Generates data used to foster students' metacognitive and metalinguistic awareness	Generates data used for formative purposes	Generates data used for summative purposes
Occurs on an ongoing basis, facilitated by teachers with gradual release of responsibility to students	Occurs on an ongoing, continuous basis between teachers and students	Occurs at designated time intervals
Is internal to student learning	Is internal to instruction and teacher learning	Is focused on the accrued learning at the end of a cycle
Uses original student work as data sources	Uses student work and a variety of instructional methods and response formats for data sources	Uses tests as the primary data source, with multiple-choice and short-answer questions or constructed-response formats
Encourages coconstruction by students and teachers	Encourages teachers to create tasks and determine shared criteria for success with students	Encourages departments, programs, and districts to create or select measures

Source: Adapted from Gottlieb (2016).

What Is Formative Assessment?

Let's begin exploring the concept of formative assessment, in general, by—what else?—taking a quick multiple-choice quiz.[2]

Which of the following matches your perception of formative assessment?

A. It's a set of measures internal (and sometimes external) to instruction.

B. It's a set of instructional practices.

C. It's a reflective process.

D. It's a component of a system.

E. It's all of the above.

(Gottlieb, 2016, n.p.)

Did you agree with more than one response? Actually, each of these perspectives of formative assessments has support in the research and literature. (A) Testing companies and publishers view formative assessment

---

2. Adapted from Gottlieb (2016).

as a set of measures internal (and sometimes external) to instruction. (B) Stiggins (2005) defines it as a set of practices. (C) Others view formative assessment as a reflective process (Heritage, 2010; Moss & Brookhart, 2009; Popham, 2008). (D) Frey and Fisher (2011) and Marzano (2010) see it as a component of system. (E) Gottlieb (2016) notes that formative assessment is really "all of the above." Further, Noyce and Hickey (2011) share that formative assessment, in general, is "the process of monitoring student knowledge and understanding during instruction in order to give useful feedback and make timely changes in instruction to ensure maximal student growth" (p. 1).

What Does the Research Say on Assessment for ELs in General?

Before we home in on formative assessment for ELs, we will explore the issues of assessment in a broader sense for ELs, focusing first on summative assessments, or assessments that occur at the end of a unit of instruction or academic year. These summative-assessment scores are usually compared against a standard or other benchmark. Research has clearly demonstrated that summative assessments designed mainly for native English speakers may not be as reliable and valid for ELs (Abedi, 2006). In fact, average scores for ELs on the 2013 reading and math National Assessment of Educational Progress (NAEP), or "nation's report card," in Grades 4, 8, and 12 were significantly lower than average scores for native speakers of English, and the gap in scores widened with increases in grade level (Office of English Language Acquisition, 2015).

Our work with ELs and their teachers is based in an advocacy framework in which the concept of *scaffolded advocacy*—or providing just the right amount of advocacy on the basis of students' strengths and needs—is crucial to support their academic achievement (Staehr Fenner, 2014). And nowhere do advocacy and equity for ELs play a more important role than in assessment, which can have detrimental consequences for ELs if not designed with ELs' unique attributes in mind. On the flip side, if teachers design assessments taking ELs' strengths into consideration, formative assessment holds great promise as a way for ELs to demonstrate what they know and can do in content as well as language. Gottlieb (2016) writes, "If assessment is reliable, valid, and fair (for ELs) from start to finish, then it can serve as the bridge to educational equity" (p. 1).

What Is the Role of Formative Assessment With ELs?

Assessment of ELs is more complex than assessing non-ELs. In addition to assessing ELs' content knowledge, it is necessary to assess their acquisition of academic language. As a result, because all teachers of ELs are teachers of academic language, all teachers should also assess ELs' academic language.

In a recent convening of teachers, administrators, policy makers, and researchers hosted by TESOL International Association, participants described the need to rethink testing for English learners, the amount of time that is being spent on testing them, and how assessment data are being used for them. The convening participants underscored that the purpose of assessment for English learners should be to ensure that teachers have the information they need about the students with whom they work in order to develop appropriate instruction (TESOL, 2016). The educators noted that formative assessments are one effective, efficient way to provide data to teachers that they can use in planning for EL instruction. Unlike summative-assessment measures, formative assessments should not take time from classroom instruction and should be seamlessly integrated into instructional routines. Formative assessments have the benefit of fostering student involvement in their own learning and acquisition of language. For example, you can develop student-friendly checklists, rubrics, and other formative-assessment tools to keep ELs abreast of their own content learning and language development. For ELs learning in two languages, such as in a dual-language program, students should be given formative assessments in the language in which they receive instruction. For example, if native speakers of Arabic receive mathematics instruction in Arabic, then they should be assessed on mathematics content in Arabic.

How Do I Structure the Formative-Assessment Process for ELs?

The ultimate benefit of using formative assessment for ELs is that it provides teachers with ongoing insights into students' learning and supports teachers in adjusting their instruction. Teachers can structure the formative-assessment process in three basic steps, shown in Figure 9.2.

Figure 9.3 provides more details around each of these steps and describes how each step is unique for teachers of ELs. We apply these steps to one classroom and one student in particular later in the chapter.

FIGURE 9.2 Formative-Assessment Process for ELs

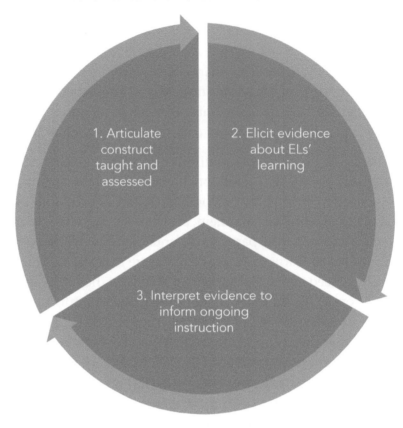

1. Articulate construct taught and assessed

2. Elicit evidence about ELs' learning

3. Interpret evidence to inform ongoing instruction

Source: Adapted from Alvarez, Ananda, Walqui, Sato, and Rabinowitz (2014).

FIGURE 9.3 Three-Step Process to Structuring Formative Assessment

Step to Structure Formative-Assessment Process for ELs	Explanation for Teachers of ELs
Step 1: Articulate the construct being taught and assessed: teacher and/or student articulate learning goals and success criteria	• Teachers consider what is being taught, whether language and/or literacy are part of the learning goals or success criteria, and what aspects of language or literacy are relevant. • Teachers also consider whether content is being assessed. • Teachers should refer to content and language objectives in this step to ensure assessment alignment. • Teachers' use of rubrics or a set of criteria to help teacher and students determine how well something has been learned is essential.

Step to Structure Formative-Assessment Process for ELs	Explanation for Teachers of ELs
Step 2: Elicit evidence about ELs' learning: teacher gathers evidence to determine where the student is in relation to learning goal	• Depending on the learning goal from Step 1, teachers can decide how language dependent the formative assessment task will be. If the focus is content knowledge, teachers may choose to use tasks that are less language dependent (e.g., visual or performance tasks). • Consider the use of open-ended tasks that allow students at various level of understanding to demonstrate learning. • Consider tasks that have multiple strategies to demonstrate learning (e.g., an assessment involving writing, drawing, or use of home language).
Step 3: Interpret evidence to inform ongoing instruction: teacher and/or student look at evidence to provide feedback on the status of student learning	• Student interpretation can be done through peer assessment and self-assessment using a student-friendly rubric or checklist. • Interpretation of evidence also informs subsequent teaching and learning activities. • Language and content are closely linked, but it may be useful to analyze the two separately when looking at student work.

Source: Adapted from Alvarez, Ananda, Walqui, Sato, and Rabinowitz (2014).

How Can I Interpret Formative-Assessment Evidence to Inform Instruction of ELs?

In our work with teachers of ELs, we often find that Step 3, interpret evidence to inform ongoing instruction, is one of the most challenging areas. After teachers collect evidence from a formative assessment, they may be unsure as to how to actually use the evidence to make changes to their instruction of ELs. To provide guidance to teachers on this important step, we created a checklist (Figure 9.4), which details instructional supports you can use that are tailored to the three levels of academic language (word, sentence, and discourse). Further, the checklist provides detail on certain types of scaffolds and supports you can use to help ELs at one level of ELP move to the next proficiency level at the word, sentence, and discourse levels. These scaffolds and strategies are suggestions, not mandates, so we encourage you to use this checklist as a starting point and adapt it for your context.

FIGURE 9.4 Instructional Scaffolding and Strategies Checklist by ELP Level

Level of Academic Language	Beginning ELP Scaffolds	Intermediate ELP Scaffolds	Advanced ELP Scaffolds	Scaffolds for All ELP Levels
Word Level of Academic Language	☐ Word walls and word banks	☐ Word walls and word banks	☐ Thesauri	☐ Bilingual and/or English glossaries ☐ Dictionaries ☐ Direct vocabulary instruction ☐ Pretaught vocabulary ☐ Visuals
Sentence Level of Academic Language	☐ Quick minilesson to introduce new basic sentence structure ☐ Sentence frames ☐ Pretaught phrases	☐ Quick minilesson to introduce new compound or complex sentence structure ☐ Sentence frames	☐ Quick minilesson to introduce advanced grammar structure	☐ Sentence stems
Discourse Level of Academic Language	☐ Paragraph frames	☐ Paragraph frames ☐ Paraphrasing activities (for fluency and register)	☐ Paraphrasing activities (for fluency and register)	☐ Graphic organizers ☐ Shared writing
All Levels of Academic Language (Word, Sentence, Discourse)	☐ Home language text and/or instructions ☐ Reduced linguistic load for language of instruction	☐ Home language text ☐ Supplementary text or video	☐ Supplementary text or video	☐ Access to text or video in home language, as well as in English, as appropriate ☐ Cloze activities ☐ Concise instruction of background knowledge ☐ Repetition ☐ Structured pair and small-group work ☐ Teacher and/or peer modeling ☐ Teacher-led small groups

APPLICATION ACTIVITY 9.1

Formative-Assessment Brainstorm

Let's now take a look at the variety of formative assessments you may wish to consider for your ELs. Figure 9.5 provides a sample of different categories of formative assessments and some examples of each. We have provided a space for you to indicate which types of formative assessments have been effective for your ELs. You may be surprised at the types of activities already part of your practice that you could use for formative assessment.

> Brainstorm a list of the various types of formative assessments that you already use in your classroom. What categories would you divide those assessments into?

FIGURE 9.5 Categories of Formative Assessments and Examples

Category of Formative Assessment	Examples	My Notes on the Effectiveness for ELs
Physical demonstration	• Hands-on tasks • Acting out concepts • Gestures • Other: _____	
Pictorial products	• Drawings • Models • Graphs • Other: _____	
Graphic organizers	• Charts and tables • Venn diagrams • Webs • Other: _____	
Written products	• Captions of images • Content area logs • Reading response logs • Other: _____	
Oral assessments	• Oral interviews • Reports • Retelling • Role plays • Audio or video recording • Other: _____	

What Is Assessment Validity for ELs, and How Can I Ensure My Formative Assessments Are Valid?

Imagine a first-grade teacher assessing all of her students' understanding of word-ending sounds. Ms. Aponte shows her student, Gao-Jer, a Hmong speaker at a beginning level of English language proficiency, the picture seen here at left.

Ms. Aponte asks Gao-Jer to identify what other word has the same ending sound: *wish*, *hat*, *hop*, or *pan*.

- What may be standing in the way of this student demonstrating what she knows on this question?

- What could the teacher do to make this assessment more valid for Gao-Jer?

Source: © iStockphoto.com/ DNY59

The mop question is an example of validity, which generally refers to how accurately a conclusion, measurement, or concept corresponds to what is being tested. Validity is defined as the extent to which an assessment accurately measures what it is intended to measure (American Educational Research Association, American Psychological Association, National Council on Measurement in Education, Joint Committee on Standards for Educational and Psychological Testing, 2014). For example, if you weigh yourself on a scale, the scale should give you an accurate measurement of your weight. If the scale tells you that you weigh 200 pounds, and you actually weigh 150 pounds, then the scale is not valid. If an assessment intends to measure achievement and ability in a particular subject area but then measures concepts that are completely unrelated, the assessment is not valid. In the example of the mop, if Gao-Jer does not know the English word for mop, she will not be able to correctly determine which of the four words has the same ending sound. As a result, it is her knowledge of English vocabulary rather than her knowledge of ending letter sounds that is being assessed. Within the larger umbrella of validity, there are categories of construct validity, content validity, and predictive validity, among others.

You don't need to be an assessment expert to work with ELs, but you should have a sense of how the concept of validity can affect ELs differently than non-ELs. In addition, you should have a plan for addressing different types of validity when you design assessments for ELs to make them more valid. You should also know where to go and with whom to collaborate to better support your ELs in assessment. Figure 9.6 provides an overview of different aspects of validity, their definition, and examples that are specific to ELs.

FIGURE 9.6 Type of Validity, Definition, and Example for ELs

Type of Validity	Definition	Example for ELs
Construct validity	The degree to which a test measures what it claims, or purports, to be measuring	A math test which involves word problems in English may be more of an assessment of language proficiency than of mathematical knowledge
Content validity	The extent to which an assessment represents all facets of tasks within the domain being assessed	A multiple-choice vocabulary quiz that is supposed to measure not only ELs' understanding of meaning but their ability to use the words in context
Predictive validity	The extent to which a score on an assessment predicts future performance	How well an EL's score on the annual state English language proficiency assessment predicts his or her performance on the state English language arts assessment

APPLICATION ACTIVITY 9.2

Why Is Validity a Concern for ELs?

Imagine you are in fourth grade, and your family has moved to Germany for a year for your mother's career. You are enrolling in the German public school system. To determine your mathematics class placement, you are given an assessment to see how much you know in mathematics. In fact, you were in advanced math in the United States and love the topic. You sail through the multiplication problems and the long division until you come to this problem:

Schreibe den richtigen Namen unter die entsprechende Darstellung!

Versuche anschließend zu entscheiden, ob die angeführten Aussagen wahr (w) oder falsch (f) sind. Kreuze Entsprechendes an!

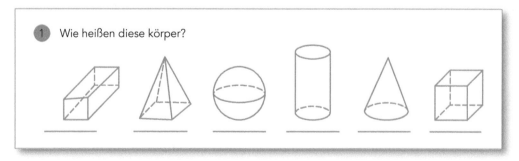

1   Wie heißen diese körper?

Aussage	w	f
Der Würfel hat 10 Ecken.		
Die Kugel hat keine Kanten und keine Ecken.		

Source: Staehr Fenner (2014).

- Is this a valid assessment for you? Why, or why not?

- Is the main issue at hand construct, content, or predictive validity?

- What kind of support could you have to help you show what you know and can do in geometry?

How Can I Ensure That Formative Assessments Are Valid for ELs of Varying Proficiency Levels?

There are several areas that pose validity considerations for ELs, from the instructions to the format to language to cultural bias. We will next take a deeper look at six areas that may have an impact on validity for ELs.

Area 1. **Assessment instructions.** Let's start with the instructions for the assessment. They need to be clear and easy to understand. You may wish to consider communicating the directions orally, as well as in writing, and have a visual cue for students to refer to. You can also communicate the directions in the students' home language and/or have students translate them for each other, if needed.

Area 2. **Format and use of technology.** The assessment should be in a familiar format. Multiple-choice format should not be used for the first time when assessing. The technology used, if any, needs to be familiar as well. Consider the format used and whether the student has had ample time to practice with the technology in class. Bear in mind students have various levels of access to technology outside of school. Later in this chapter, we will provide more information on the use of technology in assessment.

Area 3. **Linguistic accessibility.** The instructions to the content need to be linguistically accessible for ELs. Look for opportunities to reduce the *linguistic load* in all areas that aren't being directly accessed. For example, you can avoid constructing sentences in the negative and using unnecessarily complex vocabulary and grammatical structures. Teachers should double check their language—both in the assessment and any oral prompting or instructions they give—to avoid the use of idioms, which are often confusing for language learners. We also encourage teachers to share a draft of their assessments with another teacher to have a set of "fresh eyes" take a look at it for linguistic accessibility.

Area 4. **Cultural bias.** Cultural biases are often a hidden problem, as teachers may be unaware of these biases themselves. We recommend selecting content for the formative assessment that is something familiar to all students' shared experience, not topics students may not have had access to in their culture, education, or life experience. For example, American fairy tales, summer camp, vacations in the mountains, and the beach may not be familiar to all students. Shared experiences, such as class field trips and stories students have read or shared in class, can be used instead as context in assessments.

Area 5. **Scoring**. Finally, scoring needs to be based on the assessed construct only. Assigning points for spelling and grammar when they aren't the targeted skill or knowledge (on a test on the water cycle, for example) being assessed reduces the validity of the assessment. To determine what construct you're assessing, refer back to your lesson's content and language objectives.[3]

Area 6. **Scaffolds**. ELs need appropriate modifications and supports in assessments, from differentiated assessments to scaffolds that enable students to demonstrate their knowledge and skills in content while their language is still developing. The assessment does not need to look the same for all students. For beginning levels, nonverbal assessments, such as sorts and picture matching, may be used to demonstrate understanding of the concept. For students at higher levels of proficiency, you can provide glossaries and sentence stems as supports so that ELs can demonstrate what they know and can do.

How Do I Scaffold Formative Assessments for ELs?

In addition to ensuring formative assessments are valid for ELs, you should also consider scaffolds on these assessments, as we mention in Area 6. Providing scaffolds on formative assessments increases their validity for ELs. Let's look at an example of one way to scaffold formative assessments for ELs. Suppose that students have had the Chinese folktale "Tikki Tikki Tembo" read aloud several times, have read it themselves, and have discussed it in small

---

3. See Figure 9.3 for steps to develop formative assessments for ELs.

FIGURE 9.7 Students' ELP Level and Differentiated-Assessment Tasks

ELP Level	Differentiated-Assessment Task
Beginning	Place pictures of the story in order. Describe the pictures orally using sentence frames. Answer questions about the central message in writing in the home language or English using sentence frames and a word bank.
Intermediate	Place pictures of the story in order. Describe the pictures orally and in writing using sentence stems. Answer questions about the central message in writing in English using sentence stems and/or a word bank.
Advanced	Describe the events of the story orally in small groups using sentence stems. Answer questions about the central message in writing in English using sentence stems and/or pretaught vocabulary.

groups. Their third-grade teacher, Mr. Leonato, would like students to now demonstrate that they can recount the events of the story and determine the central message. Based on his students' level of proficiency, Mr. Leonato has devised a sketch of what the formative assessment might look like for his ELs who are at three general levels of proficiency, as outlined in Figure 9.7. All assessment supports allow his ELs to show they can recount the events of the story and determine the central message, but his students are demonstrating their content knowledge in different ways.

APPLICATION ACTIVITY 9.3

Validity and Scaffolding Formative Assessments for ELs

As we introduced earlier in the chapter, formative assessments can take many forms: physical demonstrations, pictorial products, graphic organizers, written products, and oral assessments, to name a few. Look at the formative-assessment examples in Figures 9.8 through 9.11. Answer the following questions for each assessment:

1. What questions or comments do you have about the formative assessment related to using it with your ELs?

2. How can you increase the validity of this assessment for ELs?

3. How could you scaffold this assessment for ELs at varying English proficiency levels?

FIGURE 9.8 Exit Slip

Name _____

Write one thing you learned today.

_____

_____

_____

_____

_____

_____

FIGURE 9.9 Learning Log

Project: Student: Date:
I had the following goals:
I accomplished the following:
My most important questions are these:
My next steps are these:

FIGURE 9.10 Make a Math Connection

Mathematical Problem	Everyday Example
Representation (diagram, graph, picture)	My Explanation

FIGURE 9.11 T-Chart

How Does the Formative-Assessment Process for ELs Unfold in a Classroom?

Now that we've given you some food for thought in terms of formative assessments for ELs, we're going to show you how each of the three steps in Figure 9.3 might look "on the ground" in one fourth-grade classroom that contains ELs. For each step, we'll apply that information to one classroom and one student in particular. As you read through the steps and application, think about how you could adapt this formative-assessment process for your own context.

Step 1: Articulate the construct being taught and assessed.

In this case, the ESOL teacher, Ms. Broady, and fourth-grade science teacher, Ms. Cortez, decided to develop a formative-assessment rubric that would capture their ELs' acquisition of academic language at the word, sentence, and discourse levels while working on complex content. They developed a rubric specific to their ELs' levels of proficiency, which were high beginning, low intermediate, and high intermediate. To develop the rubric, they looked at the WIDA writing rubric in Grades 1–12 and made a version just for Grade 4 at their class of ELs' three levels of English language proficiency. For this assessment, they wanted to focus on how well their ELs were acquiring academic language in writing through an instructional unit on roadrunners. For purposes of this assessment, they were not assessing their ELs' knowledge of roadrunners per se, but rather, the focus was on language as a vehicle to their ELs describing their understanding of content. Figure 9.12 displays the rubric that Ms. Broady and Ms. Cortez developed. You will note that they found the sociocultural context for learning to be particularly important, so they included a space to describe the context in which the learning took place.

Step 2: Elicit evidence about ELs' learning.

In Step 2, the teachers had Cong, a Mandarin speaker, complete an open-ended task to describe how roadrunners are different from other birds as part of a unit of instruction on roadrunners. To complete the task, Cong was encouraged to look at a word wall in his classroom and to brainstorm a draft of the writing using a mind map. He produced the following writing sample (Figure 9.13).

FIGURE 9.12 Formative-Assessment Rubric for Roadrunner Assignment

Description of Sociocultural Context for Learning:

Academic Language Level	High Beginning ELP	Low Intermediate ELP	High Intermediate ELP
Word Level	Writing contains mostly Tier 1 vocabulary (familiar, everyday words) and occasionally Tier 2 vocabulary (words which appear across disciplines)	Writing contains Tier 1 vocabulary and some Tier 2 words and/or Tier 3 words (technical language related to the content area), with some accuracy	Writing contains some Tier 2 words and some Tier 3 words, mostly with accuracy
Sentence Level	• Writing contains phrases and short sentences • Some amount of text may be copied or adapted • Writing includes a minimal amount of details	• Writing contains simple and expanded sentences • A small amount of text may be copied or adapted • Writing shows emerging complexity that provides detail	• Writing contains a variety of sentence lengths of varying linguistic complexity • A minimal amount of text may be copied or adapted • Writing contains emerging cohesion used to provide detail and clarity
Discourse Level	• Writing is generally comprehensible when text is adapted from a model or source text or when original text is limited to simple text • Writing may contain some attempt at organization • Errors often impede comprehensibility	• Writing is generally comprehensible • Writing contains an attempt at organization • Errors may impede comprehensibility from time to time when attempting to produce more complex text	• Writing is usually comprehensible at all times • Writing is generally organized • Errors do not impede the overall meaning

Source: Adapted from the WIDA Consortium, Grades 1–12 Writing Rubric (2007).

Step 3: Interpret evidence to inform ongoing instruction.

In this step, Ms. Broady and Ms. Cortez collaboratively analyzed the student's work using the rubric they developed (Figure 9.12). They analyzed the writing sample's strengths at the word, sentence, and discourse levels and made a direct connection to the supports needed for this student to move to the next level of proficiency in each level of academic language, drawing from the support checklist provided in Figure 9.4. Figure 9.14 shows their analysis and link to future instructional supports for this student.

How can you adapt the analysis template for ELs to your context? How does framing the writing's strengths allow you to note which supports are needed in instruction?

FIGURE 9.13 Student Writing Sample

ROADRUNNERS

Roadrunners are unusual birds in many ways. Tell how Roadrunners are different from other birds.

> facts about roadruns
> Other bird don't eat liseldt like
> roadruns do.
> the roadrun's don't fly good like
> other bird do. roadrun's build there
> nest olny on cacdes cause they don't
> fly high. When the mother roadrun's
> grunding the nest the father
> roadrun goes out and hing out
> for a litle when the fathe comes
> back the mother goes out.
> the roadrun olny livd in Desert
> not like other birds. they run faster
> then ather bird.

Source: Maureen McCormick, Laurel Ridge Elementary School ESOL Teacher, Fairfax, VA.

FIGURE 9.14 Student Sample Analysis Template

Dimension	Notes on student writing (What *can the student do* in each of these dimensions?)	Teacher supports for student to reach the next level of proficiency in this area
Word level	The student uses Tier 2 vocabulary, such as *build* and *grunding* [guarding]. The student uses Tier 3, specific vocabulary related to the content area, such as *roadruns* [roadrunner], *desert*, and *cacdes* [cactus].	The student uses more specific vocabulary in this writing sample and seems ready for technical words to describe the habitat and life cycle of the roadrunner (e.g., scrub brush, arid, perch, hunt, incubate, predator, and defend). The teacher may support this push to use more technical vocabulary with direct vocabulary instruction, as well as the use of bilingual glossaries, word walls, and word banks (which will also facilitate spelling for this student).
Sentence level	The student's writing contains simple sentences, such as, "They run faster than other bird." The student also uses a compound sentence, "Roadrun's build there nest olny on cacdes cause they don't fly high."	The student may be ready to use additional sentence structures for comparison. The teacher may introduce a few sentence structures in a minilesson and create a poster of sentence frames for this student and others to refer to.

(Continued)

FIGURE 9.14 (Continued)

Dimension	Notes on student writing (What *can the student do* in each of these dimensions?)	Teacher supports for student to reach the next level of proficiency in this area
Sentence level (continued)	The writing includes an expanded sentence, "When the mother roadrun's grunding the nest the father roadrun goes out and hing out for a little." The writing repeats a comparative structure to contrast roadrunners and other birds—"not like other birds."	The student is ready to use more detail and descriptive language. This can be accomplished through minilessons on how to expand sentences in a teacher-led small group. Reinforcement of this concept can be provided through teacher and peer modeling.
Discourse level	The student's writing is generally comprehensible. The writing is on topic—all facts are about roadrunners. Errors do not impede the overall meaning.	The student is ready to begin organizing ideas within a paragraph. The teacher can demonstrate the use of a graphic organizer to group ideas on the same topic together. Another way to practice this skill would be to have students cut up the sentences, sort them, and rearrange them. The student is ready to begin writing a topic sentence at the beginning of a paragraph. This could be practiced through a small-group minilesson and with teacher and then peer support in recognizing the main idea of the paragraph (roadrunners are not like other birds) and turning it into a topic sentence.

APPLICATION ACTIVITY 9.4

Developing a Formative-Assessment Action Plan

Now that you have seen the three-step formative-assessment process in action, it's time for you to consider how you might incorporate formative assessment into your own instructional planning.

Directions: Using a lesson you give to your students, work collaboratively to plan instruction that incorporates formative assessment and reflection on data into the lesson design.

- Part 1: Complete the "Formative-Assessment Action Plan" template (Figure 9.15).

- Part 2: Develop the formative-assessment task that is appropriate to the lesson (e.g., a speaking task and oral language development rubric).

- Part 3: Self-assess your assessment using the "Assessment Checklist" (Figure 9.16).

- Part 3b (optional): If possible, review another team's assessment using the "Assessment Checklist." If completing this step, revise your "Formative-Assessment Action Plan" based on the feedback you received.

Directions: Complete the Formative-Assessment Action Plan.

Part 1: Formative-Assessment Action Plan

FIGURE 9.15   Formative-Assessment Action Plan Template

Grade Level:	ELP Level(s) of Students:
Description of lesson:	
Content standard(s): English language proficiency or development standard(s):	
Content objective: Language objective:	

Assessment Plan

1. What construct will you assess? (e.g., academic language, content, or both)
2. How will you share your assessment expectations with your students?
3. At what point(s) in the lesson will you assess the construct?
4. What assessment method(s) or tool(s) will you use? Why?
5. How will you evaluate the information you collect?
6. How will you use the data you gather to inform your instruction?

Part 2 Directions: Drawing from the information in Part 1, develop your authentic formative-assessment task, such as a rubric or a checklist.

Part 3 Directions: Review your assessment or another team's assessment that was developed in Part 2. For each question, answer yes or no. If your answer is no, provide a recommendation for improving the assessment.

FIGURE 9.16 Formative-Assessment Self-Assessment or Peer Assessment Checklist

Criterion	Yes	No	Action
1. Is the assessment aligned to the standards and objectives of the lesson?			
2. Are the assessment directions easy to understand for students?			
3. Are the students aware of the teacher's expectations that will be evaluated in the assessment? How?			
4. Is the format of the assessment familiar to students? (For example, if it is an oral presentation, have students had practice giving presentations?)			
5. Are the assessment questions or prompts linguistically accessible to ELs? The assessment should not include unfamiliar vocabulary, idioms, or complex sentence structures.			
6. Are the questions, tasks, or prompts free from cultural bias? There should be no references to aspects of culture that may be unfamiliar to students from another culture.			
7. Does the assessment include appropriate scaffolds for ELs of varying proficiency levels (e.g., word bank, sentence stems, and pictures)?			
8. Does the scoring of the assessment directly correlate to the construct being assessed (e.g., grammar and spelling are not taken into consideration when evaluating students' knowledge of content)?			
9. If technology is used, have students had sufficient practice with the technology prior to the assessment?			
10. Is the assessment information shared with students? How?			
11. Is the assessment used to inform instruction? How?			

Source: Adapted from Abedi, J. (2010). *Performance assessments for English language learners.* Stanford, CA: Stanford University, Stanford Center for Opportunity Policy in Education. Retrieved from https://scale.stanford.edu/system/files/performance-assessments-english-language-learners.pdf

Take a fresh look at your own assessment and/or the feedback from your colleagues if you're engaging in this activity with colleagues. Revise your "Formative-Assessment Action Plan" based on the self-feedback or peer feedback. Consider the following questions:

- In what ways was the feedback helpful?

- What new insights emerged for you in terms of assessment for ELs?

How Can I Support My ELs on Computer-Based Formative Assessments?

In addition to being able to design your own formative assessments that are applicable to ELs or to assist your colleagues to ensure their assessments are effective, you may also find your ELs taking computer-based formative assessments. As many states fully implement computer-based tests to measure students' progress toward reaching CCRS, it is an opportune time to take a closer look at how computer-based assessments might affect your ELs in particular. There are many key considerations for schools and districts to address in their planning and implementation of computer-based formative assessments. In this section, we explore which aspects of computer-based assessment might prove to be especially challenging for ELs and will provide some resources to support ELs' access to computer-based formative assessment.

One of the biggest challenges for ELs in adjusting to computer-based assessment that we cannot overlook is the *digital divide* that exists between students from low-income homes (currently two-thirds of ELs nationwide [NEA, 2008]) and students whose families can afford ample access to technology in the home (Staehr Fenner, 2016). This divide also tends to exist in terms of students' more limited access to technology in schools that serve low-income neighborhoods. In addition to less access to technology, in general, ELs also might not be fully versed, or *literate*, in the use of technology necessary for them to navigate formative-assessment test platforms, in particular. For example, ELs may be very familiar with smartphones, to which they may have access, but may not feel as comfortable with certain kinds of tasks on a computer, like clicking and dragging numbers to a number line or typing an extended answer. In addition, ELs arrive in schools at all points of the school year, and in many cases, they will still need to take content formative assessments, even though they may not be privy to the same training on the test platform that other students are given, let alone exposure to the content in English. Regardless of their arrival dates, ELs will need to understand all of the online test features—especially accessibility tools, supports, and accommodations, when applicable—and know how to use them.

The guidelines in Figure 9.17 provide a starting point from which you can advocate for ELs' access to specialized support for computer-based content assessments. There are certainly many more considerations, but these can be used as a checklist to begin to decide where to take action. While some educators may claim that these suggestions constitute "teaching to the test," we would argue that they are a way of positioning ELs to have a better chance at focusing on the content of the assessments instead of getting frustrated by the language unique to the platform. The first three supports can benefit non-ELs as well.

FIGURE 9.17   Computer-Based Assessment Recommendations for Teachers of ELs

Recommendation	Explanation
1. **Teach the terms ELs will need to know to navigate the platform.**	Some platforms contain the terms *item*, *toolbar*, *select*, *deselect*, and *icon*. These are all examples of terms you can teach to your ELs. We would also focus on some specific uses of terms for computer-based testing, such as to *flag an item*. One way to reinforce the terms is by posting a word wall of the terms, their meaning, an image, and a home language translation, if possible.
2. **Devote time to practicing test items and navigating the test platform with ELs.**	After preteaching necessary terms for ELs to navigate the platform, have students apply these terms by working through the test platform together, trying out some test items, and making sure that they know how to use any accommodations, tools, or supports that are available to them. The teacher could model how he or she uses the technology while also doing a think-aloud of how he or she answers the content using EL supports, where available. Once the teacher has modeled practice items, ELs could work on them together, in pairs, noting their questions on the platform, as well as content for the teacher.
3. **Make sure ELs have access to keyboarding skills.**	Computer-based assessments assume that students can type their responses to questions. It is important to ensure that ELs gain experience using keyboards with an instructor who is attuned to the linguistic scaffolds ELs will need to learn typing skills. With practice in typing, they will be less likely to be slowed down by developing typing skills.
4. **Collaborate with content teachers and test specialists on the use of accessibility tools, supports, and accommodations.**	It is essential that ESOL teachers work with grade-level or content teachers, as well as their school's testing coordinator, to ensure that ELs receive the appropriate supports and are also given access to the supports that they are allowed on any formative computer-based assessments.[4] ELs should be given only those supports that are appropriate for their background and level of proficiency[5]. (For example, a student not literate in her home language should not use a bilingual dictionary or translated online glossary.) ELs should be trained on and given these same appropriate supports during classroom instruction throughout the academic year.
5. **Make sure EL parents and caregivers are aware of the test requirements and platform.**	EL parents and caregivers (as well as the ELs themselves) should see the platform their children will use and should also be aware of how the assessment results will be used. Testing could be the topic of an EL parent meeting, either in school or in a place convenient for parents to meet, such as a community center.

Source: Adapted from Staehr Fenner (2015), http://www.colorincolorado.org/blog/computer-based-common-core-testing-considerations-and-supports-ells.

---

4. ELs must also be given regular access to accommodations during instruction that they are allowed on summative computer-based or paper-and-pencil assessments.

5. For more on instructional design from accommodation to accessibility, see Shafer Willner & Monroe, (2016).

What Is the Role of Collaboration in Creating and Using Formative Assessments for ELs?

As we have detailed throughout the chapter, collaboration among content and ESOL teachers is crucial in order to integrate formative assessments into your instructional loop. One way in which teachers can work toward equity, advocacy, and leadership within the framework of formative assessments is to serve as facilitator of discussions about EL formative-assessment results. Teachers and administrators can set up a time to collaboratively interpret the results and determine next steps in terms of instructional supports to help ELs reach the next level of language proficiency and/or content. Content teachers could share upcoming instructional units, standards, and content objectives to be addressed, and ESOL teachers could suggest instructional scaffolds based on proficiency level, as well as EL performance on formative assessments. For their part, administrators can demonstrate their commitment to their ELs' equity by setting aside a regular time and place for collaborative planning to support the analysis of ELs' formative-assessment results. By doing so, they set the tone in their buildings that collaboration is crucial to the success of ELs.

What Is the Role of Equity, Advocacy, and Leadership in Creating and Using Formative Assessments for ELs?

One important step teachers in a school or even a district can take to advocate for more equitable assessments for their ELs is to form a committee that includes the ESOL teacher, content area teacher(s), guidance counselor, assessment specialist, administrator, the student's parents or caregivers, and even the student. The committee can meet throughout the year to keep track of how well formative assessments are providing a means by which ELs can demonstrate what they know and can do in language and content. The committee can also discuss any tools, supports, and/or accommodations to be used on summative content assessments on a case-by-case basis and make sure those supports are also used throughout the academic year, during instruction as well as formative assessment. In addition, the committee can work together at the building level to conduct a needs analysis of where ELs could use additional technological support and also offer a time and place for ELs to practice using computer-based formative assessments. Further, a collaborative team could make certain that parents of their ELs are aware of formative assessments and any computer-based platforms used.

What Are the Next Steps to Design Formative Assessments Specific to My Context?

We recently worked with one of the largest urban school districts in the United States to create formative-assessment rubrics for ELs in speaking and writing in Grades K–12 that teachers across content areas and grade levels can use. When the year-long project was complete, we had developed sixteen rubrics total in speaking and writing in Grades K–12. The rubrics highlight ELs' strengths in academic language at the word, sentence, and discourse levels and also provide teachers with guidance in instructional planning and scaffolding. They integrate principles of Universal Design for Learning (Rose & Meyer, 2002) and are framed around the state's content standards, ELD standards, and annual ELP assessment performance-level descriptors. All teachers in this district can use the rubrics as part of their everyday instruction without taking away precious instructional time.

Equally as important as the actual formative-assessment products, the development process itself is worth mentioning, as it's one you can replicate, even with limited resources. To create the suite of rubrics, we recruited a group of twenty-five diverse cohort teachers who represented Grades K–2, 3–5, 6–8, and 9–12 in English language arts, mathematics, science, social studies, ESOL/bilingual, and special education. These were teachers who were experienced in working with ELs and who were interested in improving their EL assessment skills. During the course of the academic year, we held three meetings on weekends with teachers from across the district. The purpose of each of the meetings is displayed in Figure 9.18.

FIGURE 9.18 Teacher Cohort Meetings and Purposes

Meeting	Purpose
1	• Facilitators frame project • Facilitators share research and features of academic language with teachers • Facilitators set parameters to collect EL samples in speaking and writing • Facilitators design Version 1.0 of rubrics with teachers' input
2	• Teachers provide feedback on Version 1.0 of rubrics • Teachers bring in and discuss EL samples in speaking and writing • Facilitators and teachers begin to draft Version 2.0 of rubrics
3	• Teachers provide feedback on Version 2.0 of rubrics • Teachers bring in and discuss more EL samples in speaking and writing • Teachers use Version 2.0 of rubrics to assess ELs' work and refine rubrics • Teachers suggest revisions for Version 3.0 of rubrics

Even if you don't have the "bandwidth" to completely recreate the process we just described, you can replicate some aspects of our work within a framework of distributed expertise (Edwards, 2011) to bring together colleagues to collaborate around creating formative assessments for ELs. Figure 9.19 walks you through some considerations to do so.

FIGURE 9.19   Next Steps for Replicating the Collaborative Formative-Assessment Creation Process

1. My plan to develop or adapt formative-assessment rubrics for ELs in our school or district with content or grade-level colleagues

   Overall plan:

2. How I will draw from teachers' expertise

Type of Educator	Unique Expertise	Role
Content teacher		
ESOL/bilingual teacher		
Special education teacher		
Guidance counselor		
Administrator		
Librarian		
Other: _____		

(Continued)

FIGURE 9.19   (Continued)

3. Steps for putting my plan into action

Step	Timeline	Stakeholders
1:		
2:		
3:		
4:		
5:		

4. My summary of how this process provides insight into ELs' assessment *for* learning

Summary:

Conclusion

In this chapter, we presented an often overlooked aspect of the EL instructional loop, which is formative assessment for ELs. Some topics we explored were assessment *for* learning, the validity of ELs' formative assessments, and considerations for using computer-based formative assessments. We shared many examples of creating formative assessments, as well as how to use them to adapt instruction for ELs. Finally, we provided some structure for you to replicate a collaborative process to create formative assessments for your ELs.

Reflection Questions

1. How has your thinking evolved on formative assessment for ELs by reading this chapter?

2. Which ideas would you like to implement from this chapter?

3. What are your biggest challenges in doing so, and how can you address these challenges so your ELs will benefit?

References

Abedi, J. (2006). Psychometric issues in the ELL assessment and special education eligibility. *Teachers College Record, 108*(11), 2282–2303.

Alvarez, L., Ananda, S., Walqui, A., Sato, E., & Rabinowitz, S. (2014, February). Focusing formative assessment on the needs of English language learners. WestEd. Retrieved from https://www.wested.org/wp-content/files_mf/1391626953FormativeAssessment_report5.pdf

American Educational Research Association, American Psychological Association, National Council on Measurement in Education, Joint Committee on Standards for Educational and Psychological Testing (U.S.). (2014). Standards for educational and psychological testing. Washington, DC: AERA.

Edwards, A. (2011). Building common knowledge at the boundaries between professional practices: Relational agency and relational expertise in systems of distributed expertise. *International Journal of Educational Research, 50*(1), 33–39. doi:10.1016/j.ijer.2011.04.007

Frey, N., & Fisher, D. (2011). *The formative assessment action plan.* Alexandria, VA: ASCD.

Gottlieb, M. (2016). *Assessing English language learners: Bridges to educational equity.* Thousand Oaks, CA: Corwin.

Heritage, M. (2010). *Formative assessment: Making it happen in the classroom.* Thousand Oaks, CA: Corwin.

Marzano, R. J. (2010). *Formative assessment & standards-based grading: Classroom strategies that work.* Bloomington, IN: Marzano Research Laboratory.

Moss, C. M., & Brookhart, S. M. (2009). *Advancing formative assessment in every classroom: A guide for instructional leaders.* Alexandria, VA: ASCD.

National Education Association. (2008). *English language learners face unique challenges* (NEA Policy Brief). Retrieved from www.nea.org/assets/docs/HE/ELL_Policy_Brief_Fall_08_%282%29.pdf

Noyce, P. E., & Hickey, D. T. (Eds.). (2011). *New frontiers in formative assessment.* Cambridge, MA: Harvard Education Press.

Office of English Language Acquisition. (2015). *English learners (ELs) and NAEP* (OELA Fast Facts). Retrieved from www.ncela.us/files/fast_facts/OELA_FastFacts_ELsandNAEP.pdf

Popham, W. J. (2008). *Transformative assessment*. Alexandria, VA: Association for Supervision and Curriculum Development.

Rose, D., & Meyer, A. (2002). *Teaching every student in the digital age*. Alexandria, VA: ASCD. Retrieved from http://www.cast.org/teachingeverystudent/ideas/tes

Shafer Willner, L., & Monroe, M. (2016). Using a "Can Do" Approach to Ensure Differentiated Instruction Intentionally Supports the Needs of Language Learners [Web log post.] Colorin Colorado. Retrieved from http://www.colorincolorado.org/article/using-can-do-approach-ensure-differentiated-instruction-intentionally-supports-needs

Staehr Fenner, D. (2014). *Advocating for English learners: A guide for educators*. Thousand Oaks, CA: Corwin.

Staehr Fenner, D. (2015). Computer-based Common Core testing: Considerations and supports for ELLs [Web log post]. Colorín Colorado. Retrieved from http://www.colorincolorado.org/blog/computer-based-common-core-testing-considerations-and-supports-ells

Staehr Fenner, D. (2016). Fair and square assessments for ELLs. *Educational Leadership, 73*(5). Retrieved from http://www.ascd.org/publications/educational-leadership/feb16/vol73/num05/Fair-And-Square-Assessments-for-ELLs.aspx

Stiggins, R. J. (2005). *Student-involved assessment FOR learning* (4th ed.). Upper Saddle River, NJ: Pearson.

TESOL International Association. (2016). The preparation of the ESL educator in the era of College- and Career-Readiness Standards. Alexandria, VA: Author. Retrieved from https://www.tesol.org/docs/default-source/advocacy/ccr-standards-convening_final2.pdf?sfvrsn=2

Valdez Pierce, L. (2003). *Assessing English language learners*. Washington, DC: National Education Association.

WIDA. (2007). Writing rubric of the WIDA Consortium: Grades 1–12. Retrieved from http://www.njtesol-njbe.org/handouts15/WIDA_Writing_Rubric.pdf

Index

taught language and content simultaneously, 17, 18 (figure)

teacher collaboration and, 18–20

teachers leveraging advocacy and leadership skills for, 20–23

See also Culturally responsive teaching

Equity

academic language promotion and, 140–141

in creating text-dependent questions, 225

role in creating and using formative assessments, 253

role in developing culturally responsive classrooms, 52–53

role in developing scaffolded materials, 78–80

role in oral language development, 108

role in teaching academic vocabulary, 167–168

in teaching background knowledge, 198–199

Errors, interplay between scaffolds, academic language and, 117–118

"Evolution of the Grocery Bag, The," 211–213, 216–220

Expectations, cultural, 35

Eye contact, 37 (figure)

False cognates, 165

Fillmore, C. J., 131

Fisher, D., 178, 182, 205

Floca, Brian, 128

Formative assessment, 229–230

action plan, 248–250

assessment as, for, and of learning and, 230, 231 (figure)

brainstorm, 237

collaboration on, 253

computer-based, 251, 252 (figure)

cultural bias in, 241

defined, 231–232

designing context-specific, 254–255, 255–256 (figure)

evidence interpretation informing instruction, 235–237

format and use of technology, 240

instructions, 240

linguistic accessibility and, 240–241

process in the classroom, 245–250

process structure for ELs, 233, 234–235 (figure)

research on ELs and, 232

role of equity, advocacy, and leadership in creating and using, 253

role with ELs, 233

scaffolds, 241–242, 243–244 (figure)

scoring, 241

validity of, 238–241

Four-step framework for teaching background knowledge, 190–194

Frames

paragraph, 64, 65 (figure)

sentence, 64

Frayer Model, 156

Frey, N., 178, 205

Funds of knowledge, 14

Gallery walks, 160

Games and activities to develop vocabulary, 160–161

Gee, James, 126

Gesturing, 37 (figure)

Gibbons, P., 60

Gladwell, Malcolm, 203

Glossaries, 62–63, 160

Gonzalez, N., 14

Gottlieb, Margo, 230, 231, 232

Graphic organizers, 61–62

Guiding principles for ELs

getting started using the, 23–25

shifts in content standards and, 12, 13 (figure)

teacher collaboration, 18–20

teachers leveraging advocacy and leadership skills, 20–23

teaching ELs in a welcoming and supportive climate, 15–17

teaching language and content simultaneously, 17, 18 (figure)

Guthrie, J. R., 177

Hickey, D. T., 232

Hiebert, E., 164

High-context cultures, 37 (figure)

Home language

materials in, 64

use of, 49–50

Identity, cultural, 31, 32–33

Independent learning, 37 (figure)

Individualist cultures, 36–37 (figure)

Information gaps, 159

Interactive word walls, 158–159

Interplay between scaffolds, errors, and academic language, 117–118

A SAGE Publishing Company

Solutions you want. Experts you trust. Results you need.

AUTHOR CONSULTING

Author Consulting

On-site professional learning with sustainable results! Let us help you design a professional learning plan to meet the unique needs of your school or district. www.corwin.com/pd

INSTITUTES

Institutes

Corwin Institutes provide collaborative learning experiences that equip your team with tools and action plans ready for immediate implementation. www.corwin.com/institutes

ECOURSES

eCourses

Practical, flexible online professional learning designed to let you go at your own pace. www.corwin.com/ecourses

READ2EARN

Read2Earn

Did you know you can earn graduate credit for reading this book? Find out how: www.corwin.com/read2earn

Contact an account manager at (800) 831-6640 or visit **www.corwin.com** for more information.